Beyond Explanation

Beyond Explanation

Religious Dimensions
in Cultural Anthropology

Mark Kline Taylor

ISBN 0-86554-165-5

Library of Congress Cataloging-in-Publication Data
Taylor, Mark Kline, 1951–
Beyond explanation.

Abstract of thesis (Ph.D.)—   University of Chicago
Divinity School.
Includes index.
1. Ethnology—Religious aspects. 2. Ethnology—
Religious aspects—Christianity. 3. Lévi-Strauss,
Claude, 1908– —Criticism and interpretation.
4. Harris, Marvin, 1927– —Criticism and interpretation.
I. Title.
BL256.T36   306'.6'01   85-13770
ISBN 0-86554-165-5   ∞™

Contents

Dedication

*To my parents
and to my daughters*

Preface

Anthropologist George Peter Murdock lamented his discipline's tendency to invoke principles resembling what "we know as mythology or perhaps as philosophy or even theology."[1] Cultural anthropologists may study religions, but they view it as an intrusion if religious interests show up in their own methods and concepts. The appearance of religious interests in anthropologists' paradigms may lead to accusations that they are not sufficiently anthropological.[2]

It is true that religious interests may stand in a relationship of tension with contemporary anthropological ones. Religionists, for example, often find anthropology's functional, structural, or symbolic analyses to be uncomfortably "reductionist," while anthropologists may view religionists and theologians as provincial and ethnocentric. One can offer several historical and intellectual reasons for this mutual suspicion, but it is not a necessary feature of the relationship between religious and anthropological interests. In this book I suggest that a "religious dimension" may be discerned in anthropologists' discourse, so that this discourse may be viewed as driving beyond explanation, beyond the methods, descriptions, and theories usually seen as constitutive of this social-science discipline. The presence of such a dimension

---

[1]George Peter Murdock, "Anthropology's Mythology," *Proceedings of the Royal Anthropological Institute of Great Britain and Ireland* (1971): 18.

[2]Compare David Kaplan, "The Anthropology of Authenticity: Everyman His Own Anthropologist," *American Anthropologist* 76 (1974): 828.

may serve as a focal point around which religionists and social scientists, theologians and anthropologists, may converse. I hope to move toward that conversation without co-opting anthropological concerns into those of the fields of religious studies and theology.

This conversation may have a twofold significance. First, it involves a field of inquiry that is increasingly important in contemporary times. As scholars often speak of our common lot in a global or world community,[3] the increasing interaction of different cultural-linguistic groups reveals the need for cultural anthropology's cross-cultural approach. Nurtured by its ethnographic and comparative impulses, cultural anthropology is essential for addressing the concerns of *world* community while accenting also the *cultural specificity* of the world's peoples. Few can afford to ignore this field, which Arnold van Gennep once proposed as "the foundation on which a new philosophical conception of humanity will be built," even if, as in Richard Rorty's *Philosophy and the Mirror of Nature*, the philosophy it helps to foster is one that calls into question all foundationalism.[4]

Second, discernment of a religious dimension in this intercultural field is also a way to advance general discussion of the place of religion in contemporary life. In particular, this project shifts the locus of religious experience away from views that take it as one "field" that is coordinate with other fields of activity such as art, kinship, social life, and economics. Religious experience, placed in this way, is often marked

---

[3]Note, for example, discussions of "worldwide global culture" in John Hick, *God and the Universe of Faiths* (London: Macmillan, 1973) 146; Ninian Smart, *Beyond Ideology: Religion and the Future of Western Civilization* (New York: Harper and Row, 1981) 11; and Wilfred Cantwell Smith, *Towards a World Theology: Faith and the Comparative Study of Religions* (Philadelphia: Westminster Press, 1981) 112ff. Note also that Stephen Toulmin, after arguing for serious acknowledgment of cultural and historical relativity, nevertheless speaks of "our common humanity." Stephen Toulmin, *Human Understanding: The Use and Evolution of Concepts* (Princeton: Princeton University Press, 1972) 493-94, 499-500. See also David Tracy's treatment of the "culture of pluralism." In this discussion he also speaks of "authentically global consciousness" or "Global humanity." David Tracy, *The Analogical Imagination: Christian Theology and the Culture of Pluralism* (New York: Crossroad, 1981) 342, 425, 450. Among anthropologists, one also occasionally notes commitments to this "world culture struggling to be born." Cf. Dell Hymes, ed., *Reinventing Anthropology* (New York: Vintage Press, 1969) 19.

[4]Richard Rorty, *Philosophy and the Mirror of Nature* (Princeton: Princeton University Press, 1979). See esp. 70-127, 385.

off from other fields as a special activity dealing with the supernatural, with spiritual beings, or perhaps, with the special emotional states of ritual participants. Appropriate as these understandings may be, this project considers the locus of religious experience to be a "dimension" of a variety of possible human activities.[5]

My concern is to bring into focus any religious dimension that might attend the activities of the anthropologist who works on the boundaries of cultures. What kind of experiences may be called "religious," and what forms does such a "religious dimension" take in this contemporary social science? In sum, the significance of this work lies in its attempt to understand both the crucial inquiry of cultural anthropology and the place of religious experience among those anthropologists who describe the culturally diverse character of humankind.

This book is a revision of a doctoral dissertation written for the University of Chicago Divinity School. In spite of the number of revisions a dissertation endures, it is hard to let it go to print. Ultimately, it remains a witness to my early engagement with a set of issues that—however differently I might approach the issues now—will unquestionably influence my later work. Just as no "Preface" deceives careful readers into thinking that it was written first, so no later revisions really deceive readers into thinking that a text's first virtues and flaws have been expunged. I may be inclined now, for example, to integrate insights from critical praxis theory with this book's largely hermeneutical investigation into what anthropologists do. While these new insights, and those of others, refine, develop, and even may challenge this earlier work, they remain subjects for later research.

I wish to thank the committee of scholars who guided the original formulation of this work: David Tracy, Langdon Gilkey, Stephen Toulmin, and George W. Stocking, Jr. Their support and criticism were invaluable and appreciated throughout the project. I especially thank the chairperson of the work's original committee, David Tracy, for the example of his interdisciplinary vision, theological commitment, and timely criticisms.

---

[5]For discussion of the tradition in philosophy of religion that examines religious experience in this "dimensional" way, see David Tracy, *Blessed Rage for Order: The New Pluralism in Theology* (New York: Seabury, 1975) 91-118.

This work is indebted not only to persons but to institutions. I wish to thank the Institute for the Advanced Study of Religion at the University of Chicago Divinity School, which provided a context for the refining of this project and enabled my full-time research. Thanks must also go to Princeton Theological Seminary where colleagues in teaching—both faculty and administrators—have in one way or another provided criticism and support for this work. Some of the writing in this book has appeared elsewhere. I gratefully acknowledge permission given by editors to quote from the following sources: "Lévi-Strauss: Evolving a Myth about Myths," *Religious Studies Review* 9 (April 1983): 97-105; "Religion among the Anthropologists," in Marilyn R. Waldman and Hao Chang, eds., *Religion in the Modern World*, Papers in Comparative Studies 3 (Columbus OH: Center for Comparative Studies in the Humanities, Ohio State University, 1984) 55-69; and "Symbolic Dimensions in Cultural Anthropology," *Current Anthropology* 26 (April 1985): 167-85. It would be difficult to name all those whose support I have received along the way, but among many friends, companions, and colleagues, I thank especially Anita Kline Taylor.

Introduction
A Hermeneutical Approach
to a Theology of Culture

An attempt to discern a religious dimension in the discourse of cultural anthropology can be introduced by a critique of what Paul Tillich termed a "theology of culture." Tillich formulated this notion early in his career, but throughout his lifework he retained an interest in it as an attempt to analyze the "theology behind all cultural expressions."[1] Though subject to various criticisms and suspicions, Tillich's theology of culture continues to stimulate theological interest in the interplay of religion and culture.[2]

What "theology of culture" is will emerge more clearly in the following discussions of its ambiguities and of a hermeneutical approach to it. The fundamental orientation of a theology of culture was set by Tillich in his well-known essay on "Religion as a Dimension in Man's Spiritual Life." In that work, he advances his position that religion is not to be identified with the functions of morality, aesthetics, or feeling with which it is often confused. Nor is it Tillich's concern to carve out

---

[1]Cf. Paul Tillich, "On the Idea of a Theology of Culture," in *What is Religion?* ed. James Luther Adams (New York: Harper and Row, 1969) 155-81, and Paul Tillich, *Systematic Theology*, 3 vols. (Chicago: University of Chicago Press, 1967) 1:39-40.

[2]See, for examples, John Morgan, "Religion and Culture as Meaning Systems: A Dialogue between Geertz and Tillich," *Journal of Religion* 57 (October 1977): 363-75, and John J. Carey, ed., *Theonomy and Autonomy: Studies in Paul Tillich's Engagement with Modern Culture* (Macon GA: Mercer University Press, 1984).

a separate realm or function for religion. Rather, religion's "home" is in the dimension of depth in all cultural functions.[3] In this dimension one encounters what Tillich, throughout his work, refers to as elements of ultimacy, ultimate concern, infinity, the unconditioned. Elsewhere, he refers to this depth as the "soil" out of which cultural creations emerge. It is the "substance" out of which both a culture's subject matter and form grow.[4] In this work, I view the practice of cultural anthropology as a cultural function, and suggest that in its "depth," to use Tillich's term, one can find a religious dimension proper to it.

Though this project may be an appropriation of Tillich's theology-of-culture interest, theology in this last quarter of the twentieth century works in a context different from Tillich's. Thus, what is important is not only how this work is indebted to a theology-of-culture approach, but also how it is different from Tillich's. I will describe my approach to a theology of culture as, in general terms, hermeneutical—"hermeneutical" in the senses of H.-G. Gadamer's and Paul Ricoeur's hermeneutical theories. The hermeneutical approach checks some potential misappropriations of Tillich's theology-of-culture analyses. Contemporary appropriations of Tillich's perspective encounter two major ambiguities signaled in the very phrase "theology of culture."

Ambiguities in a "Theology of Culture"

The first ambiguity is generated by Tillich's use of the term *culture* in singular form. On the one hand, this use suggests that the theological analyst of culture faces a realm that, however diverse its parts, constitutes a unity theologians may address.[5] Use of this singular form conjures up memories of an older view of "culture" or "civilization," in contrast to contemporary anthropological or other pluralist apprecia-

---

[3]Paul Tillich, "Religion as a Dimension in Man's Spiritual Life," in *Theology of Culture*, ed. Robert C. Kimball (Oxford: Oxford University Press, 1959) 7.

[4]Tillich, *Systematic Theology*, 3:60.

[5]For Tillich's understanding of the various functions that constitute "culture," see his *Systematic Theology*, 3:57-68.

tions of the diversity of cultures.[6] Anthropologists Kroeber and Kluckhohn draw the contrast:

> The [Matthew] Arnold-[John] Powys-[Werner] Jaeger concept of
> culture is not only ethnocentric . . . it is absolutistic. It knows per-
> fection, or at least what is most perfect in human achievement and
> resolutely directs its "obligatory" gaze thereto, disdainful of what is
> "lower." The anthropological attitude is relativistic, in that in place
> of beginning with an inherited hierarchy of values, it assumes that
> every society through its culture seeks and in some measure finds
> values, and that the business of anthropology includes the determi-
> nation of the range, variety, constancy and interrelations of these in-
> numerable values.[7]

To guide theology toward discussion of "culture" in the singular
suggests advocacy of a position that overlooks today's healthy suspicion
that the human situation is marked especially by groups that display, as
Clifford Geertz puts it, "their oddities." This suspicion would also be
forthcoming among those who, like Peter Winch, argue that sociocultural life is fundamentally constituted by often incommensurable, culturally specific "forms of life."[8]

On the other hand, while Tillich's use of "culture" in the singular
does not seem to do justice to the diversity of cultures, his description
of the task of a theology of culture frequently stresses that theological
discernment of "culture's" religious dimension is always concrete and
specific. Not only are the cultural functions analyzed concrete, but the
one who conducts the analysis also stands in a circle that "has no particular existence apart from the cultural groups that surround it and the

---

[6]For an account of the rise of the contemporary anthropological formulation of the
notion of cultures, see George W. Stocking, Jr., "Franz Boas and the Culture Concept
in Historical Perspective," in *Race, Culture and Evolution: Essays in the History of Anthropology* (New York: The Free Press, 1968) 195-233.

[7]A. L. Kroeber and Clyde Kluckhohn, *Culture: A Critical Review of Concepts and
Definitions*, Papers of the Peabody Museum of American Archaeology and Ethnology,
Harvard University, vol. 47, no. 1 (Cambridge MA, 1952) 9, 150. Cited in Stocking,
"Franz Boas," 72.

[8]Peter Winch, "Understanding a Primitive Society," in *Rationality*, ed. Bryan R.
Wilson (Oxford: Basil Blackwell, 1970) 78-111.

creative acts of the past on which it rests."[9] Language of this sort suggests that Tillich wished not only to discern the religious dimension in culture, but to study a particular aspect of the religious dimension in culture, its entry into the peculiarities and relativities of cultural life. On the basis of Tillich's view, then, a religious interest in an absolute or in the unconditioned must always be focused in the relativized and concretized realms. That Tillich believed this is also suggested by the culmination of his *Systematic Theology* in an analysis of spirit as present in "history bearing groups" (note the plural).[10] Volume 3 is laden with admonitions to analyze spirit amid the relativities, ambiguities, and multiplicities of human life.

Tillich himself saw the ambiguity in his stressing concretion while speaking frequently of singular culture. His awareness is especially apparent in his last formal address, "The Significance of the History of Religions for the Systematic Theologian." Tillich discovered in the history of religions an emphasis on the particular that indicated the need for a new "more intensive period of interpenetration of theology and religious historical studies" than was displayed in his three-volume systematic theology. His realization came both as "apologia yet also self-accusation."[11]

What would the application of this new understanding mean for the theology of culture figuring so prominently in his *Systematic Theology*? It would mean that religious symbols would need to be examined for "roots in the totality of experience including local surroundings, in all their ramifications, both political and economic."[12] Such a study of religious symbols, intensified by the cross-cultural and interreligious approaches of history of religions, points the way for Tillich toward a new theological anthropology engaging religiocultural functions in a more diverse way than did his *Systematic Theology*. *Systematic Theology*'s chief concern, Tillich acknowledges, was with theology's and re-

---

[9]Tillich, "On the Idea of a Theology of Culture," 156.

[10]Tillich, *Systematic Theology*, 3:308-13.

[11]Paul Tillich, "The Significance of the History of Religions for the Systematic Theologian," in *The Future of Religions*, ed. Jerald C. Brauer (New York: Harper and Row, 1966) 91.

[12]Ibid., 93.

ligion's relations to the scientific and philosophical, secular culture of the West.[13]

In this "post-liberal" or "post-modern age" of pluralist sensibilities and consciousness of cultural specificity, continuing the tasks of a theology of "culture" sounds anachronistic.[14] It might be far more appropriate to say that at best one might formulate several, perhaps many, theologies of cultures by drawing from fields like history of religions and cultural anthropology. And many of the current attempts to focus theological issues for diverse cultures (African, Oceanic, Asian, Mesoamerican, and so forth) or subcultures (Afro-American, masculinist, feminist, urban nomadic, and so forth) suggest just how varied the tasks are for those who would continue to appropriate Tillich's theology of culture.

The theology-of-culture approach of this project focuses on the particular culture or subculture of those conducting cross-cultural inquiry. In other words, one can move toward a "theology" of cross-cultural scholars' cultural experience. In their experiences of the culturally other, what might count as religious and serve as occasion for theological conversation? By taking up these kinds of issues, a theologian of culture respects the value of enterprises that increase current pluralistic and culturally specific sensibilities, and asks about any religious dimensions to those enterprises. Such a religious dimension would lie not simply in the cross-cultural scholar's own culture, nor would it lie only in the culture entered or studied. It is a dimension to be sought among the cultural functions that involve *intercultural* encounter. It is this dimension that will be sought by examination of enterprises in cultural anthropology. If this project is characterized as a "theology of culture," the culture about which it is concerned is not "culture" in general. It focuses instead on the culture of those who have situated themselves be-

---

[13]Ibid., 91. On the evolution of Tillich's interest in comparative religions and its bearings on his theology, see Terence Thomas, "On Another Boundary: Tillich's Encounter with World Religions," in *Theonomy and Autonomy*, 193-211.

[14]For two different discussions of these sensibilities as characteristic of the post-liberal or post-modern period, see the cultural-linguistic approach of theologian George A. Lindbeck, *The Nature of Doctrine: Religion and Theology in a Postliberal Age* (Philadelphia: Westminster, 1984) 112-38; and Cox's link of postmodern theology to the phenomenon of "global spiritual heterogeneity," Harvey Cox, *Religion in the Secular City: Toward a Postmodern Theology* (New York: Simon and Schuster, 1984) 222-39.

tween cultures, in the realm of cross-cultural fieldwork, comparison, and generalization. This might be a very specific "culture," and yet be one that, by way of its intercultural activities and knowledge, seeks some transcendence of the sheer multiplicity of cultures.

A second ambiguity arises from the kind of genitive phrase "theology of culture" is taken to be. Is "theology" the subject that addresses or deals with culture? Or is "culture" the subject of the phrase, the possessor and generator of a theology? The tasks Tillich describes as proper to a theology of culture suggest that his main concern here is with culture as the subject. It is culture that possesses a theology or a religious dimension and that invites theological reflection. John Morgan shows how theology, according to Tillich, is proper to culture: "A theology of culture is a systematic analysis of the substance of *culture* in an attempt to discover *culture*'s religious core."[15]

Tillich's commitment to an analysis of culture's theology has elicited Karl Barth's well-known criticisms, which are based on the belief that theology itself has distinctive resources (tradition, Scriptures, the "Word of God") for addressing and transforming culture. But just as Barth's work can also include a "theology of culture,"[16] so also can Tillich's analysis of culture, in search of a theological or religious dimension, be seen as the completion of distinctive theological interests.

Tillich himself suggests that the theology of culture is not simply a description of culture that is only later to be used by systematic theologians. To be sure, he often presents his theology of culture as "analytic rather than synthetic" and as "historical rather than systematic," and all this as "a preparation for the work of the systematic theologian."[17] But while these modes of presentation highlight the primary tasks of a theology of culture, they do not set theology of culture outside of what Tillich called "the theological circle."

---

[15]Morgan, "Religion and Culture," 374.

[16]See Robert J. Palma, *Karl Barth's Theology of Culture: The Freedom of Culture for the Praise of God* (Allison Park PA: Pickwick Publications, 1983); see Karl Barth, *Church Dogmatics*, 1.2, trans. G. T. Thompson and Harold Knight (Edinburgh: T & T Clarke, 1956) 280-81, and Karl Barth, *Evangelical Theology: An Introduction* (Grand Rapids: William B. Eerdmans, 1963) 63-84.

[17]Tillich, *Systematic Theology*, 1:39.

By means of this notion, Tillich stressed that however much a theologian may be an analyst outside the circle of theological concerns, he or she is also always inside it. Theologians of culture do not set out to analyze the religious dimension of a cultural function as some already-out-there-now-real phenomena. If a theologian discovers a religious a priori in cultural functions, through some "scientific" analyses, for example, its discovery is possible only because it was present from the very beginning. No religious philosopher or theologian totally escapes the circle. "Every understanding of spiritual things (*Geisteswissenschaften*) is circular."[18]

According to this reading of the introduction to Tillich's *Systematic Theology*, theologians' analyses and explanations of culture may be viewed not only as an attempt to take cues from culture—to watch it, listen to it, describe it—but also as the completion of a theological tradition in which the theologian as analyst of cultural functions stands. This work's discernment of a religious dimension in the cultural activity of being a cultural anthropologist will, therefore, begin with discussion of the theological traditions that motivate the discernment. To be sure, acknowledging a motivation from a theological tradition is no warrant for *what* one is motivated to claim about cultural anthropology. Any validity to the claim that there is a religious dimension will have to come from conversation and engagement with the perspectives of cultural anthropology; this will be the concern of subsequent chapters.

"Theology of Culture" and Hermeneutics

With this commentary on the ambiguities that attend Tillich's theology of culture, one may turn to the ways that hermeneutical theory, whether that of Gadamer or Ricoeur, provides helpful correctives. Concerning the first ambiguity—Tillich's tendency to speak monolithically of culture and its theology while urging concrete and specific analyses of cultural functions—hermeneutics instills a healthy respect for particularity and difference in a way that yet fosters relation among particulars so that events of understanding occur. Gadamer's work, especially, stresses that "we understand in a different way, if we under-

[18]Ibid., 9.

stand at all."[19] Understanding entails, and here one may include the theological understanding of culture, allowing one's subject matter to be other and to be specific. It means acknowledging the multiplicity of cultural phenomena and functions, not simply taking the other as a typical representative of some general type.

If in this book cultural anthropology is to be investigated, then a hermeneutical approach will encourage treatment of cultural anthropology not just as a discipline but also as a set of particular encounters. A hermeneutical theology of culture, applied to cultural anthropology, will require a sojourn in the particularities of ways of being a cultural anthropologist, and amid those particularities any "religious dimensions," "elements of transcendence," or "ultimate concerns" will have to be discerned. The only sense of "the infinite," or "ultimate concern," to use Tillich's term, that a hermeneutical sensibility respects is that strange kind that emerges amid the play of finite particularities.[20] Actually, it is that kind of "infinity" or "ultimate" that does justice to the relativized absolute or spirit that Tillich sought within the conditions of life's ambiguities.

Without a methodological sojourn in the particularities of cultural functions, a theology of culture, which discerns "religious dimensions" in other disciplines or cultural realms, easily becomes the biased imposition of one discipline's concerns upon another's, or in other words, the forcing of interdisciplinary conversation. It may become a form of theological imperialism that Tillich never urged. In his language, the imposition would set theology and cultural anthropology into a "heteronomous" relationship: one in which an alien theological principle rules over the cultural function. For Tillich, the relationship between a cultural activity (here, the practice of cultural anthropology) and its theology should be "theonomous": the theology must be developed from the depth of a cultural function's own subject matter, form, and substance.[21] A significant aim of a hermeneutical approach to a theology of culture is to keep the theologian's gaze directed toward the particularities of cultural experience. If one then watches for a religious dimen-

---

[19]H.-G. Gadamer, *Truth and Method* (New York: Seabury, 1975) 264.

[20]Ibid., 416.

[21]Tillich, *Systematic Theology,* 1:83-86.

sion, it needs to be found by attending to the specific activities of cultural anthropological experience.

A hermeneutical theology of culture also speaks explicitly to the second ambiguity. Hermeneutical theory, especially that of Gadamer and Ricoeur, would confirm that theologians may be both analysts of culture and appropriators of their theological traditions. What in Tillich's "theology of culture" is an ambiguity—the tension between the theologian as analyst of culture and as faithful appropriator of theological tradition—is in hermeneutics a fundamental principle developed at great length.[22]

Hermeneutical approaches remind one that this tension is inherent not only in a theological understanding of culture, but also in events of understanding generally. The subject matter analyzed is approached through the preunderstanding or foreunderstanding of interpreters. By no means does this process imply that eventual understanding is reduced to the prejudgments and anticipations of interpreters, but it does depend upon turning reflexively to prejudgments, putting one's prejudices "into play" or "at risk," as Gadamer puts it.[23] Or, in Ricoeur's terms, the event of understanding moves necessarily from the naive guesses of preunderstanding, on through careful analysis or "explanation." Appropriating one's preunderstanding is necessary to understanding, but understanding is not reducible to preunderstanding.[24]

In sum, a hermeneutical theology of culture would aim at discerning what Tillich called "a theology behind cultural expressions," or the religious dimension in cultural expressions and functions. But a hermeneutical approach stresses the discernment of this, first, through attention to the *particularities* of cultural functions, and then through attending *reflexively* to the preunderstandings of the theologian analyzing a given cultural function. Because of the first factor, this work, in order to move toward the final chapter's discussion of religious dimensions, must devote three chapters to detailing the cultural and anthropological enterprise. Because of the second factor, this work must begin

----

[22]Gadamer, *Truth and Method*, 235-74.

[23]Ibid., 266, 350.

[24]Paul Ricoeur, *Interpretation Theory: Discourse and the Surplus of Meaning* (Ft. Worth TX: Texas Christian University Press, 1976) 71-95.

with a reflexive turn into the theological tradition motivating the theological attempt to delineate a religious dimension in cultural anthropology.

Style and Hermeneutical "Understanding"

Once hermeneutics is allowed to qualify a theology of culture in these ways, one can see what is perhaps its more significant contribution to the tasks of a theology of culture. In particular, the hermeneutical theorist's focus on *Verstehen,* or "understanding," provides a way to advance Tillich's important notion of "style." Ultimately, I do not find Tillich's notion of style very helpful for the task of articulating religious dimensions. At best, his notion is suggestive, but the task he thereby indicates is better performed by attending to "understanding."

"Style" was a notion that Tillich stressed when suggesting a method that theological analysts of culture might practice.

> Concerning the method of such a theological analysis of culture the following might be said. The key to the theological understanding of a cultural creation is its style. Style is a term derived from the realm of the arts, but it can be applied to all realms of culture. There is a style of thought, of politics, of social life, etc. The style of a period expresses itself in its cultural forms, in its choice of objects, in the attitudes of its creative personalities, in its institutions and customs. It is an art as much as a science to "read styles," and it requires religious intuition, on the basis of an ultimate concern, to look into the depth of a style, to penetrate to the level where an ultimate concern exercises its driving power.[25]

Three observations on this passage may serve to show how the notion of style is a suggestive term, but one for which the notion of hermeneutical *Verstehen* may be substituted.

First, whatever style's precise nature is, it seems to be at once ubiquitous and elusive throughout cultural functions. If one were to ask where to find a "style," Tillich states that it is not limited to any single aspect or activity of culture. Nor is style limited to any particular operation of thinking, or even to thinking generally. Styles may be found in theory and in practice, and be expressed in whole periods, institu-

---

[25]Tillich, *Systematic Theology*, 40.

tions, groups, or particular personalities. Though Tillich seems to draw the term mainly from the realm of art, he urges reflection on it in thinking, ethics, law, social life, politics—"in all other functions" of cultural life.[26] Given Tillich's invitation to theologians of culture to move into the often-elusive "depth" of cultural life, it may be appropriate that his notion of style is correspondingly ubiquitous and elusive. It is not surprising, then, that Tillich urges theologians of culture to use their "religious intuition" and own "ultimate concern" as part of their methods of reading styles.

This passage does not specify what style is, though the significance of "reading styles" is stressed. Tillich's discussions of style in the area of art perhaps provide some insight into what it is that theologians of culture read and then look more deeply into when they focus on style. In Tillich's discussions of art, his major claim is that style is a particular way that an expressive form is modified by its substance. Substance here is not subject matter, but rather "meaning" or import.[27] Substance is "the soil" out of which both the selection of subject matter and the creation of form arise.[28] It is primarily in the interplay of substance with form that one may read a style. As James Luther Adams summarizes, "style is the general determination of the aesthetic forms according to the way in which the import is grasped."[29] In order to read styles, then, one watches for the ways in which the substance of a cultural activity qualifies its forms.

Second, Tillich's use of the term *read* for the theologian's study of culture suggests the linguistic character of analyses in theology of culture. Reading styles, or studying ways that the substance of cultural functions qualifies their form, is especially a matter of studying the language of culture. Language, according to Tillich, "is fundamental for all cultural functions."[30] Language, one might say, has an omnipres-

---

[26]Ibid., 3:60-61.

[27]Adams, *What is Religion?* 78-90.

[28]Tillich, *Systematic Theology,* 3:60.

[29]Adams, *What is Religion?* 80.

[30]Ibid., 3:58.

ence (extending through all functions and endlessly variable)[31] that registers for the theologian of culture the style of a cultural activity, group, or creative personality. One who would read styles should study a culture's linguistic functions—not only the language of description and analytic explanation, but especially that of myth, symbol, and poetry. Tillich's commitment to the study of language is clear:

> Language reveals the basic characteristics of . . . cultural activities and affords a useful approach to their nature and their differences. If taken in this larger sense semantics could and should become a door to life in the dimension of the spirit.[32]

Third, it is "style" so conceived that is, as Tillich suggests in this passage, "the key" to discerning a religious dimension. However, the style that a theologian of culture may read is not necessarily the religious or theological element of the culture, though it might be the key to it. Elsewhere, Tillich states more clearly the nature of style's relation to the religious dimension. Style is the "immediate expression" of a cultural activity's religious concern.[33] Once one has read the style, it still remains necessary to "look into the depth of a style." It is in the style's depth that the religious or spiritual dimension is to be discerned.[34]

In the hermeneutical approach of this book, Tillich's theology-of-culture method of "reading styles" becomes a matter of studying the "understanding" (*Verstehen*) that is manifest in cultural anthropology. In the body of the text I will discuss in more detail the notion of "understanding" and its relationship to contemporary enterprises in "explanation" (*Erklären*). Introduced here are some fundamental features of *Verstehen* in terms of my three observations concerning Tillich's notion of style.

First of all, what hermeneutical theorists discuss as "understanding" reflects on style (style being that ubiquitous and elusive modification of cultural forms by their substance). Like style, *Verstehen* is not properly attributable to any one cultural realm or activity. As Paul Ri-

---

[31]Ibid.

[32]Ibid., 3:58-59.

[33]Tillich, *Theology of Culture*, 42-43.

[34]Ibid., 3-9.

coeur formulates it, understanding, whether borne by creative individuals or groups, "precedes, accompanies, closes, and thus envelopes"[35] cultural functions in which it is manifest. Ricoeur has especially attended to understanding as it occurs in the interpretation of texts, action, and history.[36] In each of these distinctive and complex realms, Ricoeur wields *Verstehen* as a term rich in ambiguity. It possesses a "density" that can designate the relation of cultural inquirers to "the whole of what is."[37] Although present in the methods and actions of a culture's inquirers, it thrives in its "non-methodic" realms; it "testifies, in the heart of epistemology, to a belonging of our being to the being which precedes every objectification, every opposition between subject and object."[38]

While "understanding" of this sort has occasionally been stressed in opposition to the practice of rigorous methods, it is Ricoeur's contribution to have articulated "understanding" *in* the manifold forms of disciplined explanation that characterize scholarly work.[39] Ricoeur's discussion of "understanding" has been fused with careful analyses of the explanatory functions of a culture's scholars. Hence, through the study of understanding one is able to advance Tillich's suggestion that styles are read in order to approach the ways a culture's "substance" (its fundamental import or meaning) engages its "form."

Second, the hermeneutical stress on "understanding" also distinguishes Tillich's concern that language be a focus. Hermeneutics endorses the belief that language is fundamental to the human cultural situation. According to Gadamer, language is fundamental to understanding and determines the hermeneutic object.[40] Ricoeur, though preserving a greater distinction between language and being, takes lan-

---

[35]Paul Ricoeur, *The Philosophy of Paul Ricoeur: An Anthology of His Work*, ed. Charles E. Reagan and David Stewart (Boston: Beacon Press, 1978) 165.

[36]Ibid., 149-66.

[37]Ibid., 165.

[38]Ibid.

[39]For further discussion of the *Verstehen* tradition in the social and human sciences, see Fred R. Dallmayr and Thomas A. McCarthy, eds., *Understanding and Social Inquiry* (Notre Dame: University of Notre Dame Press, 1977).

[40]Gadamer, *Truth and Method*, 408.

guage as essential for discerning how humans "have their world." Ricoeur therefore has exactingly analyzed metaphor, symbol, and narrative as linguistic forms that through a wealth of variations "give rise to thought." The metaphors and symbols of language have, for Ricoeur, not just semantic features, but nonsemantic ones as well.[41] The semantic and nonsemantic features are so related to each other that a scholar can be directed through the experience of language into the nonsemantic depths of existence. For Ricoeur, it becomes apparent that symbols have "rootedness" in a nonsemantic grasp of the cosmos, of the whole. Possessing these semantic and nonsemantic moments, language and especially symbol have a fundamental role in "understanding." It is the symbol that, in fact, gives birth to understanding so that *Verstehen* is always *in* and *beyond* the symbol. If the task of a theology of culture means discerning "understanding" in the hermeneutical sense, then the terms that function symbolically to nurture that understanding will need to be given special attention.

Third, in referring to the nonsemantic and deep, cosmically oriented features of symbols, I have perhaps already signaled that "understanding" may serve, as "style" did for Tillich, as the key to discernment of a "religious dimension" in a cultural activity. As with Tillich's notion of style, to discern the *Verstehen* of a cultural function is not necessarily to discern what is "religious" about that function. It will still remain necessary, therefore, to define the religious in a way enabling the theologian of culture to label an element of *Verstehen* "religious." As I will suggest in the final chapter, however, identifying the "understanding" will serve as the key to discernment of the religious dimension. In this project attention to "understanding" serves as the way into the "depth" or into the guiding orientations and attitudes of the cultural anthropologist who employs a number of fieldwork techniques, explanatory theories, cross-cultural comparisons, and generalizations.

In sum, attention here to the hermeneutical notion of *Verstehen* facilitates study of what Tillich called the "style" of a cultural activity. First, attending to *Verstehen* focuses on the elusive nonmethodic element in all cultural activities. Second, it encourages an approach to cul-

---

[41]Ricoeur, *Interpretation Theory*, 57-63.

tural functions that is focused especially on the linguistic forms nurturing *Verstehen*. Finally, it provides access to the fundamental postures and attitudes of a cultural activity, which provides a key context within which discernment of a religious dimension might occur.

Within the framework of positions characterizing a hermeneutical approach to theology of culture, I will discuss the activities of cultural anthropology in the following manner.

In chapter 1 I will examine those strands of theological tradition motivating and enabling this work's major claim. In what ways can Christian theological tradition be appropriated so that one might expect a religious dimension in cultural anthropology? How can this tradition still be appropriated in light of contemporary anthropology's often valid and necessary suspicions and criticisms of the Christian theological enterprise? Here I will argue that some long-standing theological concerns may be critically appropriated in the contemporary period with the aid of Ricoeur's notions of understanding and explanation. In this manner, the hermeneutical approach to discerning religious dimensions in cultural anthropology properly begins by turning reflexively to the tradition and preunderstanding that motivate the task.

Chapters 2, 3, and 4 together provide a portrait of cultural anthropology that displays the cultural anthropological world in some detail, while highlighting particular modes of "understanding." Chapter 2 sketches the main lines of cultural anthropology and explains my reasons for selecting Claude Lévi-Strauss and Marvin Harris as representative figures of it.

Chapters 3 and 4 constitute the work's center. There, my appropriation of strands of theological tradition and my general sketch of cultural anthropology issue in a presentation of Lévi-Strauss's and Harris's works. Chapter 3 focuses on what I will call, for reasons set forth below, these anthropologists' "horizontal hermeneutic"—their intercultural, interpretive reach "out" toward contemporary others. Chapter 4 takes up their "vertical hermeneutic"—their intracultural, interpretive reach "down" into the past of their own traditions. Together, these two chapters display the two thinkers' approaches to the pluralism of other contemporary cultures and to the pluralism of positions in the history of their own cultural tradition.

On the basis of this exploration of the particular field of cultural anthropology and of two anthropologists, I then attempt, in chapter 5, to specify the religious dimensions manifest in Lévi-Strauss's and Harris's enterprises. This specification will require two distinct moves. First, I explicitly discuss the kind of "understanding" that attends these anthropologists' explanations and thereby move closer to examining the "depth" of their work. It will still be necessary, second, to ask how it is that anthropological "understanding," as here studied, can be demarcated as "religious." The aim of the work, then, is to show how this discernment of a religious dimension is possible, not simply by discoursing on religious themes of ultimacy or the unconditioned, but by immersing oneself in particularities—the particularity of a selected discipline (cultural anthropology), and the particularity of a focus on Lévi-Strauss's and Harris's anthropological activities.

Chapter I

Religious Traditions
and Anthropological Suspicions

Theologians all to expose,
'tis the mission *of primitive man.*

Edward Burnette Tylor

Tylor penned this bit of doggerel during the West's rising consciousness of distant and "alien" peoples. For him, newly discovered religious practices and different cultural forms foreshadowed damning
criticism of any Western theologians prone to universal pronounce-
ments in their theological "anthropologies." Such theological pro-
nouncements, so this early ethnologist suspected, would soon be the
subject of a grand exposé accomplished by ethnology's knowledge of
the primitive "others."

Tylor's suspicion led the way for a number of suspicions held by
twentieth-century ethnologists and cultural anthropologists who ap-
praised Western religious thought and practice from their cross-cultural perspective. James G. Frazer, in his *Golden Bough* (1890),
compares Christian beliefs to "venerable walls mantled over with ivy
and mosses" that will crumble in the light of ethnology's comparative
knowledge of other peoples. Social anthropologist Evans-Pritchard
summarized the early ethnological suspicion: "One religion goes and
another comes, and seen from the point of view of rationalism and science they are all much alike, all children of fancy." One or more of
Christian theology's essential features—the resurrection of a man-God,

the Mass—are shown to be analogous to beliefs and practices found in other societies.[1]

The demonstration of this book's claim must begin with an acknowledgment of the long-standing suspicions of anthropologists concerning religion. For the theologian, this means acknowledging not only the *presence* of anthropological suspicion of Christian religion, but also the *value* of that suspicion. The intercultural and global character of contemporary human life makes it increasingly difficult to formulate theological language and doctrine without something like the anthropologist's suspicions concerning the culturally relative character of religion and theology. Theologians are increasingly called to make an anthropological or cross-cultural turn in their discourse, and this in part means acknowledging the critique of Western religion and theology that exposes the culturally bounded nature of their work. This acknowledgment is a condition for Christian theology's entry into intercultural conversation.

To acknowledge the presence and value of anthropological suspicions, however, is not necessarily to reduce "religious experience" to the social, political, or economic categories of the cultural anthropologist's disciplined inquiry. One can appropriately acknowledge the value of anthropological suspicions while still exploring the possibility that there is a persisting "religious dimension" to cultural anthropology's own inquiry.

The major task of this chapter is to show how a theological tradition might foster discernments of a religious dimension to human experience while respecting the valuable critique emerging from contemporary anthropological suspicion. Accordingly, this first chapter consists of three major sections. The first section summarizes the general structure of cultural anthropology's hermeneutics of suspicion concerning the category "religion." The second section explicitly discusses a strand of Christian theological tradition. I will attempt here to indicate why this theological tradition *partly* warrants the negative critique of anthropological suspicion, but also why it can survive that criticism to nurture cross-cultural inquiry. Critical retrieval of such a

---

[1]E. E. Evans-Pritchard, "Religion and the Anthropologists," *Blackfriars* 41 (1960): 110.

tradition suggests, at least, the possibility of a properly religious dimension to cross-cultural inquiry. The chapter's third section explores contemporary modes of reflection by which philosophical theologians discern a religious dimension to human inquiry generally. This section will provide a model for discerning a religious dimension to the contemporary field of cultural anthropology, and hence sets the agenda for the rest of the book.

Anthropology's "Hermeneutic of Suspicion"

The aim here is to describe the nature of the suspicions that guide cultural-anthropological interpretation of religious phenomena. These suspicions ground valuable critique, but they also are potentially reductive of religious experience. Anthropology's hermeneutic of suspicion[2] is an interpretive posture by which theology's "failures" in cross-cultural contexts are diagnosed, and by which theology's presumptions are, in Tylor's sense, "exposed." This suspicious posture involves, first, a preunderstanding of the emergence of cultural anthropology as critically transcending "folk anthropology." Second, anthropology's hermeneutic of suspicion includes a particular mode of inquiry into religious experience.

Critically transcending "folk anthropology"

To discuss cultural anthropology's preunderstanding, one must deal with anthropology's view of its own emergence in the West.

The development of what is known in the United States as contemporary "cultural anthropology" or, on the British scene, as "social anthropology," is relatively recent. This newness is stressed by a number of cultural-anthropology historians, who focus on the new contexts in Western culture enabling cultural anthropology to emerge; on cultural anthropology's new approaches to questions of human self-understanding; or on cultural anthropologists' recent and distinctive use of con-

---

[2]For discussion of "hermeneutics of suspicion" in relation to "hermeneutics of retrieval," see Paul Ricoeur, "The Critique of Religion," in *The Philosophy of Paul Ricoeur*, ed. Charles E. Reagan and David Stewart (Boston: Beacon Press, 1978) 213-22.

cepts like "culture."[3] General reflection on anthropological questions, of course, is hardly a new development. One needs, therefore, to characterize the kind of anthropological reflection that precedes the emergence of cultural anthropology and that can serve as a contrasting kind of "anthropology" to highlight what "cultural anthropology" is.

It is at this point that cultural anthropology's preunderstanding functions. Many cultural anthropologists view their discipline as defined by its critical transcendence of earlier, more provincial and cross-culturally unaware views of sociocultural phenomena. This attitude is perhaps most clearly expressed in the reflections offered by anthropologist A. I. Hallowell, for whom cultural anthropology emerges from and moves beyond what he terms "folk anthropology."[4]

To Hallowell, "folk anthropology" refers to the "body of observations, beliefs and socially sanctioned dogmas which parallel folk knowledge about other aspects of the phenomenal world." Such "folk anthropology" can take many forms and treats different kinds of anthropological questions. Hallowell, however, roots all these variations in a "universal interest in himself exemplified by man everywhere."[5] This interest is a "provincial tradition" characteristic of nonliterate cultures and the West's early cultures.

Hallowell sees the body of observations, beliefs, and socially sanctioned dogmas that constitute "folk anthropology" as inextricably bound up with mythology and religion. In Western culture, from which professional cultural anthropology was to emerge, the persons who formulated and disseminated such folk anthropologies were "priests,

---

[3]For examples of such historical summaries, see Murray J. Leaf, *Man, Mind and Science: The History of Anthropology* (New York: Columbia University Press, 1979) 78-92; and George W. Stocking, Jr., "Franz Boas and the Culture Concept in Historical Perspective," in *Race, Culture and Evolution* (New York: The Free Press, 1968) 195-233.

[4]A. Irving Hallowell, "The History of Anthropology as an Anthropological Problem," in *Contributions to Anthropology: Selected Papers of A. Irving Hallowell*, ed. with intros. Raymond D. Fogelson, Fred Eggan, Melford Spiro, George W. Stocking, Jr., Anthony F. C. Wallace, Wilcomb E. Washburn (Chicago: University of Chicago Press, 1976) 21-35.

[5]Ibid., 22.

theologians, philosophers and their equivalents."[6] Hallowell also suggests that in early Western culture "the level of knowledge represented in the traditional Christian worldview is equivalent to folk anthropology." Hallowell summarizes this Christian, folk anthropological world view as

> culturally constituted, untested knowledge about man and his world, reinforced by socially sanctioned religious values which gave it the stamp of ultimate truth. This traditional worldview of the West is the historical backdrop against which changes in the answers to anthropological questions may be plotted.[7]

On the basis of this reading, early Christian theology and tradition are essentially folk interpretations of anthropology and experience. Christian theology expresses and sanctions the "provincial" or "dogmatic" anthropologies of early Western cultures. Christian theology shares this characterization as "folk anthropology" with other mythological and religious interpretations of human experience offered by nonliterate or early literate cultures. As an anthropologist examining his own culture, Hallowell charts the progress of cultural anthropology's emancipation from this folk anthropology. He proceeds to interpret cultural anthropology in relation to "folk anthropology," and does so by means of philosophical and historical comments on humans' "universal interest" in themselves.

Philosophically, he interprets this "universal interest" as a "capacity" of humans to become objects to themselves so that they then contemplate their existence as beings living in a world conjunctively with other beings. This "capacity" is "concomitant with his [the human's] distinctive mode of cultural adaptation."[8] Hallowell sees cultural anthropology as a recent, striking example of this adaptation and as a product in Western culture of "a continuing and accelerating effort by man to obtain increasingly reliable knowledge about his own nature,

---

[6]Ibid.

[7]Ibid., 24.

[8]A. Irving Hallowell, "Personality, Culture and Society in Behavioral Evolution," in *Psychology: A Study of a Science*, ed. Sigmund Koch (New York: McGraw-Hill, 1963) 429-509.

behavior, his history and varying modes of life, as well as his place in the universe."[9] Hallowell's point is that cultural anthropology is the result of an "intellectual shift" from the provincial and socially sanctioned folk anthropologies to a

> level of systematic observations and inquiry detached from traditional beliefs and inspired by values giving prime emphasis to the search for more reliable knowledge of all aspects of human phenomena.[10]

Cultural anthropology is the "extension of science to the study of man."[11] In particular, this extension gives rise to the discipline's special task: to depict the character of the various cultures and the processes of stability, change, and development characteristic of them, and to study the similarities and differences of behavior in human groups.[12]

Hallowell, however, also interpreted this "intellectual shift," or "extension" in humans' universal interest in themselves, historically. Hallowell, who has by some been "acknowledged as the legitimate father of modern scholarly interest in the history of anthropology,"[13] does not himself provide this historical documentation.[14] For cultural-historical work on the rise of current anthropological theory, he relies primarily on such scholars as Margaret Hodgen, Frank E. Manuel, and Paul Hazard.[15] They provide him with a wealth of material illustrating

---

[9]Hallowell, "The History of Anthropology," 22.

[10]Ibid., 23.

[11]On the notion of such an extension, see also May Brodbeck, *Readings in the Philosophy of the Social Sciences* (New York: Macmillan, 1968) 2f.

[12]*International Encyclopedia of Social Science*, 1968 ed., under "Cultural Anthropology," by David G. Mandelbaum.

[13]Raymond D. Fogelson, "General Introduction," *Contributions to Anthropology*, xi. See also the qualifications and discussion of this acknowledgment offered by George W. Stocking, Jr., "Introduction," 18.

[14]When he treats the particular history of anthropology in its *American* context, then his contribution is more distinctively "historical."

[15]Margaret T. Hodgen, *Early Anthropology in the Sixteenth and Seventeenth Centuries* (Philadelphia: University of Pennsylvania Press, 1964); Paul Hazard, *The European Mind: The Critical Years—1680-1715* (New Haven: Yale University Press, 1953); Frank E. Manuel, *The Eighteenth Century Confronts the Gods* (Cambridge MA: Harvard University Press, 1959).

not only the "provincial" character of folk anthropologies, but also the contribution that the Age of Discovery made to the "transcendence" of folk anthropology and the emergence of cultural anthropology.

Hodgen's work, for example, illustrated Hallowell's characterization of folk anthropology. Moving through the classical and medieval literature, Hodgen explicated the sources of a "pre-Columbian system of ethnological thought," made up of "fragments of ancient learning and superstition, disfigured by careless repetition and invention."[16] Pliny the Elder (A.D. 23-79), Solinus (third century), Isidore of Seville's *Etymologies* (622-623), the Franciscan Bartholomeuw (1240-1260), and others all display this "pre-Columbian state of mind." They were predominantly mesmerized by the exotic, the unnatural, the "beastly," the fabulous, and other "epitomizations" of alien peoples. According to Hodgen, until the sixteenth century little effort was made to break free from the tradition of such epitomizing. "The legendary was preferred to the factual."[17] After 1502, when the Age of Discovery was accelerating, various collections of fashions and curios, though still displaying the lure of the legendary and of exotica, encouraged the collection and classification of data that contributed to the rise of a less-traditional "anthropology."[18]

Manuel's work, *The Eighteenth Century Confronts the Gods*, corresponds to many of Hodgen's perspectives. In particular, he builds on Hodgen's theme of the connection between the Christian theological tradition—whose Fathers rarely doubted or thought critically about the fabulous tales because of "the restraints of classicism and scholastic logic"—and folk anthropology. About the guardians of church life, Hodgen had remarked,

> As for man as a whole, the Fathers desired less to know him, than to save him. And this point of view, narrow as it was, communicated itself to the masses of simple folk who knelt at many altars.[19]

---

[16]Hodgen, *Early Anthropology*, 34.

[17]Ibid., 33.

[18]Ibid., 122.

[19]Ibid., 55.

Manuel carries Hodgen's analysis of the connection between folk anthropology and Christian tradition further to show how the increasing number of eighteenth-century travel reports not only called into question the fabulous tales but also "confronted the gods" and the God of Christian religion. As a result, earlier "naturalistic theories of the gods" and of religion were retrieved and consolidated to lay the groundwork for the well-known Enlightenment critique of the gods and of religion by English deists and French philosophers.[20] The eighteenth century, suggests Manuel, cultivated in embryonic form the idea that "the character of the gods was determined by socio-economic systems," or was part of a primitive mentality. Nineteenth- and twentieth-century compilations of data, he suggests, were then taken as "evidence confirming the older conceptions."[21]

Combining his philosophical comments about humans' universal interest in themselves with historical perspectives drawn from Hodgen, Manuel, and others, Hallowell suggests that a first phase in the history of cultural anthropology is "a history of the conditions, events, activities and ideas which undermined the provincial, folk anthropology." To him, the "undermining" of folk anthropology and its supportive mythologies and religion is necessary to the emergence of cultural anthropology's more independent observation, accumulation, and ordering of knowledge, which provides "more reliable answers to a wide range of anthropological questions."[22]

Although the undermining of folk anthropology was a necessary condition for the rise of cultural anthropology, it was not a sufficient one. Cultural anthropology also had to await a second stage, the development of what Hallowell calls a "comprehensive spatio-temporal frame of reference which embraces all living varieties of *homo sapiens,* as well as extinct cultures and peoples of the distant past and more ancient hominid types besides."[23] The spatial aspect of this frame of reference was provided eventually by the results of the Age of Discovery, which

---

[20]Manuel, *The Eighteenth Century Confronts the Gods,* 10-12.

[21]Ibid., 311.

[22]Hallowell, "The History of Anthropology," 25.

[23]Ibid.

made possible a "global geographical perspective." The temporal aspect, embodied later in evolutionary theories, was slower in coming due to persistent rationalizing of folk-anthropology traditions and European "ethnocentrism."[24]

Hallowell's portrayal of the rise of cultural anthropology is an example of the predominant form of self-understanding for other cultural anthropologists. They too view contemporary cultural anthropology as having emerged in the wake of newly accumulated data of exploration. It next received impetus through Enlightenment and post-Enlightenment critiques of religion and its provincial "folk anthropologies"; and most recently, it achieved coherence through the spatiotemporal frameworks provided by biology and geology. These developments continue to be revised and confirmed by anthropological fieldwork throughout the nineteenth and twentieth centuries. Historical reflections on the discipline's emergence suggest that this is a conventional view.[25]

A number of introductory texts in cultural and social anthropology present perspectives similar to Hallowell's. In 1910 A. C. Haddon viewed anthropology as not having come into its own until previous centuries of "facts and fancies" were overcome after the Enlightenment.[26] Clarke Wissler stressed the combined influences of the Age of Discovery and the Enlightenment on the experiences forming the background from which cultural anthropology developed.[27] More recent introductory texts also stress the "amazingly recent" nature of scientific

---

[24]When the temporal aspect did come, it was, according to Hallowell, due to three influences: (1) the great accumulation of data about diverse peoples that suggested a pattern of development as explanation for similarities and differences, (2) a "secularized" version of Christianity's notion of history moving along a line from creation to judgment, and (3) the expression of this linear conception of time in the disciplines of geology and classificatory biology (Hallowell, "The History of Anthropology," 25-32). Each of these influences can be seen in early anthropologist E. B. Tylor's work. See his *Primitive Culture*, 2 vols. (New York: Henry Holt and Co., 1889) 1:5-15, 25-26, 32, 58.

[25]See, for example, Leaf, *Man, Mind and Science*, ix-xii. While not a historian of the discipline, Kenelm Burridge also notes the conventionality of this view. See Burridge, *Encountering Aborigines: Anthropology and the Australian Aboriginal, A Case Study* (New York: Pergamon, 1973) 8-9.

[26]A. C. Haddon, *History of Anthropology* (London: Watts and Co., 1910) 1-2.

[27]Clarke Wissler, *An Introduction to Social Anthropology* (New York: Henry Holt and Co., 1929) 3-4.

knowledge about humanity; the influence of Enlightenment and Darwinian writings on the breakdown of "sacred dogmas"; the fact that "all that is new in anthropological theory begins with the Enlightenment"; or that "not until the age of the telegraph, the railroad and the steamship did cultural anthropology begin to become a science."[28]

Of course, this "conventional" view of anthropology's move beyond folk anthropology is not the view of all anthropologists. Increasingly, as anthropologists are influenced by the continental hermeneutics of Gadamer or by the "critical theory" of Habermas and others, there is a recognition that anthropology did not emerge simply as an extension of Enlightenment "reason" to the study of humankind. Anthropology, in its emergence, was not simply the fruit of rational deliberation over new facts turned up through encounter of other peoples. Anthropology itself emerges from a tradition.[29] In fact, as Geertz notes, this emergence entailed the throwing off of the Enlightenment notion of a "uniformitarian view of man."[30] Even the anthropologists who generate these criticisms, however, suggest that theirs is not the "conventional view" functioning in anthropology. The conventional view of anthropology's emergence is a part of the "positivist" or "scientistic" orientation that functions often as the prevailing paradigm in the social sciences.[31]

Critically transcending religion?

Anthropology's hermeneutic of suspicion includes not only a preunderstanding of its transcendence of folk anthropology, but also a

---

[28]See Felix M. Keesing, *Cultural Anthropology: The Science of Custom* (New York: Rinehart and Co., 1958) 9-10; Mischa Titiev, *Introduction to Cultural Anthropology* (New York: Henry Holt and Co., 1959) 2-3; Marvin Harris, *The Rise of Anthropological Theory: A History of Theories of Culture* (New York: Thomas Crowell, 1968) 2.

[29]Robert Scholte, "Anthropological Traditions: Their Definition," in *Anthropology: Ancestors and Heirs,* ed. Stanley Diamond (The Hague: Mouton, 1980) 53-87.

[30]Clifford Geertz, *The Interpretation of Cultures* (New York: Basic Books, 1973) 34-35.

[31]In addition to Burridge's discussion of the conventional view, see the recent work of Robert C. Ulin, *Understanding Cultures: Perspectives in Anthropology and Social Theory* (Austin: University of Texas Press, 1984) xvii, 67-70.

dominant mode of approach for studying religious experience. I should summarize this major approach of anthropologists concerning religion.

The position of Hallowell, and most of the historians on whom he draws, is that religious tradition, because of its expressing and sanctioning of provincial folk anthropology, is also "transcended." As Hallowell concluded,

> The biblical age of the world had been transcended and the way was cleared for a more objective approach to anthropogenesis, and an increasing precision in ordering and interpreting human phenomena in time and space.[32]

Given the expressing and sanctioning functions of the Christian tradition in relation to folk anthropology, it is unsurprising that Western culture's anthropologists should understand themselves, as Hallowell asserts, to have transcended also the religious tradition of their culture. Anthropologists' discussion of the historical and intellectual "transcendence" of Western religious tradition has not always been as measured and polite as Hallowell's. E. E. Evans-Pritchard, drawing upon diverse texts, summarizes anthropologists' stances toward religion, especially that of their own Western culture, as "for the most part bleakly hostile."[33]

From their writings, Evans-Pritchard presents what he sees as the predominant attitude. Herbert Spencer is said to have found religion both "untrue and useless," and God as "unknowable and otiose." Religion for E. B. Tylor was based on illusion, "a sort of hallucination brought about by the reflection of immature minds on such phenomena as death, dreams, and trance." Evans-Pritchard finds similar attitudes manifested by Frazer's contemporaries: Westermarck, Hobhouse, Rivers, Seligman, Radcliffe-Brown, Malinowski. All of these are described as at best "agnostics and positivists" in their general attitude toward the religious tradition of Western culture.

The situation was not significantly different in the United States. Lewis Henry Morgan is said to have refused to have anything to do with religion, abhorring all ritualistic religion and therefore detesting the

---

[32]Hallowell, "The History of Anthropology," 33.

[33]Evans-Pritchard, "Religion and the Anthropologists," 104-18.

Roman Catholic Church. According to Evans-Pritchard, "Among the last generation of distinguished American anthropologists, there was not one who gave assent to any creed (unless agnosticism be accounted one) or who regarded all religious belief as other than illusion." Religion, though thoroughly studied, is considered superstition and thus viewed with suspicion. "Religion is superstition to be explained by anthropologists, not something an anthropologist, or indeed any rational person, could himself believe in."[34]

How then does this "bleakly hostile" suspicion become embodied in the approach taken to the anthropological study of religion? The components of the mode of approach are: first, to focus "religion" as a set of phenomena found largely outside of Western society, and second, to study religion in what Victor Turner has called a "pragmatic" fashion.

Francis L. K. Hsu has investigated the first component explicitly; he attempts to summarize anthropology's approach to the study of Western Christianity. In 1967 he expressed the concern that his anthropologist colleagues had failed "to examine Christianity critically, in contrast to the spirit with which they have examined the belief systems of some of the other societies."[35]

Hsu ponders the possibility that this uncritical attention to Christian tradition partially accounts for anthropologists' inability to construct a "tenable theory of the relationship between culture and religion." Anthropology's many fine studies of other societies' religious life ably display its critical transcendence of earlier folk anthropologies and of much Christian thought. But anthropologists have not made a comparably critical move to study Christian tradition. Hsu is not calling for some positive appropriation or affirmation of the religious, but rather is pointing out that lack of such critical attention by anthropologists often means that "their view of religion everywhere is the Western folk view of Christianity and religion."[36] To illustrate his point, Hsu cites a number of classic texts in anthropological study, all of which he

---

[34]Ibid., 110.

[35]Francis L. K. Hsu, "Christianity and the Anthropologist," *International Journal of Comparative Sociology* 8 (March 1967): 1-19.

[36]Ibid., 3.

claims do not seriously discuss Christianity. Such texts include those by Keesing, Lessa and Vogt, Herskovits, Beals and Hoijer, Linton, Mead, Malinowski, Radcliffe-Brown, Kluckhohn and Howells.[37] One of the implications that may be drawn from Hsu is that while cultural anthropologists may display a sophisticated, critical transcendence of Western folk anthropologies and of the religious expressions that sanction these anthropologies, they often hold uncritical, "folk" views of Christian tradition. This may be a serious oversight, especially if Christian tradition is unequivalent to the folk anthropologies it has sanctioned.

There are other implications of an approach that locates religion outside of anthropologists' own culture. If cultural anthropology's "transcendence" of Western Christianity's folk anthropology results in focusing anthropological research mainly on other societies' religious phenomena, rather than on religion in the anthropologist's own society, then it also inhibits evaluating the claim of this work that there is a religious dimension to the inquiry of cultural anthropology itself. In fact, when anthropologists define or characterize religion, they often do so in ways that oppose the "religious" to their own mode of social-science inquiry. Marvin Harris understands religious belief as "any culturally patterned belief about man, culture, or nature that is not a product of scientific research" or "based on a minimum of such tests or none at all."[38] Religion, according to Harris, is one of several "other ways of knowing" subordinate to science when it comes to knowing the world in which we live.[39]

The separability of religion from the anthropologist's "scientific" inquiry is especially apparent when religion is viewed only as phenomena to be inquired about. For the purpose of having a "phenomenal referent" for anthropological study of religion, anthropologists Robin Horton, James Goody, and Melford Spiro concur that belief in helpful or harmful superhuman beings is the "core variable" in a definition of

---

[37]See Hsu, "Christianity and the Anthropologist," 4.

[38]Marvin Harris, *Culture, Man and Nature: An Introduction to General Anthropology* (New York: Thomas Crowell, 1971) 536-37.

[39]Marvin Harris, *Cultural Materialism: The Struggle for a Science of Culture* (New York: Random House, 1979).

religion that approaches universal distribution.[40] Such a definition, Spiro hastens to add, is only a "nominal definition" and not a "formal" one trying to get at what religion "really is."[41] The nominal definition is the one to be sought, because it allows formulation of hypotheses susceptible to empirical, cross-cultural testing.

When Spiro and others begin to speak of limiting themselves to "nominal" definitions, the second major component of the anthropological approach to religion begins to emerge; that is, a tendency to adopt what Victor Turner calls a basically "pragmatic" outlook for the study of religion.[42] In addition to those who fashion only nominal definitions, Turner also labels as "pragmatic" those who limit themselves to the study of the "function" of religion or of religious "conduct." He presents Clifford Geertz's work as representative of this pragmatism because Geertz limits the study of religion to "discovering just what sorts of beliefs and practices support what sorts of faith under what conditions," or how religious faith "is sustained in this world by symbolic forms and social arrangements."[43]

What is lost in such pragmatic approaches, according to Turner, is inquiry into "the ultimate roots of the faith of an individual or community." He considers his own focus on ritual as "processual" and composed of "structures of experience" as important for turning an-

---

[40]Melford Spiro, "Religion: Problems of Definition and Explanation," in *Anthropological Approaches to the Study of Religion*, ed. Michael Banton (London: Tavistock Publications, 1966) 85-126; J. Goody, "Religion and Ritual: The Definitional Problem," *British Journal of Sociology* 12 (1961): 142-64; and Robin Horton, "A Definition of Religion and Its Uses," *Journal of the Royal Anthropological Institute* 90 (1960): 201-26.

For a notable exception among anthropologists to those who limit religion to "belief in spiritual beings," see Mary Douglas, *Purity and Danger: An Analysis of the Concepts of Pollution and Taboo* (London: Routledge & Kegan Paul, 1966) 27-28.

[41]Spiro, "Religion," 91.

[42]Victor Turner, "Religion in Current Cultural Anthropology," in *What is Religion? An Inquiry for Christian Theology*, ed. Mircea Eliade and David Tracy (New York: Seabury, 1980) 68.

[43]Turner is citing Clifford Geertz in *Islam Observed* (New Haven and London: Yale University Press, 1968) 2. Other writings on religion by Geertz cannot be so properly described as "pragmatic." See "Religion as a Cultural System," *The Interpretation of Cultures* (New York: Basic Books, 1973) 87-125.

thropology to the problem of religion understood in more than pragmatic terms. Turner suggests locating religion in several "crucial phases
of human experience" that are operative in many realms. This need not
call for a "formal" definition of what religion "really is," but it does call
for one that goes beyond the pragmatic approach by locating the religious within human experience, in "crucial phases" of experience that
lie at the root of symbolic forms of expression and functions of social
arrangements. This definition would include the possibility that such
"crucial phases" might affect aspects of the anthropologist's own experience as well as the experience of those studied.[44] He states that crucial phases, such as religious experiences of "liminality," also
characterize philosophical and scientific thought.[45]

Turner's view, which places religion within human experience, is
consonant with a critical, more thorough understanding of Christian
theological tradition. In the next section I shall attempt to demonstrate
that a more critical awareness of the Western Christian tradition will
show Christianity to possess "theological anthropologies" that cannot
be wholly subsumed under, or taken as equivalent to, the folk anthropology critically transcended in cultural anthropology. Indeed, much
of Christianity, which did sanction and express provincial folk anthropologies, needed exposure to the criticism that was mounted by emergent cultural anthropology. The point is not that this criticism is
unnecessary, but rather that the Christian tradition may not be reducible to folk anthropology. Christianity's theological anthropologies tend
to relate religion to human experience in such a way that cultural anthropological inquiry does not critically transcend, or distance itself
from, theological anthropology as much as it does from folk anthropology. Not all of Christian tradition merely sanctions folk anthropology's
"superstition." Not all of the theological tradition warrants the anthropologist's "bleakly hostile" suspicion.

---

[44]Turner acknowledges, for example, the effect of Western religious tradition on
his own anthropological inquiry. Victor Turner, *Image and Pilgrimage in Christian Culture: Anthropological Perspectives* (New York: Columbia University Press, 1978) xv.

[45]Victor Turner, *Dramas, Fields and Metaphors: Symbolic Action in Human Society*
(Ithaca and London: Cornell University Press, 1974) 242.

Christian Theological Tradition:
Possibilities for Retrieval

H.-G. Gadamer has offered a sustained argument for the importance of tradition as a source of truth.[46] Contemporary quests for truth
involve not only a distancing of inquirers from a past tradition, but also
a rootedness in that tradition.[47] Tradition, with its prejudices, is her-
meneutically productive. Gadamer believes that the role of tradition in
inquiry is significant to quests for truth because of its prejudices. Since
the Enlightenment, it has been fashionable to cultivate a prejudice
against prejudice. For Gadamer, standing within a tradition of prejudices is inescapable. What matters is to understand that there may be
"legitimate" as well as "illegitimate" prejudices.

Gadamer's understanding of tradition illuminates what I attempt
in this section. Christian theological tradition may embody prejudices
that are "legitimate" or "illegitimate" in light of contemporary anthropological suspicions. I wish to show here that Christian theology, while
seeking to be appropriate to its own traditional sources, also displays
prejudices that cannot easily be dismissed by current anthropological
suspicions. This is not to deny that current anthropological critique does
lay bare many of the Christian tradition's illegitimate prejudices (its
provincialisms, dogmatisms, and ethnocentrisms), and I shall attempt
to signal some of these along the way. But the tradition also possesses
prejudices that are legitimate in the light of the cross-cultural scholar's
suspicions. Such prejudices, in fact, may constitute part of the tradition
within which today's cross-cultural scholar works. I will view these legitimate prejudices as possibilities for retrieving that tradition in some
critically revised form.

If retrieval of a religious tradition such as Christian theology is possible in light of anthropology's hermeneutic of suspicion, then it must
display two major traits. First, it must display an openness to discoveries of human knowledge. It has already been shown how important
an Age of Discovery was to anthropology's self-understanding. Ever-
refined and increased knowledge of sociocultural phenomena, culti-

---

[46]Gadamer, *Truth and Method*, 235-73.

[47]Ibid., 241-53.

vated through human mind and sense, is basic to anthropological perspectives. Christian theological tradition, if it is to persist as a conversation partner with contemporary anthropology, must show itself open to human discovery and not closed to it. Particularly, this means showing that what the theological tradition claims is revealed by God concerning humanity does not override human discovery or prevent openness to the discoveries of natural and social science.

Second, keeping in mind anthropology's cross-cultural orientation, a retrievable theological tradition must also display a trait of openness to the "alien," to the distant other. Christian theological tradition, though mostly nurtured by European and American cultural systems, must show itself capable of critically transcending its own sociocultural frame so as to value the other. If the tradition only "sanctions and expresses" its own beliefs and practices, then it becomes reducible to the folk anthropology that contemporary cultural anthropology rightly calls into question. One will need to ask, then, how the tradition is itself oriented to others; how it relates its particular beliefs, symbols, and rituals to the universe of diverse others. Can one tradition accept the other as other, or must it always force the other into the constraining patterns of its own particular vision?

I will bring these two traits to light by reference to the classical theological systems of four theologians: St. Augustine, St. Thomas Aquinas, John Calvin, Friedrich Schleiermacher. In their works elements can be found of a theological anthropology that cannot be reduced to folk anthropology and that, hence, are not quite so easily dismissed by anthropological suspicions. Folk anthropology's provincialisms, dogmatisms, and ethnocentrisms may persist in the everyday life of Western Christians, in many intellectual figures who sanctioned Christian theologies, and indeed in the four theologians presented here. There have always been proponents of the Christian tradition who were ready to oppose the human discoveries of a Galileo, or the new sociocultural data of a Captain James Cook. Missionaries like Hiram Bingham, who viewed the native Sandwich Islanders (Hawaiians) only as potential converts existing in "a low and revolting state of society,"[48]

---

[48]Hiram Bingham, *A Residence of Twenty-One Years in the Sandwich Islands; or,*

have too frequently dominated the history of Christians' cross-cultural encounters. But the four theologians treated here, who so influenced Christian thought, each exploited the intellectual resources of their Western tradition in ways that could promote openness to human discovery and to diverse others.

Theology as open to human discovery

In the thought of each theologian considered here, openness to discovery of the new, through human mind and sense, is affirmed—but in relation to the revealing presence of the divine. The pertinent question here centers on how the tradition conceives of the divine relation to human discovery. All I wish to establish is that in the tradition as I present it, the divine presence does not override or replace powers of human discovery. Human discovery of the new is not to be resisted on the supposition that a divine illumination or revelation to believers is itself sufficient. Christian theological anthropology, in different ways, may in fact support human discovery of the new. This is in marked contrast to cultural anthropologists' view of religious folk anthropology, which stubbornly sanctions and expresses the tradition *against* the new encountered by human discovery.

St. Augustine's theological anthropology has been read as having an epistemology wherein human powers of discovery, especially by way of the senses, are negligible. Emphasis is placed instead on the presence of the divine light and the divine forms (the *rationes aeternae*) that "illumine" the human mind.[49]

Such a reading of his epistemology may be pressed to the point where St. Augustine becomes, as for Paul Tillich, an originator of one of "the two

---

The Civil, Religious and Political History of Those Islands, Comprising a Particular View of the Missionary Operations Connected with the Introduction and Progress of Christianity and Civilization among the Hawaiian People, 2d ed. (New York: Sherman Converse, 1848) 49.

For a fuller treatment of both the positive and negative contributions of missionaries to ethnographic studies, see Frank A. Salamone, "Anthropologists and Missionaries: Competition or Reciprocity," *Human Organization* 36 (1977): 407-12.

[49]For histories of theological traditions stressing this reading of St. Augustine's "illumination theory" of human knowing, see C. E. Schützinger, *The German Controversy on St. Augustine's Illumination Theory* (New York: Regent Press, 1960).

types of the philosophy of religion."[50] For Tillich, Augustine offers a true "mysticism" in which knowers experience "the identity of subject and object in relation to Being Itself."[51] On the basis of this reading of Augustine, the knowing soul, thus conditioned by the divine light, can confidently take itself as a starting point for discovering the *prius* of all existence, of all knowledge and of the good.[52] Human powers of discovery may thus seem so radically conditioned that they are lost in the divine presence. The tendency is keenly displayed in St. Bonaventure's phrasing: "For certitudinal knowledge, the evidence of the eternal light concurs as the complete and sole reason of knowledge."[53]

There can be, however, no unambiguous "illuminationist" view of St. Augustine's epistemology. As important as the "divine light" is for him—and indeed it does grant to his epistemology its distinctive mark—there are significant features that qualify descriptions of it as illuminationist, as an innatism, or as a religious a priorism.

The first of two of these qualifying features is the important role that St. Augustine allows for "knowable things" in the process of human discovery and knowing. True, one set of these "knowable things" is made up of the *rationes aeternae* that ultimately rest in the divine intellect. The human mind must be "converted," turned toward the light-filled forms so that divine illumination might have its full effect.[54] The soul's relation to this kind of knowable thing is "wisdom" (*sapientia*). Knowing by way of relation to the forms tends to support the illuminationist reading of Augustine's epistemology.

---

[50]Paul Tillich, "Two Types of the Philosophy of Religion," *Theory of Culture* (New York: Oxford University Press, 1959).

[51]Ibid., 14.

[52]Note how St. Augustine is set forth this way in the work of John E. Smith, "Self and World as Starting Points for Theology," *International Journal for the Philosophy of Religion* 1 (Summer 1970): 97-111.

[53]St. Bonaventure, *Quaestions disputatae de scientia Christi*, q.4, in *Medieval Philosophy: From St. Augustine to Nicholas of Cusa*, ed. John Wippel and Allan B. Wolter, OFM (New York: The Free Press, 1969) 314.

[54]St. Augustine, *On Free Choice of the Will*, trans. Anna S. Benjamin and L. H. Hackstaff (Indianapolis: Bobbs-Merrill Co., 1964) 97; and St. Augustine, *Confessions*, 4.30.

The "eternal forms," however, make up only one type of the "knowable things" available to the soul. The other is the "material sense object" or "temporal object" that reports to the mind.[55] Knowing by relation to these knowable things is *scientia*, a distinctive knowledge marked off from *sapientia*. Augustine stresses *sapientia* as the preferable way that "no one doubts."[56] But this is not to render the way of *scientia* negligible. *Scientia* "presents itself before" the preferred wisdom. Knowledge by the material sense object draws the soul's attention to what is happening outside of it. It is true that the message of the sense object is a "negative" one, "crying out" to the soul, "We are not God, but he made us."[57] It is true that the soul is thereby prompted to turn to the *rationes aeternae*. Nevertheless, as indicators to the soul that it should turn to the forms, the sense objects play a significant role; they draw the soul's attention to things outside of them, so that when the soul makes its next interior move, it will be a "rightly turned one," upward to God. It is this attention-getting power, referred to in Augustine's *De Trinitate* as "knowledge" (*scientia*), that "presents itself before" the preferred "wisdom" (*sapientia*).[58] *Scientia* does not provide rational demonstration as a way to God or as sufficient for human knowing, but the mind does "practice" and "exercise" itself in the lower things available to sense knowledge,[59] in the "lower trinities" of creation, for example, "in order that we might come to the contemplation of that trinity which is God" (*sapientia*).[60]

The second feature that qualifies an unambiguous illuminationist reading of St. Augustine's epistemology comes from the relatively independent status he grants the human mind. Although it is important for the mind to know by way of the divine light, this mind is distinguished by Augustine as another light, a "created light." It is a know-

[55]St. Augustine, *Confessions*, 10.6.9, and Schützinger, *German Controversy*, 21.

[56]St. Augustine, *De Trinitate*, 12.15.25.

[57]St. Augustine, *Confessions*, 10.6.9.

[58]St. Augustine, *De Trinitate*, 15.15.25.

[59]Ibid., 15.1.1.

[60]Ibid., 13.20.26.

ing light that God has made, but that is not the light that God is.[61] The knowing soul knows, not by way of an immediate presence of the divine light, but as one of the several created lights.[62] The knowing soul, then, while never moving out of relation to the divine light, has for itself a distinctiveness that is not lost in the divine presence. Martin Grabmann summarizes Augustine's "illumination theory" in a way that observes the important qualifications by which Augustine makes a place for the powers of distinctively human discovery.

> Augustine conceives the creative influence of the first divine truth upon the intellect, then, not in the sense of a mediation or depression of an already formed idea, but rather in the sense that we work together with God in the formation of the ideas. We receive from the uncreated light the illuminatory power to discern the intelligible in the sensible world which surrounds us. Although our ideas are the work of this power, it however comes from above, because these ideas in us are a light which comes from the divine light and is an emanation, a lower grade of this light.[63]

One need not labor so hard to show in the thought of St. Thomas Aquinas his valuation of human powers of discovery. There would seem to be little possibility of attributing to Thomas a notion of the divine presence or of revelation that prohibits openness to science and human discovery. The place usually marked out for Thomas in Christian tradition is one wherein the affirmation of human knowledge is primary. Theologians have in fact occasionally objected to the apparent autonomy Thomas attributes to human powers of discovery.

According to Tillich, for example, Thomas has a "sense-bound epistemology" that can only arrive at God with the help of the category

---

[61]St. Augustine, *Contra adversarium legis et prophetarium,* 1.7.10. *"Aliud est lux, quod est Deus, aliud est lux, quam fecit Deus"* ("The light which God is, is one thing; the light which God makes is another").

[62]The other created lights, in addition to the "intellectual light," are physical or sensory light and the light of angels or of grace. St. Augustine, *Confessions,* 10.4.51, and *Contra Faustus,* 22.9, 22.7. Cf. St. Augustine, *De Genesi ad litterum,* 7.15.21, cited in Martin Grabmann, *Der Göttliche Grund menschlicher Wahrheitserkenntnis nach Augustinus und Thomas von Aquin* (Muenster in Westfallen: Verlag der Baschendorffschen Verlagsbuchhandlung, 1924) 27.

[63]Translated from Grabmann, *Der Göttliche Grund,* 24.

of causality, the result being that the concept of God's existence is brought down "to the level of a stone or a star."[64] John E. Smith too tends to see Thomas as a purveyor of "the other classic Western theology" that is characterized by a starting point in the world of finite things.[65]

Throughout Thomas's writings there indeed are numerous passages that seem to support the "sense-bound" interpretation of his epistemology. Grabmann stresses the importance to Thomas, for example, of the phenomena of the senses: *"Alle geistige Erkenntnis beginnt mit Sinneserfahrung."* In addition, the human's "active intellect" seems to possess an autonomy greater than Augustine's intellectual light; certainly Thomas delineates its activity in more detail. Throughout his *Summa Theologica* he explicitly refers to the "created intellect." In his *Compendium of Theology* he speaks of "man's natural light."[66] Several passages suggest the autonomy of this natural light. In his commentary on Boethius's *De Trinitate,* Thomas suggests that

> the human soul, which possesses in itself the active and passive potency, is completely equipped for the knowledge of natural truth and no new divine light is necessary for it, since the light of reason is fully sufficient.[67]

Thomas attempts even to enlist St. Augustine's support, suggesting that St. Augustine appreciated a certain "sufficiency" of the created intellect.[68] In his *Summa Theologica,* he therefore uses Augustine to remind readers that not all knowledge is due to participation in the "eternal exemplars" or in "the unchangeable truth."[69]

---

[64]Tillich, "Two Types of the Philosophy of Religion," 18.

[65]Smith, "Self and World as Starting Points for Theology," 104.

[66]St. Thomas Aquinas, *Compendium of Theology,* trans. Cyril Vollert (St. Louis: B. Herder Book Co., 1955) 136-37.

[67]St. Thomas Aquinas, *Boethius de Trinitate,* q.1, a.1, cited in Grabmann, *Der Göttliche Grund,* 58.

[68]For a discussion of the ways in which St. Thomas frequently seeks to harmonize his own thought with St. Augustine's, note Schützinger, *German Controversy,* 39-47.

[69]St. Thomas Aquinas, *Summa Theologica,* 1, q.84, a.1. Quotations from *Summa Theologica* are taken from *Basic Writings of St. Thomas Aquinas,* 2 vols., ed. and annotated with an intro. by Anton C. Pegis (New York: Random House, 1945).

Passages and perspectives like those mentioned above demonstrate Thomas's strong affirmation of human knowledge and discovery. The main question that arises now is whether his affirmation of an allegedly "sufficient" intellect still stands in any meaningful relation to the divine presence. A careful reading of Thomas's corpus reveals that Thomas indeed qualifies his notion of the human intellect's sufficiency. Therefore, it hardly does Thomas's theory of knowledge justice to say only that he begins with "world" (Smith) or that he has a "sense-bound" epistemology (Tillich).[70] While it has been pointed out that Thomas's theological anthropology readily displays an appreciation for human powers of discovery, it remains to indicate how this appreciation still involves qualifications of their sufficiency.

One can highlight three aspects of Thomas's thought that qualify the human intellect's sufficiency. First, for Thomas, possession of knowledge of "supernatural truth" always requires more than the natural light. In essence, a divine light needs to be added to the natural light.[71] But one need not discuss his notion of "supernatural truth" to see his qualifications of the created intellect's sufficiency. The next two qualifications concern the knowledge of "natural truth" and its relation to the divine presence.

The second qualification is apparent from Thomas's view of the intellect's encounter with the sense object. For Thomas, the human intellect does not encounter sense objects as such, but rather "abstracts" from them their "form" or kernel.[72] This form is the object that is adequate to the human mind. Grabmann rightly views this form as a copy of the divine idea (*Nachbild*), a "substantialized divine idea." Thus one might say that the divine presence is etched into the deep places of sensory knowledge, into the sense object, so that "man's natural light," though distinguishable from the divine presence, is not separate from it.

---

[70]Tillich's characterization of Thomas's epistemology in his "Two Types of the Philosophy of Religion" was formulated at a time when the neo-Thomist appropriations of Thomas were not well known. See John C. Robertson, "Tillich's Two Types and the Transcendental Method," *Journal of Religion* 55 (April 1975): 199-219.

[71]Aquinas, *Boethius de Trinitate*, q.1, a.1.

[72]Grabmann, *Der Göttliche Grund*, 47.

A third qualification of the created intellect's sufficiency can be seen in Thomas's reference to the created intellect as "participation" in the divine light. The intellect's abstracting from sense experience is described by Thomas as resting on previously received "first principles."[73] These are arrived at "without effort," "flowing in" as a "natural habit."[74] This effortless and "natural" activity of the intellect does not suggest its autonomy from the divine presence. Quite to the contrary, it suggests again just how deeply the divine presence is etched into human being and knowing. One might say that for Thomas the intellect's sufficiency is enabled by the pervasive divine presence. Thomas can show his Augustinian side then: "The very light of reason is a participation of the divine light."[75] Perhaps a passage from Etienne Gilson's eloquent *Spirit of Medieval Philosophy* accounts best for Thomas acknowledging both the created intellect's sufficiency and its conditioning by the divine presence.

> For St. Augustine as for St. Thomas, *coeli ennarrant gloriam Dei*, and if the heavens declare his glory it is because they bear His likeness; only with St. Thomas the divine likeness sinks for the first time into the heart of nature, goes beyond order, number, and beauty, reaches and saturates the very physical structure, and touches the very efficacy of causality.[76]

The tension between affirming discoveries by human intellectual powers and affirming God as the condition of all knowing is especially acute in the thought of John Calvin. At several points in his master work, *Institutes of the Christian Religion,* he lauds discoveries by the "secular writers" in matters of art and science. He seriously and frequently qual-

---

[73]Following Aristotle in *Ethics,* 6, Aquinas takes "first principles" as those principles upon which all scientific knowledge is based. See Aquinas, *Summa Theologica,* 1-2, q.51, a.1. Cf. Aristotle, *Ethics,* 6.6. 1141a-b, 31-33.

[74]St. Thomas Aquinas, *De virtutibus in communi,* q.1, a.8, cited in Grabmann, *Der Göttliche Grund,* 50; *Quodlibeta,* 10, a.7, cited in ibid., 59; *De Veritate,* q.10, a.8, cited in ibid., 55.

[75]Aquinas, *Summa Theologica,* 1, q.12, a.11. Thomas is citing Augustine's *Soliloquies,* 1.8.

[76]Etienne Gilson, *The Spirit of Medieval Philosophy,* Gifford Lectures, 1931-1932, trans. A. C. Dornes (London: Sheed and Ward, 1936) 141.

ifies this praise, however, by saying that the human mind is "fallen and perverted from its wholeness."[77] What sense is one to make of Calvin's openness to human powers of discovery in light of this stringent qualification?

Fundamental for understanding Calvin's position here is his distinction between "heavenly things" and "earthly things" as two kinds of object for the human "faculty" of understanding.[78] Generally, Calvin's valuation of the human mind's powers of discovery is strong when he considers its study of earthly things, but weak concerning knowledge of heavenly things.

According to Calvin, the human mind's ability to discern what is worthy and unworthy with regard to heavenly things is severely curtailed by humanity's "fall from uprightness" and persistence in sin.[79] True, for Calvin there is indeed a certain *divinitatis sensum* in human natural knowledge, an "awareness of divinity," a "vague general veneration for God," a "seed of religion" implanted or engraved in all people's minds that cannot be effaced.[80] But due to the Fall and persistent human sin, this *divinitatis sensum* is fleeting. It is only a "slight taste" of God's divinity, an ever-so-slight initiation into knowledge of heavenly things that is swiftly sabotaged by humanity's giddy imagination.[81] Scripture with the "witness of the Spirit," then, becomes necessary as "spectacles" for humankind's knowledge of heavenly things.[82]

---

[77]John Calvin, *Institutes of the Christian Religion*, 2 vols., ed. John T. McNeill, trans. Ford Lewis Battles (Philadelphia: Westminster Press, 1960) 2.2.15. This edition was made from the 1559 Latin text and collated with earlier editions. The numerals refer to the relevant book, chapter, and section in the McNeill and Battles edition.

[78]Ibid., 2.2.13.

[79]Ibid., 1.2.1.

[80]For Calvin's treatment of this "divine sense," see 1.2.2, 1.3.1, 1.3.2-3. The divine sense has a numinous quality, as suggested by Calvin's reference to it as a "veneration" of God. But at the same time it also has a moral tone, being integrally bound up with the "worm of conscience" that "gnaws away within" (1.3.3). This numinous and moral *divinitatis sensum* is cited by Calvin later in the *Institutes* to account for the "conception of equity" on which all people agree and which is the "seed of political order" among them (2.2.13).

[81]Ibid., 2.2.18.

[82]Ibid., 1.6.1.

Regarding "earthly things," the human understanding's distinguishing powers and its resources for marshaling knowledge are more trustworthy. This class of things includes government, household management, all mechanical skills, and the liberal arts.[83] Astronomy, medicine, and natural science "thrust themselves upon even the untutored and ignorant." Calvin joins with Seneca to argue that those who have dipped into these forms of earthly knowledge and into the liberal arts are aided in attempts to penetrate the secrets of divine wisdom.[84] He regards with "great admiration" the knowledge of the ancients, "preeminent" in their "sharp and penetrating investigation" of inferior things. Their "natural gifts," though corrupted by sin, also give off a "light which still shines in the darkness."[85] Calvin, therefore, cautions the reader not to condemn the human understanding; for its gifts display its enduring, natural captivation by love of truth.[86] Far from rejecting truth, a genuine religion, he asserts with Lactantius, must be joined with truth.[87]

Calvin does not clarify how this valuable knowledge of earthly things is related to the knowledge of heavenly things that rests so firmly on divine revelation. That the divine has some role in providing the valuable knowledge of "heathen philosophers" is clear from his discussion of the "common" or "general grace of God" (*Generalem Dei gratiam*).[88] This good knowledge of earthly things "flows from" God, and makes up the "drops of wisdom" coming from God, who is the "sole fountain of truth."[89] In all this, God is dispensing a "general grace."

As other readers of Calvin have also noted, however, it remains unclear why earthly things remain "earthly."[90] The notion of "general

---

[83]Ibid., 2.2.13.

[84]Ibid., 1.5.2.

[85]Ibid., 2.2.12.

[86]Ibid.

[87]Ibid., 1.4.3; 2.2.15.

[88]Ibid., 2.2.17.

[89]Ibid., 1.5.2; 2.2.15.

[90]For discussion of this problem, see Quentin Breen, "An Essay on Calvin's Defense of Secular Studies: His Doctrine of Common Grace," in *John Calvin: A Study in French Humanism* (New York: Archon, 1931) 165-81.

grace," which suggests that earthly things share a common source with heavenly things, makes puzzling the sharp line he draws between earthly and heavenly things. There seem to be few "heavenly reasons," or little in the way of an explicit theology, for Calvin's admiration of secular knowledge and desire that others be grateful for it as well.[91] This apparent ambiguity in Calvin's thought does not need to be resolved here. Enough has been said to indicate that this theologian of Christian tradition—trained as he was in French humanist culture—valued discoveries of the human mind, however much this valuation was strictly qualified by human sin, and however unable he was to provide a theology for the somewhat strange persistence of terrestrial goods in a "fallen world."

Openness to human discovery is also found in the theology of Friedrich Schleiermacher, the last thinker presented here who contributes to a retrievable tradition. Schleiermacher, once hailed by Wilhelm Dilthey as "the Kant of Protestant theology," set himself the task of explicating "Christian self-consciousness" (Christian "piety") as a modification of the more general human self-consciousness.[92] In so doing, he affirmed human powers of discovery and human dependence on the "nature system" generally, while insisting on the human subject's ultimate dependence on God. Schleiermacher attempted this complex explanation through two tasks. First, he delineated the ways in which God is related to finite existence. Second, he focused on how both a "God-consciousness" and a "sensuous self-consciousness" can coexist in the human consciousness.

Concerning his first task, the two ideas that Schleiermacher feels are in need of relation are "divine causality" and "finite existence." In relating them, he insists that there can be no identity. He speaks of the divine causality as "opposed to" the finite world.[93] The divine causality is something other than the forces and entities making up nature. Not only is it other, but as such it conditions, founds, or grounds the entire

---

[91]Ibid., 70.

[92]Friedrich Schleiermacher, *The Christian Faith*, ed. H. R. MacKintosh and J. S. Stewart (Philadelphia: Fortress, 1976) 3.1. Citations here and below refer to the relevant paragraph and section of Schleiermacher's *Christian Faith*.

[93]Ibid., 51.1.

finite system in its spatial and temporal aspects.[94] Furthermore, Schleiermacher had a doctrine (the doctrine of God's "eternity") formulated particularly to highlight the traditional understanding of the "opposition" of divine causality and finite world.[95]

Schleiermacher stresses, however, that this opposition is only an "opposition in kind."[96] In terms of "compass," "scope," or "comprehension," the divine causality is "equal to the finite." The divine causality "is completely presented in the totality of *finite* being."[97] Here too, Schleiermacher had a particular doctrine (divine omnipotence) that expressed this view of the divine causality as equal in compass to the sum total of the natural order.[98] Schleiermacher's critics could take this as grounds for crying "pantheism." Schleiermacher would insist, however, that his first doctrine, which stressed "opposition in kind" of divine causality and finite order, exempted him from the "hullabaloo" of pantheism charges.[99] For Schleiermacher's thought, as for many a "pan*en*theism," God and world are integrally related without being identical. How this is so is made clearer by what here has been called Schleiermacher's second task, his explication of human self-consciousness.

Basic to this second task is Schleiermacher's claim that an explication of the nature of human self-consciousness will reveal the presence there of a "sensuous self-consciousness" and also a "God-consciousness." Both of these "belong to human nature originally."[100] God-consciousness, if dominated by the sensuous self-consciousness, never reaches its pure and highest stage, which for Schleiermacher is a "feeling of absolute dependence." But experiencing this highest stage

---

[94]Ibid., 52, 53, 54.

[95]Ibid., 15.1, 15.2, 52.

[96]Ibid., 51.1.

[97]Ibid., 54.1 (emphasis mine).

[98]Ibid., 51.1.

[99]Ibid., 8, postscript 2. On the issue of pantheism, see Schleiermacher's footnote regarding his "Second Speech" on "The Nature of Religion," Schleiermacher, *On Religion: Speeches to Its Cultured Despisers* (Philadelphia: Fortress, 1958) 115-16. Cf. Friedrich Schleiermacher, *On The Glaubenslehre: Two Letters to Dr. Lücke*, trans. James Duke and Francis Fiorenza (Chico CA: Scholars Press, 1981) 47-51.

[100]Schleiermacher, *The Christian Faith*, 94.2.

of God-consciousness does not mean simply throwing off a dominating sensuous self-consciousness. It means to experience the fluctuations of sensuous self-consciousness in a certain way—in all its feelings of freedom and dependence.[101] This experiencing allows God-consciousness (a feeling of absolute dependence) to thrive *in relation* to sensuous self-consciousness. Both nature *and* God ultimately conspire to produce the highest God-consciousness, a feeling of absolute dependence.

All the activities and experiences that a human subject has in the nature system, then, may be "excitations to God-consciousness." God-consciousness as a feeling of absolute dependence is "dependence" neither on God alone nor on nature alone. Although Schleiermacher does term God the "whence" of the feeling of absolute dependence, God in his theology has structured the feeling so that humans experience dependency upon both nature and God. Accordingly, Schleiermacher has two important doctrines to express the coworking of sensuous consciousness with God-consciousness in human experience. His doctrine of the "Original Perfection of the World" portrays the world as an "abundance of stimuli" that give the proper "conditions by which the God-consciousness can realize itself." His doctrine of the "Original Perfection of Man" portrays the human person as possessing the necessary "faculty" or "inner impulse" that amounts to a "predisposition to God-consciousness." Original perfection of "world" and of "man" are two doctrinal ways to express how both the nature system and the divine causality develop in humans the feeling of absolute dependence.[102]

If the nature system plays such a crucial role in exciting God-consciousness, it is not surprising to find Schleiermacher markedly open to human activities, experiences, and discoveries in the finite world. All of these experiences in the world, whether "life-hindrances" or "life-enhancements," may excite God-consciousness.

> For it is only in connection with his organs that man realizes his sovereignty over the world, of which he can only be conscious as some-

---

[101]A substantial portion of the introduction to *The Christian Faith* examines how a "feeling of *absolute* dependence" emerges from the dynamic interplay of relative feelings of dependence and freedom. See esp. 5-16.

[102]Ibid., 57.1-60.3.

thing based on the divine omnipotence; and it is only inasmuch as the simple activity of spirit is expressed through the medium of space and time that it awakens as a copy thereof, the consciousness of the divine causality.[103]

God-consciousness, according to Schleiermacher, is radically misunderstood if it is opposed to experiences of change, development, and discovery. The early Schleiermacher perhaps most eloquently spoke, even for the mature Schleiermacher, on the mutual excitation that characterizes the relation of God-consciousness and human learning through experience and discovery.

> What can man accomplish that is worth speaking of either in life or in art that does not arise in his own self from the influence of this sense for the Infinite? Without it, how can anyone wish to comprehend the world scientifically. . . . What is all science, if not the existence of things in you, in your reason. . . . Wherefore you will find every truly learned man devout and pious.[104]

The theological anthropologies of each of these four theologians display, insofar as they treat human knowledge, a characteristic synthesis of human discovery with divine presence. The first element of this synthesis—openness to the powers of human discovery—has been the more important concern here with regard to anthropological suspicions that subsume theological anthropology within a folk anthropology that allegedly resists the new and opposes revelation to human knowledge.

In sum, although Augustine's theory of illumination has been sometimes interpreted to render human sense discovery negligible, I have suggested the persistence of an Augustinian *scientia* for knowledge of sensible things and have attempted to qualify arguments claiming an unmediated presence of the divine light and forms. Although Aquinas's "active intellect" and his concern with sense experience seem to weight the synthesis in the other direction, suggesting to some a "sense-bound epistemology," I have suggested the importance of divine presence as that in which both the "active intellect" and its sense objects partici-

---

[103]Ibid., 59.2.

[104]Schleiermacher, *On Religion*, 39.

pate. Although Calvin presented human understanding as limited by sin and its "giddy imagination," and thus in need of a fundamental renewal by God, he insisted that the Ancient and Renaissance humanists offer knowledge and truth that Christian tradition must value and accept. And although Schleiermacher traditionally affirmed the opposition "in kind" of divine causality and finite existence, he also, in less traditional fashion, equated them "in scope" so that in human self-consciousness, sensuous self-consciousness and God-consciousness mutually give rise to or "excite" one another.

Indeed, it is true that the divine presence is never separated from powers of human discovery in any of these theologians. God, for these theologians, may be the illumination, source, or ground of the powers of human discovery. But in none of these cases do they disparage the distinctive contribution made to knowledge of existence and of God by the powers of human discovery. To the contrary, there is a valuing of such human knowledge and an openness to what is discovered through it. For example, there is Augustine's *scientia*, which "presents itself before" cognizance of eternal things; Thomas Aquinas's "active intellect," which abstracts from sense phenomena; Calvin's "natural gifts," manifested by the Ancients and other scholars; and Schleiermacher's "sensuous self-consciousness," which excites God-consciousness. This openness to human discovery is what I have identified as the first trait a Christian theological tradition must display in order to be retrieved in light of anthropological suspicion.

Granted, these four theological anthropologies show an openness to powers of human discovery. When the newly discovered are "strange" peoples and "alien" cultures, however, how open do these theological anthropologies remain?

Theology and the alien

When squarely facing the history of Christian tradition and theology, there can be no easy claim that Christian theology has valued and affirmed the alien. Indeed, theologians might readily insist that any genuine consideration of the tradition in this light must entail confession and a sense of enduring grief for what Enrique Dussel has aptly termed the theologians' "No-to-the-Other."[105] Generally, there is an

---

[105]Enrique Dussel, *A History of the Church in Latin America: Colonialism to Liberation* (Grand Rapids: Eerdmans, 1981) 8-13.

ontology of domination in the European tradition that the Christian theological tradition did sanction and fail to critically examine.

The problem is not that Christian theology in the West took up its faith in the particular terms and concepts of European tradition. Such an intensification of its own place is an inextricable part of any theological interpretation.[106] What is lamentable is how that intensification is bound up with a language of domination of others. In other words, provincial and ethnocentric impulses accreted to the theologians' particularly Western and European visions. This accretion is undeniably reflected in the theological anthropologies discussed here.

From the very beginning, then, one must acknowledge the ethnocentric impulses that taint the theological anthropologies examined here. Part of the ethnocentrism may be because at least three of the four theologians lived and wrote at a time prior to the Age of Discovery, which cultural anthropologists see as very significant to their own other-affirming orientation. As historian of anthropology Margaret Hodgen observes, however, St. Augustine and other church fathers of his time exhibited "far less interest in barbarian types of culture than had the Greeks and the Romans."[107] Augustine was prone to strike analogies between "primitives" and children.[108]

Similarly, Thomas Aquinas compounded the continuing deficiency of sociocultural data with a "hierarchical principle" that often condoned ethnocentric impulses. Newly discovered "savage" peoples were "natural men" occupying a "lower estate" in the order of being. Following interpretations of Aristotle's *Politics*, the hierarchical view could condone the notion that some "seem made by nature for service."[109] The hierarchical schema was one within which "natural men"

---

[106]David Tracy, *The Analogical Imagination: Christian Theology and the Culture of Pluralism* (New York: Crossroad, 1983) 205-206.

[107]Hodgen, *Early Anthropology*, 52-53. Hodgen particularly cites St. Augustine's reluctance to admit the existence of the "antipodes—people that inhabit the land where the sun riseth and go with their feet towards ours." See St. Augustine, *The City of God*, book 16, c.9. Conceivably, Augustine's "reluctance" here could also be interpreted as a resistance to the fabulous "epitomizations" of alien peoples that Hodgen also faults.

[108]Hallowell, "The History of Anthropology," 33 n. 41; and Manuel, *The Eighteenth Century Confronts the Gods*, 44.

[109]St. Thomas Aquinas, *Summa Contra Gentiles*, 3.81.

were locked into their lower estate so that, as George Sanderlin charges, "For Aquinas, natural man was an unalterable substance, which not even the redemption could change."[110]

Though the Age of Discovery may have been well on the way by 1502,[111] neither Calvin (d. 1564) nor Schleiermacher (d. 1834) was free from a theological ethnocentrism. Calvin at points displays this characteristic in his marked sense of difference from peoples of "remote civilization," and in a superiority to them expressed in his references to the "backward folk," the "barbarians," and "savages."[112] Schleiermacher, too, not only speaks of the distinctiveness of Christianity as the highest and purest form of self-consciousness (in contrast to polytheistic and fetishistic forms),[113] but also suggests that Christianity possesses an "exclusive superiority" among religious communions. Christianity is superior not because it is true and others are false, but because it is a more developed stage.[114] Schleiermacher's ethnocentric impulse might also be found in his view of "undeveloped human society" as "good natured grown-up children,"[115] or perhaps in his periodic belittling of the French in comparison to German culture.[116]

These marks of ethnocentric impulse in the theologians are but signals of a recurrent danger: that Christian theology might become, as in fact it often did, a European ideology sanctioning the domination of the alien.[117] However true this danger is, I now want to set forth aspects of these theological anthropologies capable of appropriation in light of anthropological suspicion. There are theological impulses that check

----

[110]George Sanderlin, ed., *Bartholome de Las Casas: A Selection of His Writings* (New York: Knopf, 1971) 112. Below I suggest that this is insufficient for assessing Thomas's own position. Sanderlin does not cite a text from Aquinas to substantiate this summary claim.

[111]Hodgen, *Early Anthropology*, 122.

[112]Calvin, *Institutes of the Christian Religion*, 1.3.1.

[113]Schleiermacher, *The Christian Faith*, 8.2.

[114]Ibid., 7.3.

[115]Ibid., 61.3.

[116]Schleiermacher, *On Religion*, 10, 23.

[117]See again, Dussel, *A History of the Church in Latin America*, 310-22.

ethnocentrism, and these need renewed emphasis. What are these impulses that check ethnocentrism and so display the trait of affirming the other?

In the case of each theologian, a certain view of the universality of the divine presence is what potentially checks ethnocentric impulse. I say *a certain view* of God's universality because not just any universalist claim checks ethnocentrism. For example, a notion of God's universal presence might prompt Westerners to foster among other populations the special practices and beliefs of the Western Christian tradition. What is divinely revealed by God as good in the West is carried elsewhere. Western missionary activity, recounted by anthropologists and by missionaries themselves, can display this approach and its alleged "imperialist" or "ethnocentric" abuses.[118]

In the thought of the aforementioned theologians, I try to disentangle from ethnocentric accretions another notion of the universality of divine presence—one that may check ethnocentrism. This other notion accords other peoples and groups, clothed as they may be in all their differences, a meaningful relation to God. This accordance may be done not primarily because of the alien's contact or familiarity with the particular religious beliefs and practices of Western tradition, but because of the universality of the divine presence. Such universality is independent of the West's expansion and proclamation; it flourishes in the play of different religious customs and beliefs.

One may begin again with St. Augustine and a passage in which he contests the beastly "epitomization" of other peoples characterizing so many reports of his time.[119]

> But we are not bound to believe all we hear of these monstrosities. But whoever is anywhere born a man, that is a rational, mortal animal, no matter what unusual appearance he presents in color, movement, sound, nor how peculiar he is in some power, part or quality of his nature, no Christian can doubt that he springs from that one

---

[118]Cf. Frank A. Salamone, "Anthropologists and Missionaries: Competition or Reciprocity," 407-12, and Eugene Nida, "Missionaries and Anthropologists," *Practical Anthropology* 13 (1966): 273-77, 287.

[119]Hodgen, *Early Anthropology,* 34, 122.

protoplast. We can distinguish the common human nature from that
which is peculiar and therefore wonderful.[120]

For Augustine, the "peculiar" may be not monstrous as so many Western reporters would have it, but rather "wonderful" by reason of a distinguishable "common human nature." Here St. Augustine's notion of
the common human nature means not homogeneity but the relation of
wonderful peculiars. This notion is, of course, rooted in his belief concerning the universally present, creating and sustaining God. All the
peculiar natures of humanity, "inasmuch as they are, and have a rank
and species of their own, and have a kind of internal harmony, are certainly good."[121] This unity of diverse humanity and other species by
reason of the one creating God is summarized by Augustine in *The City
of God*.

> For God, the Creator of all, knows where and when each thing ought
> to be, or to have been created, because He sees the similarities and
> diversities which can contribute to the beauty of the whole.[122]

These theological beliefs of Augustine also left their mark in the
history of Westerners' cross-cultural encounters. J.-F. Lafitau, missionary and writer of the first full-scale ethnographic monograph on the
Huron and Iroquois,[123] appropriated Augustine's notion of the one
God's universality to promote European respect for native American
religion and custom. To make his case, Lafitau drew from Augustine's
affirmations of God's universality in the *Contra Faustus*, claiming for *les
Gentiles* a "belief in the one true God."[124] On this basis Lafitau insists
that the *sauvages Ameriquains* have never lost this true belief; compares
"heathen practices" and the Eucharist; and urges that the "savages" at

---

[120]St. Augustine, *The City of God*, 16, c.8.

[121]Ibid., 12, c.5.

[122]Ibid., 16, c.8.

[123]For an assessment of Lafitau's place in the history of anthropology and ethnography, see Burridge, *Encountering Aborigines*, 64ff.

[124]Lafitau cites Augustine's *Contra Faustum*, 20, c.19.

least be accorded as much respect as the church grants to the West's own "heathen ancients."[125]

It has already been noted that in St. Thomas Aquinas's thought, there is a hierarchical principle locking the alien into a "lower estate" and that such a principle could fuel the ethnocentric impulse. But even Hodgen notes that the hierarchical principle, though potentially a tool for ethnocentrism, could actually mitigate ethnocentrism. In making a place for the "savage," the "orthodox Christian concept of the unity of mankind" accepted the savage as "a man like other men, and inserted him in a scale of being with European and other known men."[126] For Thomas, "God must be everywhere and in all things" and "in some way in contact with them."[127] True as it was for Thomas that God orders men to one another, truer still was it that they are all ordered to "one end which is God." The ordering of all peoples to God as end grants to each, in fact, a "natural tendency to be like God."[128]

Another crucial issue, relevant to discerning the value St. Thomas grants to the alien, centers on the relation he articulates between the "natural law" that God has implanted in all people, and the "human laws" that vary "according to the customs of the country [that are] adapted to time and place."[129] All human laws may be approved if they do not depart from God's natural law. If they do depart from natural law, they are not laws at all. "Consequently, every human law has just so much of the nature of law as it is derived from the law of nature."[130]

A great temptation for those Europeans approaching aliens from within Thomas's perspective on natural law is to label a peculiar and newly encountered human law as "no law at all" simply because its peculiarity cloaks its derivation from God's natural law. A sensitive read-

---

[125]J.-F. Lafitau, *Moeurs des Sauvages Amériquains, comparées aux moeurs des premier temps* (Paris, 1724). See esp. 111, 418, 455.

[126]Hodgen, *Early Anthropology*, 405, 407.

[127]Aquinas, *Summa Contra Gentiles*, 3.68.

[128]Ibid., 3.17, 21.

[129]On "natural law" and "human laws," see Aquinas, *Summa Theologica*, 1-2, q.95, aa.1-4; 1-2, q.94, aa.2, 6.

[130]Ibid., 1-2, q.95, a.2.

ing of Thomas here, however, should check any interpreter who thinks that radical peculiarity means departure from God's natural law. Quite to the contrary, for Thomas a human law appropriately derived from natural law always varies according to custom, time, and place.[131] Peculiarity, therefore, is intrinsic to a human law that is truly derived from God's natural law.[132]

Given Aquinas's universalist impulse, which valued peculiarity, it is unsurprising to find missionary Bartholome de Las Casas citing him in his fight for the lives of his Latin American peoples against the persecution of the Spanish. Las Casas looks past the potentially degrading effects of any Aristotelian hierarchical principle in Thomas and searches instead for arguments against compelling Latin American peoples to embrace Christianity.[133] Las Casas explicitly states that he sees little contradiction between the fundamentals of Aquinas's theology and the Bull *Sublimis Deus* by Pope Paul III:

> We . . . consider that the Indians are truly men and that they are not only capable of understanding the Catholic faith but, according to our information, they desire exceedingly to receive it. . . . The said Indians and all other peoples who may later be discovered by Christians, are by no means to be deprived of their liberty or the possession of their property *even though they be outside the faith of Jesus Christ;* and that they may and should, freely and legitimately, enjoy their liberty and possession of property; nor should they be in any way enslaved; should the contrary happen it shall be null and of no effect.[134]

Here again, as demonstrated in las Casas's appropriation of St. Thomas,

---

[131]Ibid., 1-2, q.95, a.3.

[132]One contemporary anthropologist suggests that Thomas Aquinas be included in an anthropologist's "personal pantheon" precisely because of his "resolution of the relation between the local and the universal in the realm of law." See Dell Hymes, "The Use of Anthropology: Critical, Political, Personal," *Reinventing Anthropology,* ed. Dell Hymes (New York: Vintage, 1969) 20.

[133]Bartholome de Las Casas, *In Defense of the Indians,* ed. Stafford Poole, CM (DeKalb: Northern Illinois University Press, 1974) 334-36.

[134]Cited in Lewis Hanke, *All Mankind Is One: A Study of the Disputation between Bartholome de Las Casas and Juan Gines de Sepulvada in 1550 on the Intellectual and Religious Capacity of the American Indians* (DeKalb: Northern Illinois University Press, 1974) 21.

the history of Christianity's cross-cultural encounters shows theological tradition checking the ethnocentric impulse.

In the theological anthropology of John Calvin, there are also universalist claims that could either condone or check Westerners' ethnocentric impulses. The main task here is to note the theological traits that might nourish appreciation of cultural variety. The point of focus should be the *divinitatis sensum* embedded universally in human understanding. About this sense and about the alien, Calvin observes, there is "no notion so barbarous, no people so savage, that they have not a deepseated conviction that there is a God."[135]

Humans possess this "deep-seated conviction" for two major reasons: first, the skillful ordering of the universe causes them to contemplate the numinous creator, God; and second, their sense of conscience, right and wrong, nourishes their moral sense.[136] There is sensed both a God of nature and a God of conscience. Calvin's notion of the *divinitatis sensum* is an awareness of a God of nature who is also a God of conscience.

In the contexts of Christians' cross-cultural encounters with others, different interpretations of this divine sense could be seen. When Christian interpreters drove a wedge between the two meanings of Calvin's divine sense, "aliens" tended not to be valued in their particularity or ably understood. This attitude is particularly evident in the theologies of missionaries to the Sandwich Islands. Less productive of cross-cultural sensitivity are those applications of Calvin's theology that focus on "moral feeling" before God as "Moral Governor," while neglecting the "God of nature" who, in Calvin's terms, drives the celestial frame and cares for each part.

Hiram Bingham, nineteenth-century missionary to the Sandwich Islands (now known as the Hawaiian Islands), made it his goal to preach God as "moral Governor" so as to cultivate the Hawaiians' "innate moral feeling," which he believed stood in close relation to the idea of God and lead directly to it. His ethnography of these "others," then, was overshadowed by a stern moralistic hermeneutic that repeatedly led him

---

[135]John Calvin, *Institutes of the Christian Religion*, 1.3.1.

[136]For these two aspects of the *divinitatis sensum*, see Calvin, *Institutes*, 1.5.1, 1.3.1, 1.3.3.

to deprecate Hawaiian culture. A descriptive anthropology presenting others as "other" was stifled in Bingham, intoxicated as he was by the conviction that "no man is better than his principles."[137]

A contrasting valuation and description of the other can be seen in William Ellis, another missionary to the same Hawaiian society in the same century. Ellis began with a conception of the "God of nature," whose divine plan was in harmony with the laws of nature. The "God of nature" was portrayed as a "gracious Deity" who propounded a law of benevolence and desired that humans live in peace with one another, thus effecting an "essential unity of mankind."[138] While Ellis never denied a universal moral feeling among all peoples, the "actual state of human nature" was not interpreted morally in terms of a set of shared standards, but simply in the fact of harmonious interchange.

> All mankind are created and upheld by the same God, descended from the same parents, subject to the same changes, are living under the same canopy of heaven, upon the same planet and therefore have a natural right to claim fellowship.[139]

Ellis criticizes both Westerners and other societies for inhibiting the "fellowship" of all peoples with God and with one another.

In his "propagation of the gospel," Ellis proclaimed the God of nature as the Hawaiians' "Almighty Friend" and abstained from "cultivation" of their moral sense and denunciations of eternal wrath.[140] Such a theology also had the effect of allowing his descriptions of Hawaiian and Polynesian "others" to remain important ethnographic docu-

---

[137]Bingham, *A Residence of Twenty-One Years in the Sandwich Islands*, 23. For an example of the theology that focused on the "moral feeling" possessed by all "uncultivated natives of America, Kamschatka, and the Caribbean Islands," see Leonard Woods, *The Works of Leonard Woods, DD*, 5 vols. (Boston: Jowett, 1851) 1:67-70.

[138]John Eimeo Ellis, *Life of William Ellis* (London: John Murray, 1873) 185, 188; William Ellis, *Polynesian Researches: Hawaii* (London: Fisher, Son and Co., 1842) 2, 188.

[139]William Ellis, Preface, in Charles Gutzlaff, *Journal of Three Voyages along the Coast of China in 1831, 1832, 1833, to Which Is Prefixed an Introductory Essay on the Policy, Religion, etc. of China by the Rev. William Ellis* (London: Westley and Adams, 1834) 1.

[140]Ellis, *Life of William Ellis*, 185; and William Ellis, Preface, 78, 85, 108, 140-41. All of these latter citations are from William Ellis's sermons.

ments.[141] He was generally more successful than Bingham in suspending his moral and theological judgments of this culture, treating Polynesian beliefs and customs not so much as moral perversions to be combated, but as diverse manifestations of the God of nature who created all humankind.[142] To emphasize this aspect of Calvin's *divinitatis sensum* is reminiscent less of Bingham's "moral Governor" and more of St. Augustine's veneration of the one Creator of all who sees diversities as contributing to the beauty of the whole.

It remains now to indicate how any universalist claims in Friedrich Schleiermacher's thought might qualify the ethnocentrism implied in his discussions of Christianity's "distinctiveness" and "exclusive superiority." Such qualifications stem from two major points in his theology: first, from his view of Christianity as a modification of a universal piety; and second, from his notion of what it means to experience God's providential care.

Take first Schleiermacher's way of relating Christianity and piety. When speaking of Christianity's distinctiveness, he stresses that "the same thing is present in all [religious communions], but present in a quite different way in each."[143] That which is present in all is "piety," a "universal element of human life."[144] Christian consciousness is a distinctive modification of this universal element. Schleiermacher uses the introduction in his *The Christian Faith* to locate Christianity within a *general* view of human self-consciousness.[145] It is not surprising, there-

---

[141]Cf. Francis K. W. Ching, "The Archaeology of South Kona," *Hawaiian Journal of Archaeology* 71 (1971): 16-17.

[142]The "ethnographic impulse" was not an unusual development among missionaries of the London Missionary Society to which Ellis belonged. The LMS's leadership had proclaimed a "funeral of bigotry," a "Catholic bias," and attempted not to impose upon their native converts unnatural habits and conventions that were erroneously supposed to represent "civilization." See C. Sylvester Horne, *The Story of the London Missionary Society, 1795-1895* (London: The London Missionary Society, 1894) 11-12, 422, 431; and Richard Lovett, *The History of the London Missionary Society, 1795-1895* (London: Henry Frowde, 1899) 747-48.

[143]Schleiermacher, *The Christian Faith*, 10.2.

[144]Ibid., 57.1.

[145]Schleiermacher carefully identifies the purpose of his introduction as not "to demonstrate Christianity apriori," but "to specify the distinctive place Christianity occupies among the various possible modifications of that common consciousness." Schleiermacher, *On the Glaubenslehre*, 76.

fore, that in his doctrines of the original perfection of "world" and "man," the term *original* does not refer to an early state of history, but rather to what is prior to all temporal development and characteristic of all finite being as such.[146] World and humans are so constituted that piety may be universally prevalent. Since piety is "excited by" and caused by both the world's and humanity's stimuli and impulses, it cannot be limited to any religious communion, however distinctive the Christian communion may be. In Schleiermacher, then, one finds little missionary zeal designed to propagate what is distinctively Christian. Instead, he speaks of piety as "self-communicating" just as the human race is "self-propagating."[147]

Turning to a second point in Schleiermacher's theology, his notion of God's providential care, one can see more explicit grounds for affirming the other. He stresses that the object of God's providential care is not the individual, but rather the whole system, the "universal relatedness" of all individuals and things.[148] If the whole is the object of providential care, then Christians experience God's providence in fellowship, in the encounter with others. Through the encounter with others, one as individual achieves not only a personal self-consciousness, but also a human "race consciousness" or "consciousness of kind."[149] Without such a consciousness of being embedded in a whole that is the human race, one does not experience the whole that is the object of God's providential care. This is not an immediate grasp or intuition of the whole, but a consciousness of the whole through concrete encounters with others in "fellowship." It is this kind of fellowship that is necessary for there to be a "living and vigorous piety."[150] The communion of the pious, then, is called not to a life of exclusivity and homogeneity, but to a "free and mobile outward life featuring the whole range of external expressions and communications."[151]

---

[146]Schleiermacher, *The Christian Faith*, 10.2.

[147]Ibid., 57.1.

[148]Ibid., 46.1.2.

[149]Ibid., 6.2, 121.3.

[150]Ibid., 60.2.

[151]Ibid.

By referring to these four theologians and to several appropriations of their theology in cross-cultural encounters, I have uncovered the kind of universalist claims about divine presence that may check Christian ethnocentrism. In Augustine's thought, God, the Creator of all, creates and sustains the being of things different and things similar in order to constitute the beauty of a whole. In Thomas Aquinas, the "human laws" that vary according to custom, time, and place express God's universal natural law in that variance. In Calvin, a loving God of nature has planted a divine sense in the conscience of all humans and in the creation that all may contemplate; and no people are so savage that they lack a "deep-seated conviction that there is a God." For Schleiermacher, although the combination of sensuous- and God-consciousness that characterizes piety varies according to kind and stage, the tendency toward such a combination is universally present and especially facilitated by selves' encounters with others in an ever-widening, multifarious communion of feeling. By means of such claims as these, one may discern in Christian tradition the second "trait" that must be displayed (openness to the "alien") if a Christian tradition is to be retrieved in light of contemporary anthropological suspicions.

Openness to the alien and openness to discovery, then, are two traits in Christian theology pertinent to the claim that there is a religious dimension to contemporary cultural anthropology. What I have tried to show is that Western religious tradition is not reducible without remainder to the provincial folk anthropology that current anthropological suspicion exposes. There are in religious tradition theological anthropologies that display an openness to human discovery and an affirmation of the alien such that ethnocentrism need not, in principle, dominate. As a consequence, these two traits point to the possibility of retrieving a religious tradition. In these two traits are grounds for considering the possibility that a religious tradition may not stifle cross-cultural discovery and affirmation of the other, but rather nurture them.

I would argue further—and my references to the "other-affirming" missionaries suggest this—that the possibility of retrieving religious tradition can be considered not only in principle but also historically. Missionaries' religious endeavors, which frequently involved theological interpretation, may have contributed significantly to the set of factors giving rise to what is now known as cultural anthropology. Hodgen, for example, noted that missionaries often returned home with stories of alien customs couched in "a realistic spirit wholly at variance with ethnological fable," and this in turn affected scholarship.[152] Anthropologist Kenelm Burridge also suggests that "it has been the collective and accumulated experience of the missionary tradition, in short, which has prepared the European mind to accept rather than reject the strange or new experience, and then come to terms with it."[153] Burridge even sees an enduring affinity between cultural anthropology and missionary endeavor: "The field anthropologists of this century, like all others involved in the expansion of the European cultural heritage, have been and are embued with missionary purpose."[154]

I am not out to show here what Burridge somewhat controversially calls the missionary character of current anthropology. Nonetheless, in considering possibilities for a claim that brings together often-opposed fields (here, religion and anthropology), Burridge's historical reflections about anthropology are significant. Anthropology's own hermeneutic of suspicion may possibly, from a historical point of view, be a function of a tradition that included the missionaries' reach for the strange and new.

A Model for Discerning Religious Dimensions

In asking how a religious dimension can be discerned in contemporary social science, it will not do to engage simply in a search for Augustinian *rationes aeternae* in *scientia;* for signs that inquirers "participate," in St. Thomas's sense, in grace; for elements of Calvin's "common grace"; or for a Schleiermacherian "God-consciousness" evident in the self-consciousness of inquirers. All these notions may partially constitute the tradition that can motivate contemporary discernments, but they are not easily related to current discussion. One must also indicate how these "religious" interests can be introduced into

---

[152]Hodgen, *Early Anthropology*, 79.

[153]Burridge, *Encountering Aborigines*, 17.

[154]Ibid., 18. For more discussion of the importance of missionary work in the early development of cultural anthropology, see E. Sidney Hartland, "Review of *Totemism and Exogamy* by J. G. Frazer," *Man* 11 (1911): 11-16; and Wilhelm Schmidt, "Is Ethnological Information Coming from Missionaries Sufficiently Reliable?" *Anthropos* 7 (1911): 430-31.

conversation with a *contemporary* field of inquiry like cultural anthropology. In this chapter's final section, I shall attempt to achieve this relation by setting out a model for discerning religious dimensions.

To make this discernment, philosophers of religion and theologians depend heavily on contemporary philosophers and philosophers of science. The works of four thinkers (Michael Polanyi, Bernard Lonergan, Hans-George Gadamer, and Paul Ricoeur) have each been influential at this point. Ricoeur's thought, for reasons to be explained later, serves as most appropriate for this work's aim.

From these writers' works and the uses made of them, a model for discerning religious dimensions can be developed consisting of three major steps. First, and this constitutes the primary tasks of theorists like Polanyi, Lonergan, Gadamer, and Ricoeur, there is a portrait given of the structure of human inquiry. Polanyi exhibits a general philosophy-of-science approach that seeks to articulate the story of scientific discovery, most notably the "story of relativity" and its implications for understanding processes of scientific discovery.[155] Lonergan's portrait of human inquiry seeks to be a "matter of fact" analysis of the "patterns of operations" constituting the experience of human understanding.[156] Gadamer's fundamental hermeneutical concern is to offer a "theory of the real experience that thinking is."[157] In each case, the concern is to make explicit the kind of experience that inquiry is.

Ricoeur's portrait of the experience of human inquiry is shaped by his whole project of "general hermeneutics," which focuses not only on interpreting written expressions, but on a "whole process that encompasses explanation and understanding."[158] Human inquiry, for Ricoeur, moves from preunderstanding as a "naive guess" or anticipation of one's subject-matter, to the disciplined and analytical task of "explanation," before issuing in the kind of understanding that Ricoeur calls

---

[155]Michael Polanyi, *Personal Knowledge: Toward a Post-Critical Philosophy* (Chicago: University of Chicago Press, 1958) vii-viii, 3-65.

[156]Bernard J. F. Lonergan, *Insight: A Study of Human Understanding* (New York: Longmans, Green and Co., 1957) xxviii, 319-47; and Bernard J. F. Lonergan, *Method in Theology* (New York: Herder and Herder, 1972) 4, 6-13.

[157]Gadamer, *Truth and Method,*, xxiv.

[158]Ricoeur, *Interpretation Theory*, 74.

"comprehension." The event of understanding refers to a possible world and to a "possible way of being in that world."[159] In portraying the process of inquiry into actions and texts—and for Ricoeur actions and texts can be approached in similar ways[160]—what is crucial is not just the subjective, intuitive grasping of an intention underlying a text or action, which has traditionally been of interest to the *Geisteswissenschaften*. Nor is inquiry distinguished by an "objective" approach that conducts analyses of a text's or an action's structure and seeks the kind of "verification" traditionally sought by the *Naturwissenschaften*. For Ricoeur, human inquiry as a dialectic of understanding *and* explanation is a process that gathers both of these traditional ideals of inquiry into one interpretive process. As I will delineate in the next chapter, the fusion of both *Geisteswissenschaften* and *Naturwissenschaften* ideals makes Ricoeur's portrait of human inquiry especially appropriate for studying a field like anthropology, which has often included in its methodology the ideals of natural history and of human science.[161] Because Ricoeur's hermeneutical portrait brings together these two methodological ideals, his mode of portraying the process of human inquiry most determines this work's approach to cultural anthropology.

Within the context of their portrayal of inquiry, discerners of religious dimensions often take a second step; they identify the "limits" of inquiry. I shall use the term *limit* in the technical sense employed by Ricoeur and others influenced by him such as David Tracy and Hugh McElwain.[162]

---

[159]Ibid., 88.

[160]Paul Ricoeur, "The Model of the Text: Meaningful Action Considered as a Text," in *Interpretative Social Science: A Reader,* ed. Paul Rabinow and William Sullivan (Berkeley: University of California Press, 1979) 73-101.

[161]George W. Stocking, Jr., ed., *The Shaping of American Anthropology, 1883-1911: A Franz Boas Reader* (New York: Basic Books, 1974) 1-20; and Stocking, "From Physics to Ethnology," in *Race, Culture and Evolution,* 133-60.

[162]Hugh T. McElwain, *Theology of Limits and the Limits of Theology: Reflections on Language, Environment and Death* (Washington: University Press of America, 1983) 1-56; David Tracy, *Blessed Rage for Order: The New Pluralism in Theology* (New York: Seabury, 1975) 92-109; and Paul Ricoeur, "The Specificity of Religious Language," *Semeia* 4 (1975): 122-45.

Crucial to this technical use of the term is its twofold meaning: first, referring to the restrictions and borders of inquiry, and second, to any limiting wholes that are invoked by inquirers as the ground of their inquiry. Tracy attempts to capture this twofold meaning in his distinction between "limit-to experiences" and "limit-of reality." Inquirers experience the limits-to their inquiry in such a way that realities at the limit-of human existence are invoked. It will be appropriate to discuss this twofold sense in more detail when addressing the "limits" of cultural anthropological inquiry. Identifying limits in this sense is not only a feature of Ricoeur's perspective, but of other contemporary writers as well.

One can find the twofold sense of limit, for example, in Polanyi's philosophy-of-science approach. Inquirers, for Polanyi, are restricted, limited by and to intensely personal passions.[163] But their personal knowledge is not thereby only restrictive in relation to their inquiries. It also facilitates the inquirer's grasp of the whole, that is, of some fundamental limit-of reality. The personal commitments of inquirers are so structured that they are dialectically related to the universal.[164]

Lonergan, too, gives explicit attention to the identification of inquiry's limits. For him, inquiry's continual questioning confronts inquirers with their "limited capacity to attain knowledge."[165] However, in this sense of restriction, inquirers know themselves to be at least ones who also raise further questions, and in this insight there is a self-transcendence into a succession of "higher viewpoints."[166] The "elementary matter of raising further questions" is a transcendence in which inquirers are "taken beyond the defined limits of particular issues."[167]

Gadamer, also, can speak of restricting limit-to experiences in his hermeneutical portrait of understanding. Humans are restricted in their understanding not simply because there are many languages and they rarely command them all, but primarily because every language is itself

---

[163]Polanyi, *Personal Knowledge*, 323.

[164]Ibid., 308-12.

[165]Lonergan, *Insight*, 639.

[166]Ibid., 637.

[167]Ibid., 636, 639.

constantly developing and being formed.[168] Nevertheless, it is part of the paradox of human finitude that language can bring into play a "totality of meaning." For Gadamer, "All human speaking is finite in such a way that there is within it an infinity of meaning to be elaborated and interpreted."[169] Language speculates about such a totality or infinity and so invokes amid all restrictions an encompassing "limit-of reality."

For Ricoeur, the twofold limit-situation of inquiry arises, as for Gadamer, from his probing the linguisticality of the experience of inquiry for its nonlinguistic character. The twofold understanding of limit is apparent in his study of symbols. The symbols that inquirers employ to nurture their preunderstandings, explanations, and comprehension have a text-focused, semantic character. As such, they are finite and restrictive; yet they also have a nonlinguistic side, being rooted in a nonsemantic order: in short, they are bound to the cosmos.[170] Symbols, bearing their nonsemantic features, "plunge us into the shadowy experience of power," into the depths of human experience. In this function, symbols invoke and make present a "limit-of reality" although their semantic and text-focused features are finite and restrictive. Symbols often display this rootedness in the nonsemantic by their connection to some vision of the whole of what is, to a possible world and way of being in it.

Ricoeur also displays, then, within the context of his portrait of human inquiry, an attempt to identify the limits of human inquiry as both limit-to experience and limit-of reality. The last chapter will contain any further explication of how his mode of identifying limits contributes to the task of discerning a religious dimension in cultural anthropology.

While theologians and philosophers of religion may take the notion of limit as a "key characteristic" of a religious dimension, many of them also stress that not all limit-situations are religious.[171] A third and

---

[168]Gadamer, *Truth and Method*, 415.

[169]Ibid., 416.

[170]Ricoeur, *Interpretation Theory*, 60, 65.

[171]Tracy, *Blessed Rage for Order*, 93, 96, 111 n. 11.

distinctive step is usually necessary—a step that involves distinguishing what it is about a given limit-situation that is properly "religious."

The philosophers and philosophers of religion discussed in this section are careful about clothing their respective visions of inquiry's limits in religious terms. But each thinker does take definite steps toward distinguishing a religious dimension in relation to his views of inquiry's limits. For Polanyi, the personal passions that restrict and yet disclose the universal for the scientific inquirer provide a "cosmic field." This latter is not God but the "clue to God,"[172] and tends to "align religion with the great intellectual systems such as mathematics, fiction and the fine arts which are validated by becoming happy dwelling places of the human mind."[173]

Lonergan, by way of a multistage process of reflection, attempts to move from the fact of an inquirer's continual questioning to the "question of God." In this process he seeks to show that the self-transcending impulse to raise further questions is a distinctively religious dimension.[174]

Gadamer does not articulate his notions of infinity and totality, which are brought into play by finite language, in ostensibly religious terms. He does, however, see this infinity as pointing to a "universal ontological structure," the disclosure of which rests on a "metaphysics of the beautiful," and a "metaphysics of light." In this, he admits the continuing influence of Augustine and converses with theologians Thomas Aquinas and Nicholas of Cusa, but insists that this metaphysics can be detached from that of Neoplatonism and Christian thought.[175]

Ricoeur is particularly clear about the importance of limit-experiences for discerning the religious dimension. While he too would af-

---

[172]Polanyi, *Personal Knowledge*, 324, 379, 405.

[173]Ibid., 280.

[174]Lonergan, *Insight*, 655, 657-86.

[175]Gadamer, *Truth and Method*, 440-41. Theologian Wolfhart Pannenberg notes that Gadamer's discussion of the "totality of meaning" is of great significance for theologians since, historically, confidence in a total semantic whole and thematic treatment of it has been embodied in the religions. Pannenberg is, therefore, engaged in an effort to demarcate Gadamer's "totality of meaning" as a notion that is properly "religious" and then also theological. See Wolfhart Pannenberg, *Theology and the Philosophy of Science*, trans. Francis McDonagh (Philadelphia: Westminster Press, 1976) 105.

firm that not all limit-situations are religious, he claims that limit-situations are the "ultimate referents" of explicitly religious discourse.[176] Religious language refers to and re-presents these situations in a language ("limit-language") that joins an "odd" linguistic character (intensification, superabundance) with a sense of total commitment and universal significance.[177] It is when a limit-language of this sort projects its "radical vision of existence that a religious dimension to ordinary experience and inquiry becomes discernible."[178]

While Ricoeur's thought, which has been only briefly presented here, will be most apparent in this work, I have discussed his mode of discerning a religious dimension in relation to Polanyi, Lonergan, and Gadamer in order to show that my model emerges not just from Ricoeur, but from several contemporary thinkers who are concerned with the religious dimension. My reason for choosing Ricoeur is not that he alone exhibits the three steps in the model for study of religious dimensions, but that his tendency to portray human inquiry (in the first step of the model) in terms of understanding and explanation is especially appropriate for the field of cultural anthropology. The next three chapters are devoted to providing that kind of portrait of cultural anthropology.

Conclusion

In this chapter I have laid the groundwork necessary for the conversation with cultural anthropology that next transpires. This project is not simply a matter of "taking a look" at anthropology's inquiry and pointing out what is "religious" in it. Rather, it is a matter of discerning those dimensions by retrieving key aspects of a religious tradition, all the while remaining conscious of the particular suspicions that are obstacles to such retrieval. Readers of other traditions and disciplines may judge the cogency of this discernment by the quality and nature of the conversation that discloses it.

---

[176]Ricoeur, "The Specificity of Religious Language," 122.

[177]Ibid., 107, 128.

[178]Ibid., 128.

I have prepared the way for this conversation by moving through three major phases of discussion relevant to discerning religious dimensions in cultural anthropology. I first addressed anthropology's "hermeneutic of suspicion" about the "religious." Anthropology's suspicion entails a preunderstanding according to which cultural anthropology emerged as a critical transcendence of "folk anthropology." This transcendence was often viewed as including a critical transcendence of religion and theology. Anthropology's hermeneutic of suspicion then also involved marking off religion as subject matter for anthropological study, but rarely acknowledging it as a feature bearing upon anthropologists' lives and discourses. In any conversation with contemporary anthropology, such a hermeneutic of suspicion is a force to consider when one seeks to discern enduring religious dimensions.

The second major phase of this chapter displayed strands in a religious tradition that make it possible to retrieve a sense of the religious in light of anthropological suspicions. I attempted this retrieval by examining Christian theological tradition (embodied in the works of Augustine, Thomas Aquinas, Calvin, Schleiermacher) for traits making it irreducible to provincial and dogmatic "folk anthropology." I emphasized two significant traits: the tradition's openness to new human discovery and its potential for affirming the alien. The two traits do not in themselves make Christian theology a ready conversation partner with current anthropology; but they do suggest that theological traits or enduring "legitimate prejudices" make discernment of a religious dimension possible in anthropology.

Still, the groundwork for conversation with genuinely *contemporary* cultural anthropology was not laid until, in the chapter's final phase, a model for discerning a religious dimension in current forms of inquiry was considered. That model consists of three steps derived from a study of available modes of reflection used for discerning religious dimensions. The three steps—portrayal of human inquiry, identification of limits, demarcation of limits as "religious"—characterize the major moments of reflection in the approaches of Polanyi, Lonergan, Gadamer, and Ricoeur. Those three steps guide the subsequent agenda.

Chapter II

Anthropological Inquiry:
The Understanding
and Explanation of Others

If I did not somewhat fear the reproach of exaggeration, I would say that in the twentieth century ethnography will be the foundation on which a new philosophical conception of humanity will be built.

Arnold van Gennep

Though theologians may wish to resist the "bleakly hostile" personal attitudes and "reductive" explanations of religion offered by anthropologists, they must nevertheless find their place *within* a horizon marked by what Hallowell termed the "intellectual shift" in human self-understanding—from the provincial and socially sanctioned folk anthropologies of their particular societies to a "level of systematic observations and inquiry detached from traditional beliefs and inspired by values giving prime emphasis to the search for more reliable knowledge of all aspects of human phenomena."[1]

If in cultural anthropology there has occurred an extension of "science" to the cross-cultural study of humanity, then theologians do well to understand that science—its processes of interpretation, its particular modes of understanding and explanation—before identifying any religious dimension to it.

---

[1]A. Irving Hallowell, "The History of Anthropology as an Anthropological Problem," in *Contribution to Anthropology: Selected Papers of A. Irving Hallowell*, ed. with intro. by Raymond D. Fogelson et al. (Chicago: University of Chicago Press, 1976) 22.

A Portrait of Anthropological Inquiry

The subsequent focus, in chapters 3 and 4, on two particular anthropologists is necessary because of the difficulties of generally portraying anthropological inquiry by reference to cultural anthropology as a "discipline." In fact, as anthropologists themselves readily admit, it is difficult to characterize cultural anthropology as a discipline.[2] It fits more readily Stephen Toulmin's notion of a "would-be discipline" that diverges methodologically and institutionally from the "compact disciplines" more characteristic of physical and biological sciences. "Would-be disciplines," methodologically, lack a clearly defined set of disciplinary problems so that "conceptual innovations within them face no consistent critical tests." Institutionally, would-be disciplines lack a professional organization able to exploit fully disciplinary possibilities. The "discipline" of anthropology, along with sociology and philosophy, is particularly singled out by Toulmin as such a would-be discipline due to its "diversity of approaches of a kind unparalleled in physics."[3] Because anthropology can be viewed as a would-be discipline, the portrait of anthropology here will depend less on carefully defined disciplinary boundaries and more on certain intellectual ideals and commitments held by its practitioners.[4]

Some preliminary steps toward construing anthropological inquiry have already been taken. In the first chapter, for example, in discussing anthropologists' self-understanding of the rise of their discipline, I have generally referred to cultural anthropology as an "undermining" of earlier folk anthropology; as the development of a "comprehensive

---

[2]Note, for example, Eric Wolf, "They Divide and Subdivide and Call It Anthropology," *New York Times*, 30 November 1980, sec. 4, p. 9, and frequent notes in the discipline's introductory texts, which highlight the diffuseness of anthropological interests that always threatens disciplinary unity. Cf. Maurice Freedman, *Main Trends in Social and Cultural Anthropology* (New York: Holmes and Meier Publishers, Inc., 1978) 5-18.

[3]Stephen Toulmin, *Human Understanding: The Use and Evolution of Concepts* (Princeton: Princeton University Press, 1972) 378-95. On anthropology, see esp. 380-82.

[4]On the fragmentation of anthropology as a "discipline," see Dell Hymes, ed., *Reinventing Anthropology* (New York: Vintage Press, 1969) 3-7.

spatio-temporal frame of reference which embraces all living varieties of *homo sapiens* as well as extinct cultures and peoples of the distant past and more ancient hominid types besides"[5]; or as a depicting of various cultures, their processes of stability and change, their similarities and differences.[6] Most anthropologists would affirm the breadth of such concerns in spite of their tendency to prevent a scholarly consensus that might raise cultural anthropology above the status of a "would-be discipline." The spatial and temporal diversity of peoples and cultures studied, and the diverse tools borrowed from other disciplines for this study, are usually viewed as strengths of anthropology, whatever the present hazards to disciplinary unity. It is by means of such broad concerns that the "discipline" hopes to make its fundamental contribution to integrating the study of human behavior and thought.

> Anthropology is the only discipline that offers a conceptual schema for the whole context of human experience. To use Tylor's image, it is like the carrying frame onto which may be fitted all the several subjects of a liberal education, and by organizing the load, makes it more wieldy and capable of being carried.[7]

However true it is that anthropology is characterized by commitments to diversity and to a "whole context of human experience," I have still left unaddressed the precise nature of this anthropological inquiry. How do anthropologists study diverse peoples, especially when the others are radically "other," that is, identifiable by different languages and cultures? By what kind of inquiry do anthropologists relate the study of diverse others to what De Laguna termed a "conceptual schema for the whole context of human experience"? And upon what kind of inquiry is discernment of this holistic conceptual schema founded?

---

[5]Hallowell, "The History of Anthropology," 23-25.

[6]David G. Mandelbaum, *International Encyclopedia of Social Science*, 1968 ed., under "Cultural Anthropology," 319.

[7]Frederica De Laguna, "Presidential Address—1967," *American Anthropologist* 70 (1968): 469-76, 475. De Laguna has no "blueprint" for this "carrying frame" nor can she yet see the whole frame, "yet it is always there to be discovered anew." For a statement similar to De Laguna's, see Muriel Dimen-Schein, *The Anthropological Imagination* (New York: McGraw Hill, 1977): "Anthropological theory contains a totalizing view of the world that replicates the fully integrated quality of life as it goes on at any given moment" (18).

In order to address such basic questions, I will generally present anthropological inquiry in terms of the dialectical relation between "understanding" (*Verstehen*) and "explanation" (*Erklären*), two ideals for the study of human thought and action. While this dialectic certainly is not the only rubric by which anthropological inquiry can be explicated, I employ it not only because of its use in reflecting upon the social and human sciences taken together, but also because it encompasses many of the intellectual tensions and commitments traditionally addressed by anthropologists.

Understanding and explanation

The distinction between "explanation" and "understanding" is traditionally a German one, often discussed in terms of Wilhelm Dilthey's analysis of the differences between *Naturwissenschaften* and *Geisteswissenschaften*, between sciences dealing with physical nature and those dealing with "spiritual" activity. The relevance of the distinction should not be limited to the German context, however, if for no other reason than that the term *Geisteswissenschaften* was employed and opposed to *Naturwissenschaften* within the German context as a result of the German translation of an English text. The German translator of John Stuart Mill's *System of Logic* in 1849 rendered Mill's "moral sciences" as *Geisteswissenschaften*. Dilthey's distinction, then, may be viewed as a debate with the logical demand of Mill's famous last chapter in the *Logic*, wherein "the backward state of the moral sciences" was to be remedied by applying natural-science methods to them.[8]

The encompassing and subsuming capacities of the understanding-and-explanation rubric for construing Western knowledge is especially illustrated by Georg Henrik von Wright's book, *Explanation and Understanding*, in which the two ideals are posed as "two main traditions" in science, the philosophy of science and the history of ideas. Explanation is a "Galilean" way, referring to the contributions of natural scientists and to forms of "positivism" that would, with various qualifications, include the philosophies of Comte, John Stuart Mill, and Hume.[9] Understanding is an "Aristotelian" way, which refuses "to view

---

[8]H.-G. Gadamer, *Truth and Method* (New York: Seabury, 1975) 1, 8, 499 n. 1.

[9]Georg Henrik von Wright, *Explanation and Understanding* (New York: Cornell University Press, 1971) 2-4.

the pattern set by the natural sciences as the sole and supreme ideal for a rational understanding of reality."[10] Scholars of this latter tradition, for von Wright, would include German philosophers, historians, and social scientists such as Droysen, Dilthey, Simmel, and Weber.

The contrast has also been stressed in the modern period in, for example, Heidegger's distinction between "calculative" and "meditative" thought, a contrast he made as early as 1929 in his *Was ist Metaphysik?* and then more specifically in his *Gelassenheit* of 1959.[11] Heidegger's distinction, along with that of the tradition represented by Dilthey, is also expressed in Gadamer's discussion of the relationship between "truth" and "method." Still more recently, within the analytical tradition in philosophy, Stanley Rosen's *Limits of Analysis* embodies the fundamental distinction between understanding and explanation. By working with analysis and by giving an "account of what we actually do" in it, Rosen seeks to show that "analysis turns upon synthesis and intuition," and that it requires "a lucid and reasonable dream" offered by intuition in order to effect its analyses.[12]

True, each of these distinctions possesses differences, especially when considered in the contexts of its respective formulator's thought. The argument here, however, has been that whether one opposes "truth" and "method" (Gadamer), "meditative" and "calculative" thinking (Heidegger), or "intuition" and "analysis" (Rosen), one is accenting the fundamental contrast that constitutes the "understanding/ explanation" discussion. It remains to specify what this contrast is in order to better recognize it within a particular form of inquiry like cultural anthropology.

---

[10]Ibid., 4.

[11]For discussions of this contrast in English translation, see Heidegger, "What is Metaphysics?" in *Existence and Being*, trans. R. F. C. Hull and Alan Crick, with intro. and analysis by Werner Brock (South Bend IN: Regenery/Gateway, Inc., 1979) 356-59; and J. M. Anderson and E. Evans Freund, *Discourse on Thinking*, which is a translation of *Gelassenheit*, with intro. by J. M. Anderson (New York: Harper Torchbooks, 1966) 46-47.

[12]Stanley Rosen, *The Limits of Analysis* (New York: Basic Books, 1980), see esp. 3-4, 257, 259-60.

The two ideals can be set forth here, following Paul Ricoeur's analysis, as having both epistemological and ontological meanings.[13] Epistemologically, inquirers guided by *Geisteswissenschaften* ideals seek to "understand" other subjects and other minds. In doing so, they rely on a similarity between the inquirer and those inquired about, which allows them to trust using analogies for the understanding of others, analogies between their own and others' experiences. The inquirer of the *Geisteswissenschaften*, thus, epistemologically values "empathy" or "intuition"—the transference of inquiring subjects into others' psychic lives—as the principle common to every kind of understanding.[14] Ontologically, inquirers pursuing the ideal of understanding often focus on "mind" and the "intentions" of mind.[15] Others inquired about are expressions of *Geist*. This attitude does not mean that inquirers here are necessarily committed to "Absolute Spirit" in Hegel's sense. They may rather follow Dilthey, who, after Hegel, relativized *Geist* so that human others are individuals and groups that must be studied in their multiplicity.[16]

Epistemologically, inquirers, guided on the other hand by *naturwissenschaftlich* ideals, seek to "explain" other subjects. Looking to the natural sciences for models of study, inquirers explain by observing external facts, submitting hypotheses to empirical verification, covering facts with general laws, providing theories to encompass laws in a systematic whole.[17] Here too, inquirers may apply analogies from their experience to that of others. But here there is a greater suspicion of analogy.

---

[13]Note Paul Ricoeur's brief mention of these two concerns in *Interpretation Theory: Discourse and the Surplus of Meaning* (Ft. Worth TX: Texas Christian University Press, 1976) 72-73.

[14]Ibid., 73. Note also Talcott Parsons's discussion of *Verstehen* and "intuition" in *The Structure of Social Action* (Glencoe IL: The Free Press, 1949) 481.

[15]Von Wright, *Explanation and Understanding*, 102-18.

[16]Paul Ricoeur, "The Model of the Text: Meaningful Action Considered as a Text," *Interpretive Social Science: A Reader*, ed. Paul Rabinow and William M. Sullivan (Berkeley: University of California Press, 1979) 87. On the relativization of *Geist* so that it is "associated with specific historical periods or traditions," see George W. Stocking, Jr., *The Shaping of American Anthropology, 1883-1911. A Franz Boas Reader* (New York: Basic Books, 1974) 10-11, and Parsons, *The Structure of Social Action*, 473-85.

[17]Ricoeur, *Interpretation Theory*, 72.

The mind's analogical propensities must be "checked" and "tested." Ontologically, inquirers pursuing the ideal of explanation focus on "nature." Nature becomes the "common horizon" for facts, laws and theories, hypotheses and verifications. Inquirers study others whose being is part of a world made up of complex elements that are functionally or causally related.[18] Studied others act and think according to laws like those of natural science because they are a part of nature.

The nature of the epistemological and ontological differences between *Natur-* and *Geisteswissenschaften* is especially evident in the role each "science" grants to the values held by its interpreters. For adherents of the *Naturwissenschaften,* interpreters may strive for a *Wertfreiheit,* a freedom from values often based on a rigorously enforced distinction between fact and value. Interpreters who "explain" may seek to subordinate their values to the tasks of observation, hypothesis construction, and testing. For adherents of the *Geisteswissenschaften,* on the other hand, values play an important role and, for some, interpreters' "understanding" is constituted precisely by bringing studied "objects" into relationship with their own values.[19] In "explanation," the interpreter's values must be checked and controlled by observation and testing; conversely, in "understanding," they may be acknowledged and appropriated.

My work assumes that human inquiry involves not a dichotomy of these two ideals of understanding and explanation, but rather a dialectical relation between them. I have therefore not used the term *hermeneutic* to refer only to the *Geisteswissenschaften* or to the inquirers seeking "understanding," as have some writers who identify hermeneutics with the *Verstehen* tradition, opposing it to explanation.[20] Rather, I use the term *hermeneutic* following Ricoeur, for the entire process of interpretation that dialectically encompasses understanding and explanation. I

---

[18]Parsons, *The Structure of Social Action,* 481-82.

[19]See, for example, H. Rickert, *Die Grenzen der naturwissenschaftlichen Begriffsbildung: Eine logische einleitung in die historischen wissenschaften,* 2d ed. (Tübingen and Leipzig: J. C. B. Mohr, 1902) 516ff.

[20]Note, for example, von Wright, *Explanation and Understanding,* 5, 29-32, and Charles Taylor, "Interpretation and the Sciences of Man," in *Interpretive Social Science: A Reader,* ed. Paul Rabinow and William M. Sullivan (Berkeley: University of California Press, 1979) 66.

believe that this comprehensive and dialectical understanding of hermeneutics is adequate for portraying anthropological inquiry.

This dialectic consists of three moments through which human inquiry moves: (a) from "understanding" as a guess about the whole, (b) to "explanation" as a moment of testing and structuring one's guesses, and (c) back to "understanding" as comprehension. Ricoeur's hermeneutics is a theory of human inquiry that in this way dialectically relates the ideals of understanding *and* explanation, which are vital elements in the social (or human) sciences *and* the natural sciences.

In the first moment of the dialectic, there is intuitive "understanding." This is a necessary moment but one that Ricoeur characterizes as a "naive grasping." However naive and preliminary, this grasping is productive for the totality of meaning, for it draws into a whole the many particulars of an inquirer's subject matter. This is the "guess" about the whole.[21]

"Explanation," constituting the second moment, unfolds ranges of propositions and meanings about that which has been guessed. "Explanation" explores the whole that has been merely designated or intuited by "understanding" in its first moment. "Explanation" orders the whole, fills it out, identifying and relating its parts in "systems" or "structures" that are used to "verify" or "validate" the guess.[22]

In the third moment of the dialectic, "understanding" emerges as supported and elaborated by explanatory procedures. In the first moment "understanding" was but a naive grasping, a guess. Now, explanation has developed understanding toward the comprehension of a possible whole world and a preferred "mode of being-in-the-world."[23] From a naive guess, explanation now leads interpreters to "comprehend" a world having reference to the fundamental "boundary situations" and "existential conflicts" of human being-in-the-world. "Explanation" is, therefore, a mediation between the two stages of understanding.[24] Ricoeur summarizes the way these moments interplay in

---

[21]Ricoeur, *Interpretation Theory*, 75-80.

[22]Ibid., 78-79.

[23]Ibid., 80.

[24]Ibid., 75.

his hermeneutical theory: "Understanding precedes, accompanies, closes and thus *envelops* explanation. In return, explanation *develops* understanding analytically."[25]

Two ideals in anthropology

In this section I will undertake two tasks. First, I will cite various discussions within anthropology to show how several of its important tensions and commitments can generally be viewed as tensions between the ideals of "understanding" and "explanation," as these terms have been defined and related in the previous section. Then, second, I will indicate how the presence of these two ideals in anthropology is relevant to my project's discernment of a religious dimension to cultural anthropology.

The appropriateness of applying the understanding/explanation rubric to anthropological inquiry is apparent in anthropologists' self-conscious reflection on their fieldwork roles as "participant-observers" in other societies. In fact, in the notions of "participation" and "observation" are the seeds of the distinction between understanding and explanation. Anthropologists Dennison Nash and Ronald Wintrob have suggested, however, that it is only recently that anthropologists have become conscious about the ways that their roles as participants condition their observations. They account for the emergence of this self-consciousness in terms of factors internal to anthropology.[26] The basic epistemological route that Nash and Wintrob charted in anthropology moves from an early "naive empiricism" in which anthropologists sought to gain "scientific status" by turning the fieldworker into "a self-effacing creature without any reactions other than those of a recording machine," to a more recent recognition that self-conscious reflection on

---

[25]Paul Ricoeur, "Explanation and Understanding," in *The Philosophy of Paul Ricoeur*, ed. Charles E. Reagan and David Stewart (Boston: Beacon Press, 1978) 165.

[26]Dennison Nash and Ronald Wintrob, "The Emergence of Self-Consciousness in Ethnography," *Current Anthropology* 13 (1972): 527-42. These "internal" factors include (1) an increasing personal involvement of ethnographers with their subjects, (2) the "democratization" of anthropology, (3) multiple field studies of the same culture, and (4) assertions of independence by native peoples.

the fieldworker-self, the "personal" or "human" factor, is an essential
element of fieldwork and anthropological knowledge.[27]

> What we appear to be witnessing in this brief historical period of three
> decades or less in American social and cultural anthropology is the
> decline of an institutionalized scientific faith in an objective world
> which, with appropriate methods, can be discovered and an increas-
> ing "subjectivization" of the discipline.[28]

In terms of the ideals of explanation and understanding, the shift noted
by Nash and Wintrob can be viewed as one from the *Naturwissenschaften* to the *Geisteswissenschaften* paradigm.

It is not just recent discussions like this one that highlight the presence of the understanding/explanation problem in anthropological inquiry. In some earlier discussions of British social anthropology, for
example—about whether anthropology was a "humanity" or a "science"—the understanding/explanation problem is apparent. A. R.
Radcliffe-Brown's intense commitment to *naturwissenschaftlich* ideals
led him to suggest that social anthropology adopt unreservedly the "inductive" approach that has already "conquered one realm of nature after
another" (in astronomy, chemistry, physics, and biology).[29] Evans-
Pritchard found such *naturwissenschaftlich* commitments to be a "doc-

---

[27]The publication of Bronislaw Malinowski's *A Diary in the Strict Sense of the Term*
(New York: Harcourt, Brace and World, 1966) may be taken as an important indicator
of the rise of anthropological self-consciousness. Malinowski, the master fieldworker
rigorously pursuing the "natives' point of view," revealed his European ethnocentrism
and personal idiosyncrasies in that text. Cf. Francis L. K. Hsu, "The Cultural Problem
of the Cultural Anthropologist," *American Anthropologist* 81 (1979): 517-32, and Clifford C. Geertz, "Under the Mosquito Net," *New York Review of Books* 9 (September
1967): 12-13.

[28]Nash and Wintrob, "The Emergence of Self-Consciousness in Ethnology," 529.
S. F. Nadel, *The Foundations of Social Anthropology* (Glencoe IL: Free Press, 1951), is
viewed by Nash and Wintrob as exemplary of the passing "objectivist" orientation, while
the works of George Devereaux (*From Anxiety to Method in the Social Sciences* [New York:
Humanities Press, 1967]), Robert Redfield (*The Primitive World and Its Transformations* [Chicago: University of Chicago Press, 1953]), and D. Maybury-Lewis (*The Savage and the Innocent* [London: Evans, 1965]), along with Malinowski in his *Diary*, are
representative of the emerging self-consciousness of fieldworkers.

[29]A. R. Radcliffe-Brown, "The Methods of Ethnology and Social Anthropology,"
South African Journal of Science 20 (1923): 124.

trinaire positivism at its worst,"[30] and argued that social anthropology belongs more to the humanities than to the natural sciences. According to him, there is an "empirical" ingredient for which anthropology must be noted, but this ingredient entails not a commitment to inductive method, but rather an intense participation in the life of another people, characterized by a sufficiently long period of study, close contact with the people, and attention to their entire cultural and social life.[31] Evans-Pritchard especially demonstrates his preference for the *geisteswissenschaftlich* ideal of understanding when he argues that the anthropologist is not photographic but "interpretive," that the anthropologist must have "the imaginative insight of an artist," a "feeling for form and pattern and a touch of genius."[32] The conclusion is clear: "Social anthropology is best regarded as an art and not as a natural science."[33]

Moving further back into the history of anthropological thought, note the contrast between Edward B. Tylor's "rational ethnography," which was consciously modeled after the natural sciences,[34] and F. Max Müller's critique of applying such "evolutionist" perspectives to the study of humanity.[35] Müller sought to expose what he believed was the naiveté of the British philosophical milieu. He opposed "the new philosophy priding itself on its positive character, professing . . . to appeal for evidence to matter of fact only."[36] He rejected a Tylorian view that human mind and "cultural phenomena" are but the outcome of an "association of sensuous impressions." Arguing against British tendencies to think in an "anti-Kantian" fashion, Müller tried in his *Science of Thought* to prod early anthropological science toward the recognition that there are not only "sensations" and "percepts," but also "concepts"

---

[30]E. E. Evans-Pritchard, *Social Anthropology* (Glencoe: Free Press, 1951) 57.

[31]Ibid., 77-81.

[32]Ibid., 82.

[33]Ibid., 85.

[34]Edward B. Tylor, *Primitive Culture*, 2 vols. (New York: Henry Holt and Co., 1889) 1:2-4, 20.

[35]F. Max Müller, *The Science of Thought*, 2 vols. (New York: Charles Scribner's and Sons, 1887) 1:12.

[36]Ibid., 116.

("forms of intuition") and "names." As a "scientist" of human thought and language, then, Müller appropriated his own subjectivity in his studies.

Tylor may laud Müller for his philosophical brilliance and subtlety, but he still insists that the results of Müller's studies, particularly in mythology, lack the evidence of "scientific method" and "actual fact." They are the fruits of an "unbridled imagination."[37] Tylor vigorously defends, then, his *naturwissenschaftlich* approach to the study of cultural phenomena against the more intuitive approach of Müller.[38]

The pertinence of the understanding/explanation problem to anthropology is not evident simply in polemical contexts wherein anthropologists defend one of the ideals against the other. Anthropologists may also affirm both ideals as constitutive of anthropological inquiry, though they may not always indicate what the relation between them is. Margaret Mead affirmed anthropology's use of "two methods of approach":

> [There is] that of the *humanities* which focuses on the recognition of the unique character of the work of imagination, and that of the *sciences*, which attempt by careful observation, analysis and finally experiment to understand the lawfulness of the behavior involved.[39]

Fieldwork, especially, for Mead was a distinctive intellectual enterprise that combined "art" and "technology."[40] Other thinkers, also studying

---

[37]Edward B. Tylor, "Review of *Science of Language* by F. Max Müller," *Quarterly Review* 119 (1866): 424.

[38]Tylor himself did not unambiguously disparage imagination for a "science of culture." See Tylor, *Primitive Culture*, 1:274, 315. In spite of Tylor's predominant claim that analogy and poetry are vestiges of a "savage rationality" that the civilized rational ethnographer no longer needs (1:22), he himself employs an "analogical imagination" in moving from the present to a knowledge of earlier, "primitive" humanity (cf. 1:27-28, 62). Tylor also occasionally admits that the "doctrine of analogy" is not only practiced by the "savage" mind but is "universal" (1:61).

[39]Margaret Mead, "Toward More Vivid Utopias," in *Anthropology: A Human Science, Selected Papers, 1939-1960* (Princeton: D. Van Norstrand Co., Inc., 1964) 230. In the same volume, see her comments on "Anthropology among the Sciences," 6-13.

[40]Margaret Mead, "The Art and Technology of Fieldwork," in *Handbook of Method in Cultural Anthropology*, ed. Ronald Cohen and Raoul Naroll (New York: Columbia University Press, 1970) 246-65.

the fieldwork process, exhibit the commitment to both ideals in anthropology. Pelto characterizes fieldwork as both "art" and "science."[41] Georges and Jones argue that fieldworkers, "people studying people," are both "objective" inquirers and also "human" like their objects/subjects of study.[42]

The dual commitment to both *Natur-* and *Geisteswissenschaften* ideals is evident also in Gerald Berreman's claim that anthropology is frequently caught on the horns of a dilemma: between being "scientific at the expense of insight," or "insightful at the expense of being unscientific," between being "scientific" and being "humanist."[43] Like Mead, Pelto, and Georges and Jones, Berreman insists that anthropology must pursue both scientific rigor and insight.

A number of other examples of the understanding-and-explanation tension might be drawn from anthropological discussion. Discussion in which the two ideals seem opposed would include that of Clifford Geertz, for whom cultural anthropology as "thick description" has surpassed a now-dead "operationalism" in anthropology.[44] In spite of a number of mediating positions, the "rationality" debate in social anthropology also displays an opposition of the two ideals. In that debate, Alasdair MacIntyre values the rational, natural science of Western tradition as a model for the study of other cultures, while Peter Winch values for such study an "intelligible" social science of "understanding."[45]

---

[41]Pertti J. Pelto, *Anthropological Research: The Structure of Inquiry* (New York: Harper and Row, 1970) 213ff.

[42]Robert A. Georges and Michael O. Jones, *People Studying People: The Human Element in Fieldwork* (Berkeley: University of California Press, 1980) 21-22, 153.

[43]Gerald D. Berreman, "Anemic and Emetic Analyses in Social Anthropology," *American Anthropologist* 68 (1966): 346-54, esp. 346.

[44]Clifford Geertz, *The Interpretation of Cultures* (New York: Basic Books, 1973) 5.

[45]B. R. Wilson, *Rationality* (Oxford: Basil Blackwell, 1970) 15, 71. In the same volume, Stephen Lukes's contribution is a particularly helpful mediation between MacIntyre's and Winch's positions. Lukes tries to discern the appropriate roles played by the "context-dependent" criteria of rationality valued by Winch's social-scientific understanding, and by the "universal" criteria of rationality maintained in MacIntyre's commitment to scientific, universal criteria. For discussion and critique of the "rationality debates," see Robert C. Ulin, *Understanding Cultures: Perspectives in Anthropology and Social Theory* (Austin: University of Texas Press, 1984) 23-90.

In addition to Mead, Pelto, Georges and Jones, and Berreman, all of whom embrace understanding and explanation ideals, might be added Francis L. K. Hsu, who insists that the "cultural problem of the cultural anthropologist" is to hold together a scientific role as fieldworker with an "affective," positive feeling for studied subjects.[46] In these dual commitments to both ideals as well as in the tendencies to oppose them, one can observe the prevalence in anthropological inquiry of the longstanding understanding-and-explanation problem.[47]

One other important discussion in cultural anthropology, taking several different forms, requires attention because it shows strikingly what other factors are at stake in the contrast between understanding and explanation. This discussion, occurring mainly in the last decade in anthropological literature, involves an opposition of "hermeneutics" to what is pejoratively referred to as a "scientistic" anthropology. The so-called hermeneutical position is then often strengthened in its opposition to scientism when conjoined with a critical praxis theory that charges anthropologists with having neglected the integral relation between anthropological theory and praxis.[48]

An article by anthropologists Watson-Franke and Watson reveals the introduction of general hermeneutical perspectives into anthropology. They seek to draw anthropologists' attention to the importance of their having "preunderstanding," out of which questions are put to foreign others in their particular contexts of meaning.[49] Anthropology is

----

[46]Hsu, "The Cultural Problem of the Cultural Anthropologist," 520-21.

[47]Some anthropologists express their ambivalence about how or whether the two ideals are to be related. See, for example, Morris Freilich's "Reply," *Current Anthropology* 16 (1975): 254. Other texts in anthropology reveal anthropologists' ambivalence about relating the components of understanding and explanation. For more examples, see Raymond Firth's attempt to relate powers of anthropological generalization to empirical contexts in "Problem and Assumption in the Anthropological Study of Religion," The Huxley Memorial Lecture, 1959, *Journal of the Royal Anthropological Institute of Great Britain and Ireland* 89 (1960): 129-48.

[48]Robert C. Ulin's book, *Understanding Cultures,* traces the history of interpretive theory in anthropology and explicitly discusses hermeneutical theories in anthropology from the point of view of critical praxis theory; see 91-172.

[49]Maria-Barbara Watson-Franke and Lawrence C. Watson, "Understanding in Anthropology: A Philosophical Reminder," *Current Anthropology* 16 (1975): 247-62. The position taken by these authors is that the search for understanding is hermeneutical. Recall, in contrast, that in this work "hermeneutical" refers not only to "understanding," but also to "explanation" as it is bound up with "understanding."

construed as predominantly the "understanding" (*Verstehen*) of "foreign mental states." This hermeneutical stress on the anthropologist's preunderstanding undercuts any notion of the anthropological inquirer as "culture-free" or "value-free," a notion that "hermeneutical" anthropologists decry as scientism's major flaw.[50]

The "hermeneutical" position cuts more sharply into "scientistic" anthropology when it joins with critical praxis theory. The effect of this conjunction is that an anthropologist's preunderstanding is taken not simply as epistemological, but also as sociocultural. Preunderstanding, then, is not just a set of conditioning, interconnected presuppositions, but a context set historically, politically, and socially. Anthropological ethnographers from Western nations—from which anthropologists have traditionally emerged—study "primitive" or "non-literate" peoples in a highly charged sociocultural context that affects their interpretations. Bob Scholte, along with other "reinventors of anthropology" seeking to take account of these sociopolitical contexts, insists that

> the dialogue between interpreter and interpreted—the dialectic between question and answer—is a mediated reality which is rarely if ever an exchange between equals (historically, not normatively speaking). Irrespective of the ethnographer's democratic or equalitarian intent, the dialogue is situated in a historical context of conquest and oppression.[51]

Scholte earlier defended this view and argued that by becoming self-conscious and "reflexive" about these contexts, anthropology could become "emancipatory." While Scholte did not specify anthropology's emancipatory and normative "interests," he asserted that "humanism

---

[50]Supporting Watson-Franke's and Watson's application of hermeneutics to anthropology is Alfred Schutz's "interpretive sociology," in which he suggests that understanding of the alien or other (*Fremdverstehen*) occurs through a "simultaneity" of the interpreter's and the other's "stream of consciousness." In contrast to objective meaning, *Fremdverstehen* is the true comprehension of subjective meaning (and hence also of social action). See Alfred Schutz, *The Phenomenology of the Social World*, with an intro. by George Walsh (Chicago: Northwestern University Press, 1967) xxv-xxvi, 106.

[51]Bob Scholte, "Reply" to Watson-Franke and Watson, *Current Anthropology* 16 (1975): 256.

is the pre-requisite for the scientific study of humanity, . . . not the other way around."[52]

Scholte's call for a "reflexive" and "emancipatory" anthropology was the concluding essay in a volume entitled *Reinventing Anthropology*. That book offers a variety of viewpoints advocated by those whom one might term "anthropologists of understanding." The introductory essay by that volume's editor, anthropologist and linguist Dell Hymes, is especially instructive. Examining anthropologists' preunderstanding in sociological as well as logical terms, Hymes leads his fellow reinventors in calling anthropology to its "ethical" and "political" task: to serve as midwife for "a world culture struggling to be born."[53] This task entails not a radical rejection of anthropology as "science," but a radical revision of it so that it is founded on a "personal commitment" to knowledge that advances the "welfare of mankind."

> By virtue of its subject matter, anthropology is unavoidably a political and ethical discipline, not merely an empirical specialty. It is founded in a personal commitment that has inescapably a reflective, philosophical dimension. Indeed, the present surge of interest in philosophical questions among anthropologists reflects the widespread sense of political and ethical concern.[54]

The belief in the need to integrate the humanist concern for ethical and political responsibility into anthropological knowledge, in which "each anthropologist must reinvent it as a general field for him or herself following personal interest and talent where best they lead," is particularly evident in numerous essays in the *Anthropology and Humanism Quarterly* (which was founded in 1976). This journal's reflection of understanding ideals is evident in its commitment to studying the rela-

---

[52]Bob Scholte, "Toward a Reflexive and Critical Anthropology," in *Reinventing Anthropology*, 430-57. Scholte and his colleagues wishing to "reinvent anthropology" along hermeneutical and praxis lines, argue out of the hermeneutical praxis theory of Jürgen Habermas, citing, among other sources, Habermas's "Knowledge and Interest," *Inquiry* 9 (1965): 285-300, and *Toward a Rational Society* (Boston: Beacon Press, 1970).

[53]Hymes, *Reinventing Anthropology*, 19, 30, 53. Hymes is citing fellow "reinventor" Eric Wolf, *Anthropology* (Englewood Cliffs NJ: Prentice-Hall, 1964) 96.

[54]Ibid., 48. Similar arguments are offered by John O'Neill, *Sociology as Skin Trade: Essays toward a Reflexive Sociology* (New York: Harper Torchback Books, 1972).

tionship of the values of anthropological knowledge to ethnographic-scientific method.[55] Scholte and other reinventors of the discipline have used the journal as a forum for discussing "historical and epistemological alternatives" to what is viewed as the prevailing "positivistic, liberal and academic viewpoint" of anthropologists hesitant to make the reflexive, critical, and emancipatory turns.[56]

I need not further detail the position of the "reinventors" of anthropology. Many issues could be addressed. I want merely to identify them here as exemplary of a concern in anthropology with hermeneutics and with a critical praxis theory that calls into question empiricist or positivist views in anthropology. The reinventors thus in a recent and intense manner have exhibited commitment in anthropology to the *geisteswissenschaftlich* ideals of understanding.

The opposed positivism, operationalism, or scientism, however, is not dead. Particularly in the reactions to the claims of the reinventors, one can note the persistence of *naturwissenschaftlich* ideals of explanation in anthropological inquiry. Edmund Leach rather sweepingly retorted that the reinventors are "radical enthusiasts" on the order of the Diggers, Quakers, and Muggletonians who passionately defended "Holy Writ."[57] A somewhat less shocked but equally firm response by David Kaplan appeared in the *American Anthropologist*. Kaplan defends objectivity as a norm in anthropology. Whatever the merits of abandoning objectivity for consciousness raising, Kaplan says, methodologically "it would undercut any attempt at a collective systematic inquiry into sociocultural phenomena."[58] Kaplan concludes with a defense that exhibits the *naturwissenschaftlich* ideals of explanation in anthropology.

> Whether we are driven mainly by a desire to understand the world
> or by a concern to change it, we have to start by doing the same thing:

---

[55]Bruce Grindal, *Anthropology and Humanism Quarterly* 1 (April 1976): 1.

[56]Bob Scholte, "Critical Anthropology since Its Reinvention," *Anthropology and Humanism Quarterly* 3 (March/June 1978): 4.

[57]Edmund Leach, "Anthropology Upside Down," *New York Review of Books* 21:5 (1974): 33. For a reply to Leach by a "reinventor," see Stanley Diamond, *New York Review of Books* 21:16 (1974): 37-38.

[58]David Kaplan, "The Anthropology of Authenticity: Everyman His Own Anthropologist," *American Anthropologist* 76 (1974): 824-39. See esp. 828.

namely, to generate a corpus of knowledge in which we have some confidence and which bears some objective relationship to the nature of the world. Even the projection of, say, more egalitarian and humane social arrangements than we now have—if it is to be anything more than an exercise in political moonshine—ought to be grounded in some conception of the range of the possible. After all, the *logically* possible is not always the *causally* possible.[59]

I trust that anthropologists' own understanding of their inquiry has been discussed enough to indicate the appropriateness of generally construing anthropological inquiry in terms of understanding-and-explanation ideals. Sometimes these ideals are embraced together though they are in tension, as in Mead's view of anthropology as both a humanity and a science, or in Berreman's claim that anthropology is both scientific and insightful. At other times, the ideals are posited against one another, as in the difference between Radcliffe-Brown and Evans-Pritchard, or as in Geertz's claim that an "interpretative anthropology" has surpassed a now-dead "operationalism," or as in the debate between the "reinventors" and the defenders of objectivity.

Whether they choose between understanding and explanation, or embrace both, anthropologists' critique of their inquiries displays a fundamental tension between the two ideals. In the words of anthropologist Kenelm Burridge, anthropologists may show themselves partly to be caught up in the European tradition: a many times hidden, but nevertheless frequently present, dialectical engagement of "rational objectivity" (explanation) and "participation in the oneness of all things" (understanding).[60]

Granted that anthropological inquiry may be portrayed in terms of understanding and explanation, how does that portrayal relate to this work's discernment of a religious dimension? In many ways it would be most natural simply to turn to the advocates of "interpretive anthropology," those who display definite commitments to *geisteswissenschaftlich* ideals of understanding. One could then seek to articulate a religious dimension in relation, for example, to the reinventors' strong insistence

---

[59]Ibid., 828-29.

[60]Kenelm Burridge, *Encountering Aborigines: Anthropology and the Australian Aboriginal, A Case Study* (New York: Pergamon, 1973) 9-10.

on "personal commitment," "faith," or "ethical and political responsibility" in anthropology. Indeed, the close relation of the reinventors'
concerns to religious ones has been noted by their critics.

> I have the strong impression that much of the discontent with an-
> thropology expressed by the essayists in *Reinventing Anthropology*
> stems from what they see as the failure of the discipline to provide
> answers to the kinds of questions that, in other times and places, were
> provided by all encompassing religious philosophies.[61]

To use the reinventors' cultural anthropology for discerning a religious
dimension would, in a sense, be too easy and, more important, would
overlook the anthropology practiced by the reinventors' critics.

The proposal of a religious dimension to cultural anthropology
would also come too easily if other "interpretive anthropologists," such
as Clifford Geertz and Victor Turner, were made representative of cultural anthropological inquiry. Clifford Geertz's definition of religion as
a cultural "system of symbols" gives religion an all-pervading breadth
and depth of influence in cultural systems that might facilitate the find-
ing of a religious dimension in the cultural activity and symbol systems
of anthropologists themselves. Geertz hints at such when he suggests in
passing that "anthropologists are, like theologians, firmly dedicated to
proving the indubitable."[62]

Focus on Victor Turner's "interpretive" or "symbolic anthropology" would also tend to be too easy an approach for discerning a religious dimension to cultural anthropology, not only because of his claim
that his own Roman Catholic perspective has a positive role in his anthropological research,[63] but also because in his account of the Ndembu

---

[61]Kaplan, "The Anthropology of Authenticity," 828.

[62]Geertz, "Religion as a Cultural System," in *The Interpretation of Cultures*, 88. To
be sure, in spite of the pervasive character of Geertz's understanding of religion, he also
carefully distinguishes the religious perspective from that of "common sense," "science," or "aesthetics" (111-12). This distinction, however, does not lessen the strong
possibility that his notion of religion may be extended to anthropological inquiry and
activity as well.

For Geertz's view of anthropology as "interpretive," see Clifford Geertz, "Blurred
Genres: The Refiguration of Social Thought," *American Scholar* 49 (1980): 165-74.

[63]Victor Turner, *Image and Pilgrimage in Christian Culture: Anthropological Perspectives* (New York: Columbia University Press, 1978) xv.

chihamba ritual, for example, he interprets the *Kavula* symbol as an expression of the concept of "the pure act-of-being-itself."[64] To invoke this latter concept is to rely on the religious tradition of one's own culture, here Roman Catholic theology, to understand a fundamentally important symbol of a foreign cultural system.

It is true that in treating various anthropological affinities to religious concerns in the reinventors—for example, in Geertz or in Turner—there would still be the need to show that these affinities are significant or fundamental enough to their enterprises to warrant speaking of a religious dimension to their thought or to cultural anthropology. However, these affinities to religious concerns are distinctive enough to establish a *prima facie* kinship of interest between anthropology and religion, a kinship that might provide a strong starting point for discerning a religious dimension to cultural anthropology. That scholars of religion cite such "anthropologists of understanding" attests to the existence of such a kinship.[65]

This work's attempt to articulate a religious dimension to cultural anthropology, then, will not seize upon those anthropologies of understanding, in spite of their *prima facie* fusion of anthropological and religious concerns. Rather, the work focuses on the "anthropologies of explanation," in which there may be a certain suspicion of interpretive

---

[64]Victor Turner, *Revelation and Divination in Ndembu Ritual* (Ithaca and London: Cornell University Press, 1975) 19, 187. For a critique of Turner's invocation of this "theological" concept for interpreting the *chihamba* ritual, see anthropologist Robin Horton, "Ritual Man in Africa," *Reader in Comparative Religion: An Anthropological Approach*, 4th ed., ed. William A. Lessa and Evon Z. Vogt (New York: Harper and Row, 1979) 243-54.

[65]Theologians use many of the reinventors' own sources, particularly Habermas and his concern with "emancipatory interests." Cf. Joseph Komonchak, "Ecclesiology and Social Theory: A Methodological Essay," *Thomist* 45 (1981): 262-83, and David Tracy, *The Analogical Imagination: Christian Theology and the Culture of Pluralism* (New York: Crossroad, 1983) 73-75, 345. Philosophical theologians have used Geertz's discussion of religion. See David Tracy, *Blessed Rage for Order: The New Pluralism in Theology* (New York: Seabury, 1975) 92-93, and Andrew M. Greeley, *Unsecular Man: The Persistence of Religion* (New York: Schocken Books, 1972). Note also John Morgan's "Religion and Culture as Meaning Systems: A Dialogue between Geertz and Tillich," *Journal of Religion* 57 (1977): 363-75. Morgan, defining anthropology as the "systematics of culture" and theology as the "systematics of religion," strives to effect a "mutual interaction" proper to anthropology and theology. Geertz's and Tillich's joint concern with "culture as meaning" makes this interaction possible.

anthropologists' work. Not that discerning cultural anthropology's moments of understanding will not be crucial to the articulation of a religious dimension. For, as noted in the introduction, a focus on understanding (*Verstehen*) is a way into the "depth" or "limit situations" that are essential for discernment of religious dimensions. But instead of moving immediately to the moments of understanding to seek limit situations and a religious dimension, I propose in this work to display the anthropologies of explanation, to probe them for their own moments of understanding, and only then to discuss a religious dimension.

By seeking understanding *within* the anthropologies of explanation, I not only presuppose the integral, dialectical relation between understanding and explanation advocated by Ricoeur, but also hope to do greater justice to the diversity of positions in cultural anthropology, not simply to those that at first glance are significant to religious studies. This process also does greater justice to the moments of explanation and commitments to science that are not completely jettisoned by even the reinventors,[66] or other anthropologies of understanding. It is in this sense of focusing first on anthropologies of explanation, where there is suspicion of understanding, of interpretive anthropology and of religion, that the approach of this work is less easy, so to speak, than would be one that began immediately with anthropologies of understanding.

Anthropological Inquirers

I turn now to the practitioners of an anthropology of explanation. Their work provides the subject matter of the project. In this section I will lay down guidelines for approaching the work of two anthropologists, Claude Lévi-Strauss and Marvin Harris. At the same time, I will note why these two figures may be considered representative anthropologists of explanation.

The claim, of course, cannot be that Lévi-Strauss and Harris are unambiguously committed to the *naturwissenschaftlich* ideals of explanation. Such a claim would ignore the dialectical relation between explanation and understanding. Lévi-Strauss, for example, offers explanations by an aesthetic method bearing striking affinities to the

---

[66]See Hymes, *Reinventing Anthropology*, 11-12, and Scholte, "Toward a Reflexive and Critical Anthropology," 447.

geisteswissenschaftlich ideals of *Verstehen*. In both Lévi-Strauss and Harris, however, the predominant ideal or concern is to establish anthropology as a science using the tools of explanation. While this concern will emerge in later chapters through detailed analysis, one can anticipate that result with representative statements from their works.

Two modes for explaining others

Lévi-Strauss's and Harris's joint commitment to explanation is evident in several of their major works. Lévi-Strauss, for example, in the fourth volume of his structural analysis of myths, claims to be preparing the way for a "scientific anthropology" that, like any other science,

> should be able to set up experiments for the purpose of verifying its hypotheses and deducing, on the basis of certain guiding principles, hitherto unknown properties of the real world, in other words, to predict what will necessarily occur in certain given experimental conditions.[67]

Because of this commitment, Lévi-Strauss has been described as *"the* academic anthropologist—a formalist, reductionist, and 'scientific' relativist who denies the connection between theory and practice and insists on the privileged position of the Western observer."[68] He is the "natural scientist of man."[69] This "scientific" posture of his, which is then exhibited in the structuralist methods he pursues, is the basis for his being treated initially here as an anthropologist of explanation.

Similarly, Marvin Harris in his most recent works has reaffirmed his commitment to a "science of culture." Anthropology for Harris is to be a "pan-human science of society" based on "logical and evidentiary grounds." Harris's formulation of anthropology's final aim indicates his commitment to *naturwissenschaftlich* ideals.

---

[67]Claude Lévi-Strauss, *The Naked Man, Introduction to a Science of Mythology:* 4, trans. John Weightman and Doreen Weightman (New York: Harper and Row, 1981) 153. In French the work appeared under the title *L'Homme nu* (Paris: Plon, 1971).

[68]Stanley Diamond, Bob Scholte, and Eric Wolf, "Anti-Kaplan: Defining the Marxist Tradition," *American Anthropologist* 77 (1975): 872.

[69]Stanley Diamond, "Anthropology in Question," in *Reinventing Anthropology*, 402. These references to Lévi-Strauss as "scientist," however, do not stop still more scientifically inclined anthropologists from complaining that Lévi-Strauss is not "scientific" at all.

The "final aim of anthropology" . . . is the achievement of a scientific knowledge of the causes of the divergent and convergent evolutionary trajectories of sociocultural systems, which consist of behavior and the products of behavior as well as thought.[70]

Harris seeks explanations of sociocultural differences and similarities by referring to "nature." And in a recent work he explicitly rejects what he calls the "phenomenological" or "hermeneutical" attempt to separate the *Geistes-* or *Kulturwissenschaften* from the *Naturwissenschaften.*[71] Anthropology is a science of culture that, though having a unique set of epistemological problems, can be modeled after the physical sciences.[72]

However similar Lévi-Strauss and Harris may be in their commitments to *naturwissenschaftlich* ideals for anthropology, they have not been selected for this project simply because of that similarity. They also were chosen because of their markedly different modes of explanation.

Lévi-Strauss, occasionally referred to as "the world guru of anthropology," was educated at the Sorbonne and University of Paris and currently is recognized as the leader of "structural anthropology," especially in continental Europe. Though Lévi-Strauss was formally trained in philosophy, his teaching career began in sociology at the University of São Paolo, Brazil, in 1935, and included teaching in New York's New School for Social Research as well as directing studies at L'École Pratique des hautes études, and finally a chair in social anthropology at the Collège de France in 1958. Lévi-Strauss's fieldwork studies were carried out in the Mato Grosso, Brazil, with some limited investigations of the Chittagong tribes of Southern Asia. His published works include some ethnographic studies, lengthy works on kinship and mythology, and numerous articles bearing on the concerns of many dis-

---

[70]Marvin Harris, *Cultural Materialism: The Struggle for a Science of Culture* (New York: Random House, 1979) xii, 170.

[71]Ibid., 316.

[72]See Marvin Harris's earlier work, *The Nature of Cultural Things* (New York: Random House, 1964) 3.

ciplines other than anthropology.[73] Fellow anthropologists and especially laymen often characterize his works as "difficult, puzzling, sometimes incomprehensible and at other times stimulating." Lévi-Strauss's works are "delphic writings"; proper research into them might be an equivalent to anthropological fieldwork.[74]

In general, Lévi-Strauss's mode of explanation can be described as the explication of a semiotic system.[75] Lévi-Strauss attempts to postulate, deduce, display, and verify structured relationships between the basic units of kinship or myths that constitute a semiotic system. In his mode of explanation, "culture," the traditional concept of anthropological inquiry, is this system and may also be termed a conceptual scheme, code, or structure. The conceptual scheme mediates between human existence and human institutionalized organization, between praxis (human activity in its totality) and practices, between "objective conditions" and "organized behavior."[76] The particular forms of these mediating, conceptual schemes are used to explain sociocultural similarities and differences. Thus, Lévi-Strauss can refer to his mode of anthropological explanation as a mental "determinism," although this

[73]For an extensive bibliography of Lévi-Strauss's works and of secondary sources on Lévi-Strauss, see F. Lapointe and C. Lapointe, *Lévi-Strauss and Critics: An International Bibliography of Criticism (1950-1976)* (New York: Garland Pub., 1977).

For valuable introductions to Lévi-Strauss's work, see Edmund Leach, *Claude Lévi-Strauss* (New York: Viking, 1970); Ino Rossi, ed., *The Unconscious in Culture: The Structuralism of Claude Lévi-Strauss in Perspective* (New York: E. P. Dutton, 1974); Bob Scholte, "The Ethnology of Anthropological Traditions: A Comparative Study of Anglo-American Commentaries on French Structural Anthropology" (dissertation, University of California at Berkeley, 1969); Yvan Simonis, *Claude Lévi-Strauss ou la "Passion de l'inceste"* (Paris: Aubier, 1968); Octavio Paz, *Claude Lévi-Strauss: An Introduction* (New York: Cornell University Press, 1970); E. Nelson Hayes and Tanya Hayes, eds., *Claude Lévi-Strauss: The Anthropologist as Hero* (Cambridge MA: M.I.T. Press, 1970); Thomas Shalvey, *Claude Lévi-Strauss: Social Psychotherapy and the Collective Unconscious* (Amherst: University of Massachusetts Press, 1979); and Alan Jenkins, *The Social Theory of Claude Lévi-Strauss* (New York: St. Martin's Press, 1979).

[74]Marshall Sahlins, "On the Delphic Writings of Claude Lévi-Strauss," *Scientific American* 214:6 (1966): 131-36.

[75]For a statement of such semiotic explications as "explanatory," see Ricoeur, "The Model of the Text," 95ff.

[76]Claude Lévi-Strauss, *The Savage Mind* (Chicago: University of Chicago Press, 1966) 130.

determinism is always "inflected," taking many forms, according to technoeconomic conditions.[77] Lévi-Strauss stresses that he does not want to be misunderstood as opposing "mental" and "ecological" determinism, but he clearly asserts that "the world outside, that is ecology," is what it is because of an apprehension ultimately taking place in the brain.[78]

Marvin Harris is a different kind of advocate of anthropological explanation. Harris earned his undergraduate and graduate degrees at Columbia University and taught there from 1953 to 1980. During that time, from 1963 to 1966, he served as chairman of the anthropology department. In 1980 he began teaching at the University of Florida in Gainesville. He has lectured throughout the United States, and his field research has taken him to Brazil, Mozambique, Ecuador, and India.

Harris has long been disenchanted with the fragmented theories of anthropologists. His disenchantment has led to systematic reviews of the nature of anthropology, its method and its history. His writings, therefore, include not only a number of ethnographic studies, book reviews, and theoretical essays, but also a "meta-analysis" of cultural phenomena for orienting research in cultural anthropology, a wide-ranging and lengthy study of the history of anthropology, introductory textbooks to general anthropology, and more recently, an explicit statement and defense of his own commitment to theoretical explanation in anthropology. While Harris's mode of explanation is occasionally dismissed by some of his anthropologist colleagues as "vulgar materialism" or polemical,[79] the vigor of his arguments usually elicits response

---

[77]Claude Lévi-Strauss, "Structuralism and Ecology" (The Gildersleeve Lecture delivered at Barnard College, 28 March 1972), *Social Science Information* 12:1 (1972): 7-23.

[78]Lévi-Strauss, "Structuralism and Ecology," 21-22. It is for this reason that, though he admits the important role played by "infrastructure" and the need to consider ecological conditions for explaining sociocultural life, Lévi-Strauss commits himself as an ethnologist to the study of "superstructures." "Ethnology is first of all psychology." Cf. *The Savage Mind*, 130-31.

[79]For some representative critiques of Harris, see Robert Paul and Paul Rabinow, "Bourgeois Rationalism Revisited," *Dialectical Anthropology* 1 (1976): 121-34; H. D. Heinen, "Cultural Materialism, Marx and the Hegelian Monkey," *Current Anthropology* 16 (September 1975): 450-56; Elman Service, "The Prime Mover of Cultural Evolution," *Southwestern Journal of Anthropology* 24 (1969): 396-409; and the reviews of Harris's *The Rise of Anthropological Theory* in *Current Anthropology* 9 (1968): 519-33.

and discussion and allows him to serve as a contemporary spokesman for positions both within and without the anthropological discipline.[80]

The distinctiveness of Harris's mode of anthropological explanation, in contrast to Lévi-Strauss's mode, is evident in his search for causal relations in terms of regular sequences of antecedents and consequents. For Harris, culture is less a mediation between human existence and human practice, and more an effect of technoeconomic conditions of human existence. He speaks of a "material culture" in which conceptual schemes tend toward their particular forms by reason of their attachment to particular material, technoeconomic, or "infrastructural" conditions.[81] The similarities and differences in sociocultural practice and organization are not explained first by mental constraints, but rather by differences in material conditions. Thus, Harris can refer to his mode of anthropological explanation as a "techno-economic determinism." This determinism is qualified by its opposite kind (just as was Lévi-Strauss's mental determinism); for Harris does grant important functions to ideology, superstructure, and "conceptual schemes," if only as "feedback" within the causal sequences of sociocultural life.

---

[80]For his role and influence within anthropology, see Karl G. Heider, "Environment, Subsistence, and Society," *Annual Review of Anthropology* 1 (1972): 207-26, and Paul J. Magnarella, "Cultural Materialism and the Problem of Probabilities," *American Anthropologist* 84 (1982): 138-46. Andrew P. Vayda and Bonnie J. McCoy, "New Directions in Ecology and Ecological Anthropology," *Annual Review of Anthropology* 4 (1975): 293-306; Eric B. Ross, *Beyond the Myths of Culture: Essays in Cultural Materialism* (New York: Academic Press, 1980) 391-402; D. R. Gross, ed., *Peoples and Cultures of South America* (New York: Doubleday, 1973) 395-432; Eleanor Leacock, *Myths of Male Dominance: Collected Articles on Women Cross-Culturally* (New York: Monthly Review, 1981) 17, 195, 198, 299.

For discussions and appropriations of Harris by scholars in disciplines related to or outside of cultural anthropology, see Charles J. Lumsden and Edward O. Wilson, *Genes, Mind and Culture: The Coevolutionary Process* (Cambridge: Harvard University Press, 1981) 20, 50-57, 176, 352-53, 356; John C. Greene, *Science, Ideology and Worldview: Essays in the History of Evolutionary Ideas* (Berkeley: University of California Press, 1981) 95-98; Richard A. Posner, *The Economics of Justice* (Cambridge MA: Harvard University Press, 1981) 239n; Philippe C. Schmitter, *Interest, Conflict and Political Change in Brazil* (Stanford: Stanford University Press, 1971) 57, 68; Fernand Braudel, "In Bahia, Brazil: The Present Explains the Past," in *On History* (Chicago: University of Chicago Press, 1980) 165-76; and Norman Gottwald, *The Tribes of Yahweh* (New York: Orbis, 1980) 638, 713, 721, 781-85.

[81]Harris, *Cultural Materialism*, 47, 279.

Harris, in spite of all that distinguishes him from Lévi-Strauss, is also an anthropologist of explanation. However, recall that it is only in a provisional sense that Lévi-Strauss and Harris are posited as anthropologists of explanation. This positing is based on the way that both men characterize their work and the ways others view their anthropologies. In the course of this work, it will become apparent that their *naturwissenschaftlich* ideals are, in ways yet to be specified, related to *geisteswissenschaftlich* ones. I am moving through the explanatory characterization of their work toward their moments of understanding. Lévi-Strauss and Harris, amidst all their claims to achieve an anthropological "science,"[82] hint at the dialectical relation between understanding and explanation. But as in the anthropological discussions summarized above, the nature of this relation remains a problem. I seek to address that problem here by first accepting the frequent characterization of Lévi-Strauss's and Harris's anthropologies as "scientific" and "explanatory," then moving through this characterization to identify moments of understanding, so as, finally, to display the dialectical relation of explanation and understanding in their inquiry.

Again, unifying the explanatory moments of Lévi-Strauss's and Harris's anthropologies with their moments of understanding must be delayed. First, the kinds of anthropological explanation practiced by Lévi-Strauss and Harris must be examined. Lévi-Strauss's and Harris's "structuralism" and "cultural materialism," respectively, will be detailed in chapters 3 and 4. Before this detailed presentation, however, one must consider the contrast between structuralist and cultural-materialist modes of explanation in anthropology. By showing how these two modes represent a significant contrast in anthropological inquiry, I hope to show further how Lévi-Strauss's and Harris's explanatory enterprises are representative of this field of inquiry.

Structuralism and ecology
in cultural anthropology

Lévi-Strauss's and Harris's modes of explanation represent the "two paradigms of anthropological theory," noted by Marshall Sahlins

---

[82]Lévi-Strauss, for example, while concerned that the anthropologist be modeled after an "engineer" seeking "empirical satisfaction" and "proof," views social anthropology as not "opposing causal explanation and understanding" but rather as resting upon "understanding." See Lévi-Strauss, *Structural Anthropology*, 2 vols. (New York: Basic Books, 1976) 2:9.

in his *Culture and Practical Reason,* that also constitute a "founding disagreement" in anthropological theory.[83] The "founding" character of the opposition is suggested by Sahlins in a contrast of Lewis Henry Morgan and Franz Boas. For Morgan, "all species, including the human, receive immediate guidance from nature."[84] Anthropological explanations for Morgan, as for other devotees of practical reason, are oriented by a general line of argument moving "from natural constraint to behavioral practice, and from behavioral practice to cultural institution."[85] Boas moved away from such a logic, "from physics to ethnology," and stressed conceptual schemas.

> Where Morgan had understood practice and its customary formulation by the logic of objective circumstances, Boas interpolated *an independent subjective* between the objective conditions and organized behavior, such that the latter does not follow mechanically from the former. . . . For Boas the significance of the object is the property of thought, whereas for Morgan thought is the representation of objective significance.[86]

Sahlins admits that other well-known antinomies in anthropological theory should not be underestimated: history/science, society/culture, diachrony/synchrony. But "at the base" of all these oppositions is the one formulated in terms of the Morganian and Boasian points of view, between the "objective" logic of practical advantage and the meaningful logic of conceptual scheme, between utilitarian and cultural accounts, and in other terms, between ecology and structuralism. Whatever the importance of other antinomies, this is the root that often sets one functionalist against another, or one historicist against another.[87] This basic opposition, then, is not only a "founding disagreement" observable in Morgan and Boas, but also anthropology's continuing "unresolved contradiction," its "venerable conflict" be-

---

[83]Marshall Sahlins, *Culture and Practical Reason* (Chicago: University of Chicago Press, 1976) 55-125. Note esp. 73.

[84]Ibid., 61.

[85]Ibid., 60.

[86]Ibid., 69 (emphasis mine).

[87]Ibid., 73.

tween two dominant logics.[88] As shall be seen, the dominant logics manifested by Marvin Harris and Claude Lévi-Strauss together represent this founding and persistent contrast.

Not only can Lévi-Strauss and Harris be seen to represent these two kinds of dominant logic, they themselves tend to view anthropology's explanations in terms of this basic opposition and to respond to one another explicitly in its terms. Their general view of anthropology in these terms is evident especially in Lévi-Strauss's lecture distinguishing "structuralism" from "ecology" as two kinds of determinism, and in Harris's *Rise of Anthropological Theory*, which tends to partition anthropologists in terms of a materialist/idealist continuum.

Their particular characterization of one another in terms of the opposition is evidenced by Harris's vigorous response to Lévi-Strauss's "Structuralism and Ecology" lecture, in which Harris argues that structural oppositions exist "only in Lévi-Strauss's head,"[89] and by Lévi-Strauss's equally vigorous counter-response that Harris's beliefs stem from *"l'empirisme rampant qui est la maladie sénile du néo-marxisme."*[90] This is a clash of two anthropologies of explanation. That they are both advocates of explanation is evident even in their debate, as, for example, in Lévi-Strauss's concession that Harris's mode of argument is refreshing, since it places problems on their *"vrai terrain: celui des faits et de notre capacité d'en rendre compte."*[91]

Lévi-Strauss and Harris, then, serve as the two representative anthropologists of explanation attended to in this work. They are "representative" not in the sense that other advocates of explanation necessarily or openly identify with either Lévi-Strauss or Harris, but rather in the sense that their positions represent extremes among options for anthropological explanations. The choice between Lévi-Strauss's structuralism and Harris's cultural materialism may be representative for anthropologists in a sense similar to the choice noted by

---

[88]Ibid.

[89]Marvin Harris, "Lévi-Strauss et la palourde: Réponse à la Conference Gildersleeve de 1972," *L'Homme* 16, nos. 2-3 (1976): 5-22, and *Cultural Materialism*, 205.

[90]Claude Lévi-Strauss, "Structuralisme et empirisme," *L'Homme* 16, nos. 2-3 (1976): 23-39, esp. 28.

[91]Ibid., 23.

Eric Wolf between "biological reductionism" and structuralist "literary criticism" in anthropology: a choice between extremes that sets the context for anthropological theorizing, even though the choice often "prompts most anthropologists to go about their work unencumbered by theoretical consistency."[92]

By taking these two advocates of explanation as representative in anthropological inquiry, one is working with more difficult cases for discerning a religious dimension in cultural anthropology. They are more difficult not only because commitments to the ideals of *Verstehen* are hidden in their varied drives toward *Erklären*, but for an additional reason: their anthropological explanations ostensibly make religion an object or subject matter of anthropology, not an ingredient or dimension of anthropology itself. Religion is "explained" by the anthropologists of explanation in nonreligious terms. For both Lévi-Strauss and Harris, the "religious" does not have a *sui generis* character that renders aspects of it free from reduction by explanation. Religion is predominantly that which can be reduced to explanations in nonreligious terms, either the "structuralist" terms of Lévi-Strauss or the "cultural materialist" terms of Marvin Harris.

Lévi-Strauss, for example, who might best be termed an agnostic, demonstrates this prevalent commitment to the explanation of religion. In his recently translated *Naked Man*, he writes,

> I too, of course, look upon the religious field as a stupendous storehouse of images that is far from having been exhausted by objective research, but these images are like any others, and the spirit in which I approach the study of religious data supposes that such data are not credited at the outset with any specific character.[93]

Lévi-Strauss has also been questioned about any possible interplay between religious commitment and his anthropological inquiry that might make the first a dimension of the latter. When asked, for example, if he considers his passion for knowledge or his granting "absolute value" to his research a form of religious faith, Lévi-Strauss responded that this is a question he has never posed for himself from any point of

---

[92]Wolf, "They Divide and Subdivide and Call It Anthropology," 9.

[93]Lévi-Strauss, *The Naked Man*, 639.

view.[94] He would prefer to interpret his own scientific passion, even if it has affinities to religious faith, as "perfectly explicable and natural" in terms of cerebral, intellectual mechanisms.[95] Religion, like myth and kinship, is the subject matter of the structuralist's analysis, not primarily a fundamental component of the structural anthropologist as subject.

For Harris as well, more avowedly atheistic than Lévi-Strauss,[96] religion is also that which is to be explained in nonreligious terms. The "great religions" are mainly, for Harris, structural and superstructural arrangements resulting from the infrastructural or technoenvironmental conditions of old-world state societies. When political-economic exploitation resulted from imperial societies' depletion of resources, ruling elites fashioned religions as "ascetic solutions" to poverty. The religions of compassion for the weak and humble were ways to lower the costs of the elites' exploitation. Harris's anthropology of explanation, when applied to the study of religion, becomes a "demystification of the world's religions."[97] To be sure, Harris does admit the possible values of nonscientific ways of knowing, such as the religious or aesthetic modes. But these ways are to be strictly demarcated from science. Har-

---

[94]Claude Lévi-Strauss, "Un anthropologue: Claude Lévi-Strauss," in *Dieu existe-t'il? Non, Répondent Pascal Anquetil et al.*, ed. Christian Chabanis (Paris: Fayard, 1973) 71-88, 92. See esp. 72-73.

[95]Ibid., 74. This interview will be returned to since in it Lévi-Strauss, in spite of his professed personal distance from religion, admits to a similarity between his synthesizing activity as scientist and the ultimate syntheses of religion (74). However, regarding the idea of God, Lévi-Strauss writes, *"Je ne suis aucunement gêné par le mot Dieu, ou par la notion de Dieu"* (76).

[96]Marvin Harris, "Replies," *Current Anthropology* 9 (1968): 533. Here, in a response to John Tu Er-Wei, a critic of his *Rise of Anthropological Theory*, Harris replies, "If Tu Er-Wei would reread my book, he might learn the secret revealed therein, of how it is possible for me to be an atheist, a cultural materialist, historical determinist, and at the same time to believe that I have more freedom than he has."

[97]Harris, *Cultural Materialism*, 100-103. Note this also in idem, *Cannibals and Kings: The Origins of Culture* (New York: Random House, 1977) 167-89; idem, *Cows, Pigs, Wars and Witches: The Riddles of Culture* (New York: Random House, 1974) 153-77. Harris occasionally offers qualifications like the following: "By tracing the origin of religious ideas to the cost/benefits of ecological processes, I do not mean to deny that religious ideas themselves may in turn exert an influence on customs and thoughts." See Harris, *Cannibals and Kings*, 206.

ris would see little or no possibility for a religious dimension to science. The presence of religion in scientific matters usually fosters "anti-science" and "obscurantism." Religion to him remains one of the "other ways of knowing."[98]

Hence, Lévi-Strauss's "scientific anthropology" and Harris's "science of culture" reveal them both to be advocates of explanation, though the former's explanations are structuralist and the latter's are cultural-materialist. In their different modes of explanation, they represent a founding contrast, an endemic opposition in anthropological inquiry between a dominant logic of conceptual schema on the one hand, and one of practical advantage on the other. Both Lévi-Strauss and Harris, as advocates of different kinds of explanation, are difficult cases for articulating a religious dimension in cultural anthropology. Their anthropologies of explanation, therefore, must be displayed and probed for their moments of understanding before limit-situations and any religious dimension appear.

Anthropology's Hermeneutical Form

I now have come to the last of the several tasks of portraying anthropology in this chapter. Recall that in a first step, I generally explicated anthropological inquiry in terms of two ideals for the study of human action and thought: understanding and explanation. In a second step, I focused on two anthropologies of explanation, portraying these as two dominant, explanatory logics that Lévi-Strauss's structuralism and Harris's cultural materialism can represent. How is one to display the ways in which Lévi-Strauss and Harris carry out their inquiry? Addressing this question will enable one to view their explanatory enterprises within a context that will, finally, return one to the dialectical relation between understanding and explanation.

An adequate explication of Lévi-Strauss's and Harris's anthropological inquiries should be responsive to three criteria. First, it must highlight the modes of explanation unique to Lévi-Strauss and Harris, so that despite their jointly shared commitments to explanation, the differences between their structuralist and cultural-materialist programs

---

[98]Harris, *Cultural Materialism*, 5-6, 315-16.

clearly emerge. This criterion seeks to do justice to the particularity of each thinker's situation, texts, and thought.

Second, the explication must attempt to display the whole of Lévi-Strauss's and Harris's anthropological enterprises. This display, of course, need not treat every detail of their work, but must treat the relationships between the important features of their work. Thus, for example, one should not only focus on field methods involved in the traditional anthropological task of studying other peoples in foreign societies, but also on the relation of those methods to anthropologists' places within their own societies and cultural traditions. This latter focus has been described by scholars as the study of anthropology "anthropologically," or as "the ethnology of anthropological traditions."[99] This criterion, then, requires that a reflexive or critical component be built into the explication from the beginning. It demands study of an anthropologist's subjects and of the anthropologist as subject. And if this approach is "holistic," then the anthropologist as subject will at once be a thinking subject with a set of internally related presuppositions, an acting subject with a specific location in a sociocultural and sociohistorical setting, and an interpreting subject fashioning his anthropological knowledge in intercultural dialogue by means of an identifiable hermeneutic.

Third, and partially as a result of meeting the other two criteria, this explication should allow other "nonexplanatory" moments of the anthropologists' interpretations to appear: for example, any dialectically related moments of understanding wherein wholes are naively grasped or comprehensively woven together at various points in anthropologists' explanatory exercises of explication, analysis, or verification. This criterion is necessary if there is indeed a dialectical relation between explanation and understanding. It cannot be fully met until the subsequent chapters, when Lévi-Strauss's and Harris's enterprises in explanation are placed in their proper contexts.

Taken together, these criteria not only provide an explication that casts anthropological inquiry in a form susceptible to this work's thesis,

---

[99]Note, for example, Scholte, "The Ethnology of Anthropological Traditions," 4-15, and George W. Stocking, Jr., "The History of Anthropology: Where, Whence, Whither?" *Journal of the History of the Behavioral Sciences* 2 (1966): 281-90.

but they also respect the complexity of anthropological interpretation. The extent to which the explication engendered by these criteria actually displays anthropology's complexity may be gauged best after noting its applicability to the inquiries of Lévi-Strauss and Harris.

Horizontal and vertical realms

Each advocate of explanation will be displayed as an inquirer working in two realms of interpretation. I propose to call these the "horizontal" and "vertical" realms within which anthropological interpreters develop their explanations. And it is within each realm that ultimately one will ask whether and how they also seek understanding. But, again, the explanatory methods practiced in these two realms will be investigated first.

The distinction between these two interpretive realms was made by Jürgen Habermas; but as important as the distinction is to his thought, he seems not to have applied it formally and systematically. Only in passing does he explicitly refer to what for him are two "dimensions" or "levels" of hermeneutic. The horizontal level is an interpreting of cultures other than the interpreter's own, and the vertical is an interpreting of the interpreter's own past tradition.[100] The horizontal is predominantly an intercultural realm of interpretation, while the vertical is an intracultural one.

What Habermas calls "horizontal hermeneutic" is a kind of interpretation traditionally employed by anthropologists. Horizontal hermeneutic is an interpretation mediating between social or cultural "boundaries." It is an interpretation of others within anthropologists' present worlds. Anthropologists can encounter these others "in the field" and live among them so as to write texts about them that can be compared to texts about other societies.

In this horizontal realm anthropologists may interpret these others "synchronically," viewing other societies or groups as more or less integrated wholes, as structured systems. But their horizontal interpretations may also include probing the traditions of the contemporary others to discern their history. The horizontal hermeneutic of the anthropologist, then, may result in "diachronic" studies as well as "syn-

---

[100]Jürgen Habermas, *Knowledge and Human Interests*, trans. Jeremy J. Shapiro (Boston: Beacon Press, 1968) 176, 191.

chronic" ones. Both of these latter kinds of studies can find a place within horizontal hermeneutic, that is, within the anthropologists' interpretations of contemporary others.

The activity of horizontal hermeneutic carried out in the intercultural realm is complex and tends to defy characterization by conceptual schema. Lévi-Strauss's and Harris's horizontal hermeneutics are no less complex. That complexity poses difficulties for this explication of their work. Stocking's analyses of anthropological fieldwork situations indicate the diversity of factors that enter into the anthropologist's activity of interpreting others.[101] Influential factors "brought to the field" may be epistemological, metaphysical, theological, sexual, social, financial, and institutional. Determinative factors "inhering in the field" may be linguistic, technical, notational, analytical, logistical, medical, postal, reactional, and accidental. And insofar as anthropological interpretation of others continues after fieldwork, there are still other factors "flowing from the field" that also constitute a horizontal hermeneutic: systematic, presentational, retrospective, professional, and institutional.

All of these factors are rendered still more complex by the various roles and statuses that may be ascribed to the anthropological interpreter in the field. Some of these are defined by the anthropologists themselves (fieldworker, ethnologist, advocate), while others are defined by the studied society in which the interpreter appears as stranger, enemy, ancestor/god, missionary, trader, minerologist, spy, or tax collector. Even if rapport is built with a studied people, anthropologists' age, sex, and perhaps bestowed kin association affect their interpretation. Anthropologists may themselves create other roles for studied others, such as informant.[102]

Given this complexity of horizontal hermeneutic, there is an understandable tendency to eschew any conceptual schematization of it, and to remain satisfied with particular studies and accounts of anthro-

---

[101]George W. Stocking, Jr., "A Whimsical Framework for Fieldwork," unpublished document.

[102]George W. Stocking, Jr., "Anthropological Fieldwork in Historical Perspective," Course lecture, University of Chicago, 15 April 1980.

pologists in the field.[103] Moreover, and for similar reasons, advance training of fieldworkers is often considered difficult, if not impossible. The interpreters are to learn how to interpret in the field.[104] In spite of this complexity, some scholars of the discipline try to discern major components in anthropological traditions that may condition fieldwork situations.[105]

The position taken here is that the complexity of horizontal hermeneutic is indeed so intricate that the best explication of it may often be one that eschews general conceptual schematization and strives to present each single fieldwork experience in all its uniqueness. Nevertheless, since all explications of fieldwork experiences, and even the fieldwork experiences themselves, are schema-laden, it is appropriate to seek a conceptual schema for the horizontal hermeneutic characteristic of fieldwork interpretation. This schema may be especially needed if a comparison of representative anthropologists is intended.

The conceptual scheme for a horizontal hermeneutic, which will be applied in subsequent chapters to Lévi-Strauss's and Harris's work and which emerges from study of their works, is a "fundamental quadratic" of four components, each of which plays an important role in

---

[103]For this reason, perhaps, the anthropological literature seems to feature more "anthologies" of fieldwork experiences than "theories" of fieldwork. For the latter, see Pelto's *Anthropological Research*.

For representative anthologies, see A. Beteille and T. N. Madan, *Encounter and Experience: Personal Accounts of Fieldwork* (Honolulu: University of Hawaii Press, 1975); Morris Freilich, *Marginal Natives: Anthropologists at Work* (New York: Harper and Row, 1970); S. T. Kimball and J. B. Saberwal, *Stress and Response in Fieldwork* (New York: Holt, Rinehart and Winston, 1969); and G. Spindler, *Being an Anthropologist: Fieldwork in Eleven Cultures* (New York: Holt, Rinehart and Winston, 1970).

[104]Commentary on anthropologists' reluctance to train anthropology students before those students leave for the field can be found in Freilich's *Marginal Natives*, 4-37, and Paul Rabinow, *Reflections on Fieldwork in Morocco* (Berkeley: University of California Press, 1971) 46-47.

[105]For an example of one such scholar who has attempted to bring order, by means of an organizing schema, to the complexity of intercultural interpretation, see Scholte, "The Ethnology of Anthropological Traditions," 4-15, and Scholte, "Anthropological Traditions: Their Definition," in *Anthropology: Ancestors and Heirs*, ed. Stanley Diamond (The Hague: Mouton, 1980) 53-87.

shaping anthropologists' interpretations of others.[106] The four components include (a) an investigating subject (the anthropologist), (b) investigated subjects (the studied others), (c) investigated subjects' sociocultural contexts, and (d) the investigating subject's sociocultural contexts.

Use of such a scheme does not imply that there are only four major components of horizontal hermeneutic. The scheme functions only as a rubric by which the diverse factors of a particular fieldwork situation may be displayed and examined.

The first component, the investigating subject, for example, may include biographical and existential factors, insofar as they are available and appropriate.[107] The second component, the studied subjects, calls for investigation of the others encountered in their location, organization, and fundamental characteristics. The third component, studied subjects' sociocultural contexts, enables reflection on the larger whole in which the subjects live and are interpreted by the anthropologist. Under the fourth component are the various factors relating to the anthropological interpreters' place in their own societies and the nature of their relation to the studied society.

The fundamental quadratic for explicating anthropological interpretation in its horizontal dimension enables one to unify the various, important factors of fieldwork. Since in this work, however, I am concerned not just with this unity within fieldwork, but also with the whole of an anthropologist's work as revealed in his textual corpus, I must also seek a unity that goes beyond the fieldwork stage to the rest of his thought. The fundamental quadratic enables this kind of unity as well as that within the field situation. The following chapters will show that in the course of explicating the fundamental quadratic in Lévi-Strauss's and Harris's horizontal hermeneutic, certain identifiable "salient im-

---

[106]The idea of this fundamental quadratic is also formulated by Kenelm Burridge in his "quadratic relationship" that the mind intricately must "hold and map" in the study of anthropological interpretation. By means of it one can trace relationships between "the Aborigines and their culture and the investigators and their cultures." Burridge, *Encountering Aborigines*, 1.

[107]The availability and appropriateness of biographical factors are both determined by the roles they play in the anthropologist's corpus of texts. Such factors will be taken up and made part of the fundamental quadratic insofar as they are signaled in the texts.

ages" not only form a crucial center for their fieldwork, but also tend to dominate, in some form, the texts later produced.

The "salient image" that emerges when explicating the fundamental quadratic is an "image" in that it is a particular, vivid form experienced in the fieldwork situation. The "image" refers to what may be seen or heard in the fieldwork situation—perhaps more than once and perhaps in different ways—which leaves the interpreting anthropologist with a sense that he or she has encountered something uniquely characteristic about the life of the investigated subjects. The image in its very vividness is "salient," it "stands out" as unique in the field situation. But this sense of uniqueness that is left with the anthropologist suggests that the saliency of the image has to do with more than just the fieldwork situation. Whether an image is "salient" for an interpreting anthropologist, therefore, also depends on whether the image dominates that anthropologist's written texts and later theoretical discourse. Necessarily, this formulation of the "salient image" here remains vague. Salient images vary with the fieldwork situation and with the practicing anthropologist being examined. Greater specification of this notion will occur when explicating the four components of Lévi-Strauss's and Harris's fundamental quadratic so that the particular "salient images" of their interpretive work in South America appear.

The subsequent chapters on Lévi-Strauss and Harris will show that their interpretive reach toward contemporary others, their horizontal hermeneutic, is shaped by factors that can be explicated by means of a fundamental quadratic. Within this quadratic relationship will appear the salient images that begin to reveal the unity of an anthropologist's interpretations and more fundamental perspectives. But this is still only one realm of the anthropologist's interpretive activity, the "horizontal." Anthropologists also engage in interpretive activity in its "vertical" realm, though they do not as often reflect explicitly on it.

In the vertical interpretive activity, anthropologists do not so much reach out to contemporary others, but "back," or "behind" to historically distanced others. They probe "down" into their own histories and traditions for philosophical or anthropological perspectives that have aided or promise to aid them in their ongoing tasks of interpreting others. The "anthropologists of anthropology," or the "ethnologists of anthropological traditions,"[108] show anthropologists reckoning here with another kind of pluralism, one of historically distanced positions within their own cultural tradition. In vertical hermeneutic there is a kind of mediation or communication occurring not just across the "boundaries" of a culturally plural, present world, but a kind of mediation and communion that fuses this present concern with an anthropologist's past traditions.

The horizontal hermeneutic's reach toward others thus always interplays with a vertical hermeneutic. The interpretation of foreign others is bound up with anthropologists' negative and positive criticisms, evaluations, appropriations, or applications of their own cultural past. This integral relation is such that the past does not just condition the present, but its conditioning power is itself influenced by the anthropologist's present. Anthropological interpreters are in a "living relationship" to their tradition.[109] There is a "fusion of horizons." Neither the horizon of the past nor that of the present is formed apart from the other.[110] In explicating the inquiry of Lévi-Strauss and Harris, then, one must attend to their location in their own tradition and to the ways they locate themselves in their own history and tradition. For there are a variety of possible ways to fuse horizons within the culture of anthropologists.

In order best to display the complexity and richness of the anthropological inquiry of two advocates of explanation, Lévi-Strauss and Harris, one must attend to this vertical dimension of the interpretive activity practiced by anthropologists and to the horizontal dimension. Each of these realms contributes to an explication that meets the criteria set out above. Such an explication enables display of the particularity of each thinker, a holistic view of his anthropological inquiry, and lays the basis for identifying nonexplanatory as well as explanatory moments of their investigations.

Understanding and explanation in anthropology

None of the distinctions characterizing the hermeneutical form of anthropological interpretation correspond precisely to the earlier-dis-

---

[108]See note 99 above.

[109]Gadamer, *Truth and Method*, 323.

[110]Ibid., 273-74.

cussed distinction between the ideals of understanding and explanation. In particular, the distinction between horizontal and vertical hermeneutic is not the same as that between understanding and explanation. Rather, the dialectical relation between understanding and explanation may be evident in both the horizontal and vertical realms of anthropological interpretation. In both horizontal and vertical hermeneutic, there is understanding in the anthropological concern to preunderstand, grasp, or comprehend as a whole the chains of partial meanings in one act of synthesis. In both horizontal and vertical hermeneutic, there is explanation in an anthropological concern to explicate or unfold a range of propositions and meanings, to seek causes of events and of relationships between particular entities. Anthropologists' horizontal reach toward others *and also* their vertical fusing of present and past horizons feature the dialectic of understanding and explanation.

These two realms of anthropological interpretation greater complicate the understanding/explanation dialectic. In horizontal hermeneutic, for example, anthropological understanding may involve a preunderstanding or appropriation of a whole present world, a common or general humanity that enables communication across cultural boundaries, from one group or segment of the contemporary world to another.[111] Anthropological explanation in horizontal hermeneutic may include various forms of social-science technique: anthropological techniques such as "participant observation," sociological techniques such as demographic surveying, use of questionnaires and statistical analyses, and psychological techniques such as life histories.[112] Explanation in anthropology's horizontal hermeneutic would also include the structuring of others' thought and behavior in the form of ethnographic

---

[111]Examples of such a preunderstood whole will be noted later in Lévi-Strauss's and Harris's exercises in horizontal hermeneutic. Concerning the need of a "common" or "shared humanity" for understanding amid cultural relativity (which yet does not fall prey to grasping a once-for-all set of universal structures), see Toulmin, *Human Understanding*, 490-95.

[112]For use of life-histories in anthropological interpretation of others, see Victor Barnouw, *Culture and Personality* (Homewood IL: Dorsey Press, 1963) 197-235, and L. L. Langness, *The Life-History in Anthropological Science* (New York: Holt, Rinehart and Winston, 1965).

texts, and in intellectual theories that anthropologists construct and seek to test or verify.

In the other dimension of anthropological interpretation, in vertical hermeneutic, anthropological understanding involves the preunderstanding or appropriation of an anthropologist's own cultural past so that, in varying ways, there is a fusion of the anthropologist's focus on a contemporary world of cultural variety with a past tradition. This fusion may be effectively mediated logically but also *socio-logically* through sociocultural context, academic institution, international agency, and so forth. Anthropological explanation in vertical hermeneutic may involve varying forms of historical-critical research into the thought and work of past thinkers and anthropologists. Anthropologists here may discuss and unfold histories of their own particular discipline, of anthropological theories and practices, or of whole philosophies.[113]

One might pursue further a general discussion of anthropological hermeneutics. That, however, is not the major aim of this work. Enough has been offered here to enable one to explicate the anthropological inquiry of two particular anthropologists of explanation, Lévi-Strauss and Harris. Only after such an approach to these two anthropological practitioners, by which one can display an anthropologically enriched dialectic of understanding and explanation, can distinctive limit-situations in cultural anthropology be evident and signal a potentially religious dimension.

This chapter, devoted to portraying anthropological inquiry, has moved from the general to the particular, and from within the particular back to the general. After first stating the general problem of understanding and explanation in human inquiry, I placed it in the context of anthropological inquiry, illustrating how anthropologists exhibit commitments to both *naturwissenschaftlich* and *geisteswissenschaftlich*

---

[113]These forms of anthropological explanation can be observed in Lévi-Strauss's and Harris's vertical hermeneutic. Harris has written an entire book in this area, *The Rise of Anthropological Theory: A History of Theories of Culture* (New York: Thomas Cromwell, 1968). Lévi-Strauss's corpus abounds with comments that fall within the domain of historical analysis. A shorter piece of the same sort of anthropological explanation in the vertical dimension is Clifford Geertz's "The Impact of the Concept of Culture on the Concept of Man," in *The Interpretation of Cultures*, 33-54.

ideals, or debate the strength of one ideal against the other. Further particularity was gained by characterizing the proponents of *naturwissenschaftlich* ideals for anthropology, the anthropologists of explanation, in terms of two "dominant logics," one of cultural significance and another of practical utility. Lévi-Strauss's structuralism and Harris's cultural materialism were taken as representative of these two dominant logics.

Faced with the task of portraying these two particular representatives of anthropological explanation, I then began to move back to the general by offering a conceptual schema for anthropologists' interpretive activity. This activity possesses both intercultural and intracultural elements, which together give anthropological interpretation its hermeneutical form with horizontal and vertical realms. Discussion of this hermeneutical form enabled me, finally, to return to the general problem of understanding and explanation. This dialectic is operative in both realms of anthropology's hermeneutical form.

The focus of the general problem of understanding and explanation within the "anthropologists of explanation" was defended on the grounds that such a focus was a more difficult case for this work's articulation of a religious dimension. No direct moves will be made to the "anthropologies of understanding." The move will be to explanation, and then through it to its moments of understanding, and finally to limit-situations of a religious dimension. The difficulty of this route arises from the tendencies of anthropologists of explanation to neglect understanding ideals for anthropology, and from their explanations of religion in terms that make it an object or subject matter of anthropology but not a dimension of it.

Chapter III

Interpreting Brazil:
Two Horizontal Hermeneutics

Under my systematic questioning, Ali was taking realms of his own world and interpreting them for an outsider. This meant that he, too, was spending more time in this liminal self-conscious world between cultures. This is a difficult and trying experience—one could almost say it is "unnatural"—and not everyone will tolerate its ambiguities and strains.

Paul Rabinow
Reflections on Fieldwork in Morocco

The horizontal, intercultural dimension of interpretation, for both Lévi-Strauss and Harris, has as its first object or subject matter the peoples and sociocultural phenomena of Brazil. Lévi-Strauss's interpretation of Brazil began in São Paulo in 1935, from which he traveled northward into the interior. Harris's work in Brazil, in the early 1950s, was conducted in the country's central mountain zone, in the Bahia province.

I shall argue here that the horizontal dimension of their respective hermeneutics, while using different methods of explanation, consists of interpretations of Brazil that begin with the conditions of their field-work and extend to the construction of their more recent texts. I will display this horizontal hermeneutic first by referring to the fundamental quadratic, then by discussing the salient images of their field situations, before turning to the grander theoretical and philosophical aspects of their enterprises.

Claude Lévi-Strauss:
Through Ethnography to Semiology

Lévi-Strauss's horizontal hermeneutic, from the perspective of its explanatory ideals, is one that during the course of his career moves through social-science methods of explanation—particularly that of ethnography—to literary-critical methods. Throughout this particular display of his horizontal hermeneutic, then, I will not only need to state what those methods are, but also what the shift is that marks his journey through ethnographic social science to literary criticism and semiology.

Bons sauvages:
linking personal and world history

The ethnographic method of explanation, with which Lévi-Strauss began as an anthropologist, entailed fieldwork in Brazil. One can examine this field situation with the aid of the fundamental quadratic of: investigating subject, investigated subjects, investigated subjects' sociocultural context, and investigating subject's sociocultural context.

I will take up first Lévi-Strauss the individual anthropologist, the "investigating subject." His ethnographic research in Brazil may be viewed as a personal search for the "uncontaminated New World" that he sensed still existed in spite of Old World exploitation.[1] He sought *"une société réduit à sa plus simple expression."*[2] This is the thread running throughout the reflections of his autobiographical and ethnographic text, *Tristes Tropiques*.

The search for what Lévi-Strauss elsewhere calls "true primitives" must be viewed in relation to his personal inclination toward anthropology. An ethnographic method of explanation, entailing the observation and description of "true primitives," afforded Lévi-Strauss the "intellectual satisfaction" of linking his own personal history to world history. The "others" of Brazil, whether Caduveo, Bororo, Nambikwara, Mundé, or Tupi-Kawahib were never merely "alien" or "exotic." Since all were potentially human society "reduced to its simplest

---

[1]Claude Lévi-Strauss, *Tristes Tropiques*, trans. John Weightman and Doreen Weightman (New York: Atheneum, 1976) 149-50.

[2]Claude Lévi-Strauss, *Tristes Tropiques*, French ed. (Paris: Plon, 1955) 316-17.

expression," encountering them might reveal a rationale common to both world history and Lévi-Strauss's own history. So much is this the case that his field encounters are frequently described as occasions for him to view himself, and occasions for others to view themselves in him.[3]

The ethnographic method, however, can only provide this "intellectual satisfaction" through Lévi-Strauss's rejection of the philosophical tradition of his own French culture. Thus, his personal account of "The Making of an Ethnographer" provides also a rationale for his personal rejection of philosophy, both as a fundamental perspective and as a profession.[4]

The young Lévi-Strauss, after studying law and philosophy at the University of Paris, had settled on philosophy as his profession and began teaching it in 1933.[5] But his dissatisfaction with philosophy, which he felt as early as his student days at the Sorbonne, finally made him break with philosophy during his second teaching post. The break, according to Lévi-Strauss, was the result of many personal dissatisfactions with these teaching duties;[6] more important, it was due, first, to an emerging negative critique of philosophy and, second, to his discovery of anthropology "within" himself.

Essential to his criticism of philosophy was a distinction between the "rational" or "logical" level on which philosophy operated, and a "pre-logical" unconscious level largely ignored by his instructors.[7] The rational oppositions in which he was trained to think, Lévi-Strauss decries as "static," "purely verbal," and as the "gymnastics of which the dangers are especially manifest." The catalyst for this criticism of philosophy that works on a rational level was Sigmund Freud's psychoanalytic theories, which Lévi-Strauss seriously studied during his university years.[8] Freud prompted Lévi-Strauss to look "below" the surface of beings and things stressed by his professors. Only by looking

---

[3]Lévi-Strauss, *Tristes Tropiques* (Eng. ed.), 326.

[4]Ibid., 51-60.

[5]Ibid., 51-53.

[6]Ibid., 53.

[7]Ibid., 55.

[8]Ibid.

below to the category of "the meaningful" might one define and clarify beings and things.

Psychoanalysis could now take its place, for Lévi-Strauss, alongside Marx and geology, two other interests he encountered and cultivated even before his university years. Together, these *"trois maîtresses"* taught that reality was to be found beneath the surface of experience and of rationality—in the meaningful. As geology had taught young Lévi-Strauss that the "master meaning" (*maîtresens*) of a chaotic terrain is found in the hidden fault between two geological strata, and just as Marxist thought taught him that diverse social conditions could be clarified only by constructing their underlying meaningful models, so psychoanalysis now taught him that philosophy's endless rational conflicts demanded a turn to the deeper, unconscious level of the meaningful.[9]

> All three demonstrate that understanding consists in reducing one type of reality to another, that the true reality is never the most obvious, and that the nature of truth is already indicated by the care it takes to remain elusive. In all cases, the same problem arises, the problem of the relationship between feeling (*le sensible*) and reason (*le rationnel*), and the aim is the same: to achieve a kind of *superrationalisme* which will integrate the first with the second, without sacrificing any of its properties.[10]

This new orientation, aiming at a *superrationalisme*, is what Lévi-Strauss increasingly contrasts to the university philosophy in which he was trained. This *superrationalisme* prompted by Freudian psychoanalysis, combined with geology and Marx, is interpreted by Lévi-Strauss as a continuance of a basic artistic affinity that for him was especially expressed in musical composition.[11]

The break with philosophy is a result not only of this criticism, but also of his discovery of anthropology. While teaching philosophy in 1933-1934, it was *"par hazard"* that Lévi-Strauss read Robert Lowie's *Primitive Society*. It was his first introduction to specialist anthropolog-

---

[9]For more extensive treatment of Lévi-Strauss's relation to Freud's thought, see Thomas Shalvey, *Claude Lévi-Strauss: Social Psychotherapy and the Collective Unconscious* (Amherst: University of Massachusetts Press, 1979) 7-51.

[10]Lévi-Strauss, *Tristes Tropiques* (Eng. ed.), 57-58.

[11]Claude Lévi-Strauss, *Myth and Meaning* (New York: Schocken Books, 1979) 53.

ical writing, and it was *"la révélation"* for the troubled philosophy teacher. As he read Lowie's work on primitive marriage, kinship, rank, and government, he was impressed by the writer's "concrete examples," and his personal experience. Lowie's insistence that empirical analysis of multiple social forms should test general schemes freed Lévi-Strauss's mind from its "claustrophobic turkish bath atmosphere" in which his solely philosophical views imprisoned him.

> Once it [Lévi-Strauss's mind] had got out into the open air, it felt refreshed and renewed. Like a city-dweller transported to the mountains, I became drunk with space, while my dazzled eyes measured the wealth and variety of the objects surrounding me.[12]

The revelation of discovering anthropology joined with the Freudian critique he had exerted against his philosophical tutors. The *superrationalisme* toward which he aimed was to be found not only by going below the rational level, but also by going out into new fields of beings and things that were to serve as "referents" for thought. Lévi-Strauss viewed this direction as a healthy antidote for a sick philosophy that had fallen short of its true status as servant of scientific exploration. It had become "a sort of aesthetic contemplation of consciousness by itself." Lévi-Strauss, as will become clear, does not object to aesthetic contemplation in itself. Anthropology, however, must guard philosophy's aesthetic contemplation from working with signifiers unrelated to any signifieds. An ethnographic method of explanation was to provide this world of referents.[13]

With the aid of professors and administrators at the Sorbonne, particularly psychology instructor Georges Dumas, Lévi-Strauss's opportunities for practicing the ethnographic method were facilitated: he was appointed in 1935 to a sociology post at the University of São Paulo, Brazil. Lévi-Strauss, the "investigating subject," arrived in Brazil seeking to make intellectually satisfying links between his personal history and world history. When landing in Rio for the first time, for example, he could not help recalling "all those ludicrous and tragic incidents which testified to the close relations existing between the

---

[12]Lévi-Strauss, *Tristes Tropiques* (Eng. ed.), 59.

[13]Ibid., 52.

French and Indians 400 years ago." While roaming Rio's streets, he sought to recapture the mood of four centuries earlier. He was stimulated in this endeavor by a book he carried with him by a French Genevan, Jean de Léry, who, Lévi-Strauss notes, arrived at the Rio site 378 years ago to the very day he had.[14]

But the crucial link between his personal and world history was not to be found in Rio or among the elites of São Paulo's *gran fino*. These latter were only the representatives of the Old World's taint of the New. The remnants of the New World, the "true primitives," were to be found in the interior. A fuller understanding of Lévi-Strauss as investigating subject requires attention to the investigated subjects he there encountered.

The investigated subjects of Lévi-Strauss's ethnographic method are many, as any reader of Lévi-Strauss's writings knows. Discussion here will be limited to those he interpreted in Brazil,[15] and even those will be further limited. For example, Lévi-Strauss's earliest encounters in São Paulo will be put aside. He was told by the head of *L'École normale supérieure* that its "suburbs are full of Indians whom you can study on weekends."[16] Lévi-Strauss discovered only a disappointing suburbia "full of Syrians and Italians." I will not attend to his work as a "Sunday anthropologist" in São Paulo's suburbs, though Lévi-Strauss himself does discuss it.[17]

The investigated subjects deserving most attention are those he encountered on two different expeditions. The first occurred between November and March of 1935 and 1936, and corresponded to the São Paulo University vacation. Outfitted by ranchers along the Rio Paraguaya, Lévi-Strauss began his trip by descending into the river's low-

---

[14]Ibid., 81, 83.

[15]I am excluding, therefore, consideration of the one-month field trip Lévi-Strauss made to the Chittagong Hill Tracts in 1950 for UNESCO. This short stay resulted only in fragmentary, ethnographic texts. These texts include "Kinship Systems of Three Chittagong Hill Tribes (Pakistan)," *Southwestern Journal of Anthropology* 8 (1952): 40-51; "Miscellaneous Notes on the Kuki of the Chittagong Hill Tracts of Pakistan," *Man* 51 (1952): no. 284; and "Le syncrétisme religieux d'un village mogh du territoire de Chittagong," *Revue de l'Histoire des Religions* 141 (1952): 202-37.

[16]Lévi-Strauss, *Tristes Tropiques* (Eng. ed.), 47.

[17]Ibid., 29.

lands to study the little-researched Caduveo peoples in the town of Engenho, which boasted only five huts. The Caduveo, along with the Toba and Pilaga peoples of Paraguay, were the last living representatives of the Mbaya Guaicuru civilization, an aristocratic, castelike society of kings and queens that sixteenth-century explorers had likened to Central Europe's feudal lords.[18] The Caduveo living in Engenho were similar to nearby Brazilian peasants in both dress and physique, although their language was very different. The "extraordinary feature of Caduveo culture" was the graphic art Caduveo women painted on their bodies. Noticed by other explorers, this feature was particularly striking, and Lévi-Strauss collected several hundred of the designs.

After his one-month stay among the Caduveo, Lévi-Strauss devoted the rest of his university vacation to a three-month study of the Bororo, who lived further inland along the upper São Laurenco River. Lévi-Strauss conducted his studies in the village of Kejara, one of the few left basically unchanged by the missionizing Salesian Fathers. These missionaries provided anthropology with many important documents while at the same time, according to Lévi-Strauss, pursuing "systematic obliteration of native culture."[19] Kejara was important because the chief of the other Bororo villages lived there.

The Eastern Bororo whom Lévi-Strauss encountered preserved their traditional culture in the face of acculturating pressures. Lévi-Strauss was "taken aback by a society which [was] still alive and faithful to its traditions."[20] The philosopher who had become "drunk with space" on first reading Lowie's *Primitive Society*, now, as an ethnographer, became drunk with the laughter, dress, and jewels of Bororo "space":

> It was as if an entire civilization were conspiring in a single passionate affection for the shapes, substances and colors of life and, in order to preserve its richest essence around the human body, were appealing to those of its manifestations which are the most lasting or the most

[18]Ibid., 178-80.

[19]Ibid., 216.

[20]Ibid., 215.

fleeting, but which through a curious coincidence, are its privileged repositories.[21]

The Bororo of Kejara numbered 150. Their village was laid out in circular fashion, like a cartwheel: the rim being the family huts, the spokes being the paths, and the men's house being the hub. (The significance of this pattern will be clearer when other components of the fundamental quadratic are discussed.)

Lévi-Strauss's other major expedition occurred two years after his Caduveo and Bororo research, between June and November of 1938. It was on this expedition that he encountered the Nambikwara, the Mundé, and the Tupi-Kawahib.

The Nambikwara's numbers were rapidly dwindling. Members of this group lived in the northwestern Mato Grosso, in an area of narrow, fertile river valleys separated by dry savannah. They appeared to be the earlier inhabitants of this region.[22] Lévi-Strauss encountered them in the dry season when groups of them pursued their nomadic life, hunting and gathering among the savannahs and forests. He spent about three months with them, living briefly among three different groups found along a telegraph line running through the posts of Utiarity, Campos Novos, and Vilhena.

The Mundé people became Lévi-Strauss's subjects of ethnographic study in September or October of 1938. The Mundé, never studied before Lévi-Strauss encountered them, lived several days' journey up the Rio Pimento River. Encountering the Mundé was to be the "supreme reward" for this anthropologist whose encounters with *bons sauvages* linked his own history to that of the world.

> I was about to relive the experience of the early travelers and, through it, that crucial moment in modern thought when, thanks to the great voyages of discovery, a human community which believed itself to be complete in its final form suddenly learned through the effect of a counter-revelation, that it was not alone, that it was part of a greater whole, and that, in order to achieve self-knowledge, it must first of all contemplate its unrecognizable image in this mirror, of which a

---

[21]Ibid., 216.

[22]P. David Price, "Nambikwara Society" (dissertation, University of Chicago, 1972) 85.

fragment, forgotten by the centuries, was now about to be cast for me alone, its first and last reflection.[23]

Lévi-Strauss, for reasons that shall become clear, spent only one "agreeable week" in the Mundé village of about twenty-five people, noting their "Mongolian cast of countenance," their "simplicity, patience and cordiality," their gardens, and listening to (but not speaking) their "jolly language."

Unable to communicate with the Mundé and running low on provisions, Lévi-Strauss journeyed downstream to encounter the Tupi-Kawahib, residents of the tropical forest. Enlisting the aid of a Tupi-Kawahib guide at another telegraph station, he hiked into the forest and two days later met up with the Tupi-Kawahib. Their village consisted of only sixteen people, two of whom were paralyzed.[24] His visit in the village was only one-day old when one of his men shot himself and had to be immediately transported out for medical care. Lévi-Strauss persuaded the Tupi-Kawahib to camp along a river, at the forest's edge, where he later returned for two weeks of additional study. The impossibility of studying the group in their village was disappointing. He had once again hoped to be "the first white man, perhaps, to set foot in a still-intact Tupi village" and thus "bridge a gap of four hundred years."[25] But meeting with these Tupi, even if only in a tentative riverside camp, was important, since he viewed it as extremely likely that

> these Indians are the last descendents of the great Tupi communities
> of the middle and lower reaches of the Amazon, which were related
> to the coastal groups whom the sixteenth and seventeenth century
> travelers saw in their period of splendour.[26]

Evident in this quote is the interplay of Lévi-Strauss's horizontal hermeneutic with his vertical hermeneutic.

The "sociocultural contexts of the investigated subjects"—Caduveo, Bororo, Nambikwara, Mundé, and Tupi-Kawahib—also set the

---

[23]Lévi-Strauss, *Tristes Tropiques* (Eng. ed.), 326.

[24]Ibid., 346.

[25]Ibid., 335.

[26]Ibid.

field within which Lévi-Strauss interpreted Brazil. At the most general level, he encountered each group, with the exception of the Mundé perhaps, when it was experiencing acculturating pressure that was threatening its existence. Each group could testify to what Lévi-Strauss believed about the New World in general, that it was, as the title of the first English translation of *Tristes Tropiques* announced, a "world on the wane." The Caduveo's "wretched hamlets," the Nambikwara's "barrenness" on the "hostile earth," the Tupi-Kawahib as "unfortunate wretches," and even the Bororo as inflicted by disease and demographic collapse—all these conveyed to Lévi-Strauss the world of *Tristes Tropiques*, "tragic tropics," "sad tropics."[27] The precarious nature of the groups' existence would set the tone for many of his portrayals.

Aside from the context of the groups' precarious existence, it is difficult to gauge what effect their sociocultural contexts had on Lévi-Strauss's anthropological interpretation. Indeed, this difficulty has led to a criticism of Lévi-Strauss by British and American anthropologists who stress the benefits of more extensive immersion in particular societies. Edmund Leach, for example, while admitting that a trained anthropologist may in a short stay develop a comprehensive model of a social system other than his own, insists that a longer stay will certainly allow very little of an anthropologist's own social-system model to remain.[28] Lévi-Strauss's work among the Caduveo, the Mundé, and the Tupi-Kawahib was especially brief. It is only his two-month stay with the Bororo and his three-month stay among different Nambikwara groups that allows one to speak of any effect of the subjects' own sociocultural context on Lévi-Strauss's emerging anthropological knowledge.

One may note, for example, that Lévi-Strauss's access to the Bororo and residence among them was dependent on the superiority of the Kejara village's material culture. Lévi-Strauss was able to arrive in Kejara during the rainy season, when the rivers were swollen, only with

---

[27]Ibid., 11 (translator's note). For Lévi-Strauss's descriptions of his investigated subjects' context of suffering, see *Tristes Tropiques* (Eng. ed.), 173, 177, 277, 280, 346. See also Claude Lévi-Strauss, "Contribution à l'étude de l'organisation sociale des Indiens Bororo," *Journal de la Société des Américanistes* 28/29 (1936): 269-304, 270, 279.

[28]Edmund Leach, *Claude Lévi-Strauss* (New York: Viking, 1970) 12.

the aid of skillful Brazilian canoeists who risked the rivers for valuable Bororo manioc and tobacco.[29] The canoeists, anxious for trade with the wealthier Bororo, saved Lévi-Strauss's expedition from the "confused nightmare" it had become.[30]

Once Lévi-Strauss was settled in Kejara, his goods and provisions were much valued by the Bororo, especially during the rainy season, and their value opened numerous opportunities for fieldwork. The chief ordered hunting, gathering, and fishing expeditions to gather more goods so as to take full advantage of trade with Lévi-Strauss's team. The chief also assigned Lévi-Strauss to a chiefly hut where transactions were normally made. This assignment placed Lévi-Strauss within the village's parameters, in the circle of family dwellings that partially constituted its cartwheel frame. Viewed as a trader within the Bororo sociocultural context, then, Lévi-Strauss was given a place in the spatial configuration of the village. He used this configuration as the clue for unraveling Bororo views of their geographical position and for understanding their social system.[31] The isolating effect of the rainy season, the Indians' need to trade at that time, and the subsequent inclusion of Lévi-Strauss the trader within Kejara, together set sociocultural conditions for Lévi-Strauss's anthropological knowledge of the Bororo.

Lévi-Strauss's ethnographic research among the Nambikwara was also facilitated by the sociocultural place they made for the role of trader. The Nambikwara, however, who frequented the telegraph line that ran through their territory, were accustomed to living in occasional, close contact with other Brazilians and travelers.[32] Relations between Nambikwara and travelers along the line had once been good, but by the time Lévi-Strauss arrived, they had worsened.

His trading activity, however, effected good relations that, in his view, included friendship and playfulness. Lévi-Strauss reports being accepted by the Nambikwara with "immense kindness" and a "pro-

---

[29]Lévi-Strauss, "Contribution," 275-76. See esp. 275 n. 2.

[30]Lévi-Strauss, *Tristes Tropiques* (Eng. ed.), 213.

[31]Lévi-Strauss, "Contribution," 271. In this 1936 text on the Bororo, the village's "structure morphologique" is an expression of its social structure and geographical position.

[32]Lévi-Strauss, *Tristes Tropiques* (Eng. ed.), 303.

foundly carefree attitude."[33] This friendship led to his inclusion in their nightly campfire circle, to his play with children, to his conversation with chiefs, and to numerous forms of interaction with Nambikwara individuals, about whom Lévi-Strauss used the following phrases: "serious," "hard working," "vague and practically useless," "sometimes suffered from ill-humour," "loved our company," "vain, seductive," "devoted to husband and children," or "without nuance and comprehensiveness."[34] The Nambikwara acceptance included him in a range of social activities not had in the Bororo village of Kejara.

Lévi-Strauss stresses two particular occasions for involvement. When camping at Campos Novos, in Nambikwara territory, his camp became a neutral meeting place for two hostile groups who were brought together by common interest in his goods. Lévi-Strauss watched as the two groups danced at his camp, sang, and ritually acted out their mutual hostility. These actions were then followed by a "reconciliatory inspection" that ended the quarrel and began commercial exchange. Strife was replaced by barter.[35] The other occasion was at Vilhena, a post further up the telegraph line, where two Nambikwara groups were found working out a simple kinship system, a plan of intermarriage whereby the two groups would be merged by the next generation.[36] The Nambikwara made possible both of these occasions by their interaction with him as a trader and a friend.

The relations constituting Lévi-Strauss's ethnographic situation may be filled out by referring to Lévi-Strauss as "investigating subject," not just with regard to his own personal quest but also with regard to his sociocultural context. Given the limited nature of his immersion in the Brazilian subjects' contexts—at least in comparison to the standards of Leach and other Anglo-American fieldworkers—it is perhaps Lévi-Strauss's own sociocultural context that most determines his horizontal interpretation of others. This context is best set, first, in terms of the state of French ethnography at the time of his research, and

---

[33]Claude Lévi-Strauss, "La Vie familiale et sociale des Indiens Nambikwara," *Journal de la Société des Américanistes* 38 (1948): 1-31, 55-56.

[34]Ibid., 38-40, 40-46, 48.

[35]Lévi-Strauss, *Tristes Tropiques* (Eng. ed.), 303.

[36]Ibid., 306.

second, by reference to the "highly charged atmosphere" in which South American research was conducted.[37]

First, regarding the state of French ethnography, ethnography as a "scientific" or academic, professional endeavor was only just developing in France at the time Lévi-Strauss undertook his field research. Though both Durkheim and Marcel Mauss had turned to foreign fields and inspired many fieldworkers, neither undertook ethnographic research in the field. Thus, it might be expected that Lévi-Strauss would find in American Robert Lowie a model of actual ethnographic practice that awakened him to the rich world of "beings and things." But the impulse within French cultural and academic life toward ethnography—however much it might have led Lévi-Strauss to find his "revelation" in the American Lowie—was in conflict with the epistemological assumptions underlying Anglo-American field technique.

This ethnographic "impulse" may be seen as part of a "general cultural predisposition" that was integrally fused with a post-World War I surrealist movement in France.[38] James Clifford has sketched this simultaneous emergence of surrealism and ethnography in France, and while he does not draw connections to Lévi-Strauss, this context is helpful for understanding his ethnography. Lévi-Strauss himself reflects on this context:

> Of course, we [contemporary anthropologists] have acquired direct knowledge of exotic forms of life and thought, which they [Lévi-Strauss's anthropologist ancestors] lacked; but is it not also true that surrealism—that is to say, a development within our own society—has transformed our sensitivity, and that we owe to it having discovered or rediscovered at the heart of our studies some lyricism and some integrity.[39]

After the Great War had disturbed the French self's sense of any given reality, the self was cut loose to find meaning wherever it could,

---

[37]Ibid., 260.

[38]James Clifford, "On Ethnographic Surrealism," *Comparative Studies in Society and History* 23:4 (1981): 539-64.

[39]Lévi-Strauss, *Structural Anthropology*, 2 vols. (New York: Basic Books, 1976) 2:27-28.

since the war meant the end of any positivist and progressivist hopes for Western culture.[40] For the French, Africa, and to some extent Oceania and America, became reservoirs of "other forms" and "other beliefs," all of which could be embraced as serious human alternatives. The surrealist attitude, shared by literature, painting, and ethnography, was that the other must be "a crucial object of modern research."[41] This research exhibited the sensitivities cultivated in surrealist painting and literature.

Within this context, Lévi-Strauss's ethnographic research has the character of a search for *bons sauvages* who link his own history with that of the world's. His search for an "uncontaminated New World" and for "true primitives" was a search for others to point the way to an "alternative human world." Lévi-Strauss, though he may have been stimulated by Lowie's ethnographic practice, was not primarily interested in descriptions of other peoples. As indicated, he went "out" among others so as to go "below" to build a super-rationalist world that undercut usual philosophical distinctions between the rational and the irrational, the intellectual and emotional.

Lévi-Strauss's ethnographic method works in accordance with advice given by French ethnologist Marcel Mauss: "Ethnology is like an ocean. All you need is a net, any net. And then if you step into the water and swing your net around, you're sure to catch some fish."[42] This advice suggests a surrealist approach to field research that Lévi-Strauss affirmed as he was influenced by Mauss's thought. The method, means, and goal of ethnographic science, for Lévi-Strauss, is the drawing up of the greatest possible catalog of categories and then following that with the discovery of *"lunes mortes"* ("pale moons") in the "firmament of reason."[43]

Viewed in this context, then, Lévi-Strauss's ethnographic method aims not primarily at rational description of a particular society, but rather at a construction, built up from referents in the field, of a super-

---

[40]Ibid., 541.

[41]Ibid., 542.

[42]Ibid., 553.

[43]Claude Lévi-Strauss, "Introduction à l'oeuvre de Marcel Mauss," in *Sociologie et Anthropologie* by M. Mauss (Paris: Presses Universitaires, 1950) li-lii.

rationalist, alternative world. His handling of ethnographic texts bears this aim out. His early description of the Bororo, for example, while lacking the grand designs of his later super-rationalist structuralism, hints at the system to come. In that text, he directs attention to the "symmetry" and "asymmetry" of Bororo kinship, and unearths the seeds of the "logic that must exist" in the "elementary structures of kinship" which he later spells out.[44] In addition, his largely descriptive account of Nambikwara family and social life was not published until 1948, after he had finished writing his monumental *Elementary Structures of Kinship* in 1947. The search for "elementary structures" to serve as a base for an "alternative human world" had primacy over ethnographic description, whatever value there was in ethnographic description for construction of that base.

The nature and presentation of these ethnographic texts, then, is consistent with French ethnographic surrealism. Other reflections contained in *Tristes Tropiques* also suggest this relationship. These reflections exhibit the tendency among French scholars to intertwine artistic and ethnographic impulses. When he left France for the field, Lévi-Strauss had already experienced a musical world that would remain more real and more substantial to him than "the savannahs of central Brazil." Also at this time, it was Debussy's *Pelléas et Mélisande* that provided his "spiritual sustenance."[45] When Lévi-Strauss returned to Brazil from France to begin his second field expedition, he did so as a "full-fledged anthropologist" who had displayed collections and lectured in Paris, and who had received the "retrospective blessing" of Levy-Bruhl, Paul Rivet, and Marcel Mauss.[46] These last three ethnologists had in 1925 together founded the Paris Institute of Ethnology during the more intense years of 1920s Surrealism.[47]

The state of American research must also be attended to as a context for Lévi-Strauss's ethnographic approach. According to Lévi-Strauss, all American Indian research, whether archaeological or an-

---

[44]Lévi-Strauss, "Contribution," 282.

[45]Lévi-Strauss, *Tristes Tropiques* (Eng. ed.), 377.

[46]Ibid., 249.

[47]Clifford, "On Ethnographic Surrealism," 543-44.

thropological, was carried out in a "highly charged atmosphere."[48] Lévi-Strauss's study of the Bororo, during the São Paulo University vacations, convinced him of an anomaly about the South American situation that was at the same time being revealed in the writings of Curt Nimuendaju, long-time ethnographer of the Gê tribes of central Brazil. This anomaly, which Lévi-Strauss and others felt, concerned the presence of a complex social system and elaborate ceremonial life in tribes possessing a strikingly simple and rudimentary technology.[49] Lévi-Strauss's hypothesis was that these were Brazil's first inhabitants, "forgotten in the backwater" or "forced back into the poorest territories by war-like communities."[50] Thus, Lévi-Strauss's major expedition to the Nambikwara, the Mundé, and the Tupi-Kawahib was designed as a "cross-section ethnography" to encounter as yet unstudied, Western representatives of these tribes of Brazil's interior. The "cross-section" approach was taken because he was anxious to "understand America"—again a whole, alternative world—rather than "to study human nature by basing my research on one particular interest."[51]

	In contrast to English and American fieldworkers who set out to experience and interpret discrete cultural wholes of particular societies, Lévi-Strauss aimed at understanding America. His ethnographic research, awakened by the ethnographic practice of the American anthropologist Lowie, is subordinate to the ethnographic, surrealist impulse to study others as referents for constructing an alternative world. This understanding of his values does much to explain features of his ethnographic method, that is, his lack of compulsion to stay with one group beyond a three-month period, or his lack of interest in learning the native languages of groups studied.[52]

----

[48]Lévi-Strauss, *Tristes Tropiques* (Eng. ed.), 260.

[49]Ibid., 251. See also Charles Wagley, Foreword to *Dialectical Societies: The Gê and Bororo of Central Brazil*, ed. David Maybury-Lewis (Cambridge MA: Harvard University Press, 1979) xii-xiii.

[50]Lévi-Strauss, *Tristes Tropiques* (Eng. ed.), 252-53.

[51]Ibid., 250.

[52]Lévi-Strauss had no time to learn the Guaycuru language of the Caduveo (*Tristes Tropiques*, 172). He seems to have communicated with the Bororo through Portuguese-

Lévi-Strauss's commitment to this "cross-section ethnography" had for him a more disappointing result than merely a lack of time to spend with various encountered groups. This disappointing result was especially clear in his encounter with the Mundé, those most truly "savage" people who offered him the "supreme reward" of studying *bons sauvages* of the New World, untainted by Old World explorers. When he encountered them, his cross-section approach had dissipated the expedition's resources and supplies. There could be no question of remaining with this one particular group. The commitment to understand America, then, inhibited his ability to understand these particular "most authentic savages." In the Mundé, he received both his reward and his punishment.[53]

Even faced with this reality at the end of his major Brazilian expedition, however, Lévi-Strauss did not count his ethnographic research a failure. The Mundé experience, he claims, taught him that the "truly savage" or "truly human" was not to be found in a particular people. About his encounter with the Mundé, he writes,

> Was it not my mistake, and the mistake of my profession, to believe that men are not always men? that some are more deserving of our attention because they astonish us by their skin color and their customs?[54]

He later recalled that the retreat downstream from the Mundé was accompanied by reflection on the impossibility of communicating with the Mundé: "If the inhabitants were mute, perhaps the earth itself would speak to me." Now, for Lévi-Strauss, particular inhabitants are viewed not separately, but "in their entirety." The whole is now what fills him "with rapture," even though the parts may escape him. Lévi-Strauss's

---

speaking informants (ibid., 216). He learned a "rudimentary Nambikwara," a "lingua franca" of about forty words of part Nambikwara and part Portuguese. This made it possible to say everything that needed to be said, "although such basic Nambikwara did not allow for expression of very subtle ideas" ("La Vie familiale et sociale," 37). He also had too little time to learn the Mundé "jolly language," and he communicated with the Tupi-Kawahib through his Tupi-speaking guide, Abaitara (*Tristes Tropiques*, 333, 354-55).

[53]Lévi-Strauss, *Tristes Tropiques* (Eng. ed.), 333.

[54]Ibid.

eye broadens to this whole that is "over and above" or "behind the confusion of appearances which are all and yet nothing."[55]

Lévi-Strauss's field method, then, is best viewed as a surrealist ethnographer's fashioning of images in the field of others. If more empirical-minded anthropologists question the adequacy of his data—"his field time was too short," or "he didn't learn the native languages"— Lévi-Strauss would respond that the existence of the Caduveo, Bororo, Nambikwara, Tupi-Kawahib, or the Mundé cannot be fully understood from field encounters. As important as Lévi-Strauss believes the field encounters are for initiating his anthropological explanation, these others cannot be explained by that route alone. Consequently, Lévi-Strauss will not grant his own ethnographic method among South American peoples—or any supposedly more "scientific" versions of it— privileged status in his later theoretical formulations. Rather, his research provides images that fill ethnology's "ocean" of customs, myths, beliefs, rituals—an ocean also filled by other ethnographers' research. It is only within this ocean, this whole to which Lévi-Strauss's eye now broadens, that what it means to be "truly savage" or "truly human" may emerge.

Nevertheless, contrary to some persons' conclusion that Lévi-Strauss completely disregards empirical research, he does not begin interpreting this ocean of images unaffected by the images of his own fieldwork experience. His horizontal interpretation of others in the ocean does involve use of certain "salient images" from his Brazilian fieldwork.

"Faces remain in my memory"

Attention to Lévi-Strauss and to the *bons sauvages* he encountered, each within their own sociocultural context, enables one now to identify the salient images that facilitate his transition from the field to his later anthropology. The fieldwork is important to Lévi-Strauss, for he later would defend his anthropology against critics who lacked it.

All these names [and places] are associated with men and women of whom I have been fond, whom I have respected, whose faces remain in my memory. They remind me of joys, hardships, weariness and,

---

[55]Ibid.

sometimes, dangers. They are my witnesses, the living link between my theoretical views and reality.[56]

The claim is not that "faces," encounters with others in the field, alone generate and thus warrant his "macrosociology." After all, as Lévi-Strauss asserts, the "faces" remain in *his* memory; their distinction lies in their being there. The salient images identified here, then, are no mere product of either the field or of Lévi-Strauss, but of the whole set of relations characterizing the ethnographic situation laid out in the fundamental quadratic.

As a first salient image, one may take Lévi-Strauss literally and point to the faces of Caduveo women, decorated by their graphic art. These are salient for him not only because of the beauty they convey to the human face, but also because of their similarity to graphic and plastic arts among the Northwest Coast, Maori, and Chinese peoples. Unable to explain these similarities in geographical or cultural-contact terms, he turns to psychology and a structural analysis of the graphic forms.[57] Foreshadowing much of his later work, in an early essay Lévi-Strauss explains this graphic art as the placement of an "artificial harmony" upon the "natural harmony" of the human face. This is "a most profound and essential split representation" between the "dumb" biological individual and the social person whom he or she must embody. Here is not only a case of an artistic device—split representation—working a transition from nature to culture, but also a relation posited between artistic expression and social system. This latter relationship may also include the structures of myth and ritual so that, ultimately, all forms of expression are reciprocally related in one "organic whole" (*ensemble organique*). This organic whole anticipates the "total semantic field" made up of mutually convertible codes that he will later seek.

The Bororo village's spatial configuration may also be considered a salient image. Its circular form was divided by axes expressing the geographical posture of the village and its social structure. Opposed areas demarcated by these axes lead to interpretations of Bororo life in dualities. Like many other of the Gê and Bororo peoples, Kejara was a "di-

---

[56]Lévi-Strauss, *Structural Anthropology*, 1:332.

[57]Claude Lévi-Strauss, "Le Dédoublement de la Représentation dans les arts de l'Asie et de l'Amérique," in *Anthropologie Structurale* (Paris: Plon, 1958) 273.

alectical society."[58] Lévi-Strauss is prompted to a far-ranging application of the principle of "dual organization" that is discerned in the village layout, social structure, and geographical levels of Bororo life. In *The Elementary Structures of Kinship*, dual organization is described as the means of codifying in social organization a human sense of reciprocity.[59] However much Lévi-Strauss in later years would refine and correct his views on the existence of dual organization, ethnographic reflection on dialectical societies supports a theory of reciprocity.[60] But whence comes this notion of reciprocity?

Reciprocity emerges frequently in Lévi-Strauss's earliest essays. There it is an interpretive concept invoked by him in relation to three salient images derived from his work among the Nambikwara. These three are the ritualized relation between war and trade, a simple kinship system, and the phenomenon of chiefly power.

The meeting of two warring Nambikwara tribes on his campsite was especially striking. Those two tribes resolved their animosity and then moved to trading relations. This event is the subject of a 1943 article and is referred to in several other works.[61] Lévi-Strauss watched as strife became barter through one ritual of reciprocal exchange: first of angry gestures, then of reconciling words, then of goods.

His encounter with the two tribes seeking reconciliation through intermarriage, by way of a simple kinship system in which women were exchanged, is the second salient image from his Nambikwara experiences that evokes the interpretive concept of reciprocity. Not only does Lévi-Strauss see reciprocal exchange operating in this simple kinship system, he also sees a specific form of marriage (cross-cousin marriage)

---

[58]Maybury-Lewis, *Dialectical Societies*, 2.

[59]Claude Lévi-Strauss, *The Elementary Structures of Kinship*, ed. R. Needham, trans. James Harle Bell and John Richard von Sturmer (Boston: Beacon, 1969) 70-72.

[60]Lévi-Strauss, "Do Dual Organizations Exist?" in *Structural Anthropology*, 1:163.

[61]Lévi-Strauss, "Guerre et commerce chez les Indiens d'Amérique du sud," *Renaissance* 1 (1943): fasc. 1 and 2; "On Dual Organization in South America," *America Indigena* 4 (1944): 37-47; "L'Analyse structurale en Linguistique et en Anthropologie," *Word* 1: 33-53; "La Politique étrangère d'une Société Primitive," *Politique Étrangère* 2 (May 1949): 139-52; and *The Elementary Structures of Kinship*, 67.

being practiced to maximize those kinds of reciprocal exchanges that unite the society's groups most effectively.[62]

Then, third, the phenomenon of chiefly power among the Nambikwara also evokes the interpretive concept of reciprocal exchange. The chief renders care and generosity to the group in return for the group's "consent" to the legitimacy of his power.[63] In discussing consent as a form of reciprocal exchange, Lévi-Strauss explicitly cites Rousseau. This salient image, along with the other two from his Nambikwara experience, not only evokes in his early essays the interpretive concept of reciprocity, it does so in a way that shows it operating at several levels: economic, social, and political.

The "faces" remaining in Lévi-Strauss's memory, then, are related to the interpretive concept of reciprocity that will figure so prominently in his later texts. These salient images, joined to the concept of reciprocity, are easily found in his earlier essays. In his somewhat later work, *The Elementary Structures of Kinship*, however, these salient images are scattered throughout the "ocean" of others' ethnography. His images are only a few among many that suggest a basic sense of reciprocity underlying the many forms of kinship. Drawing together various ethnographic images, Lévi-Strauss seeks to construct in this text not a "picture" (*l'image*) of a particular society or even a group of societies, but a "model" of the elementary structures and basic mechanisms that underlie all known kinship systems.[64] His use of ethnography in fashioning this model is twofold: first, he gleans ethnographic examples from many ethnographic sources, including his own, that allow him to hypothesize about the nature of the model.[65] The latter part of the book then undertakes a more thorough analysis of specific regions: South Asia, China, and India.

---

[62]Claude Lévi-Strauss, "The Social Use of Kinship Terms among Brazilian Indians," *American Anthropologist* 45 (1943): 398; and Lévi-Strauss, "La Vie familiale et sociale," 17-35.

[63]Claude Lévi-Strauss, "The Social and Psychological Aspects of Chieftainship in a Primitive Tribe: The Nambikwara of Northwestern Mato Grosso," in *Comparative Political Systems*, ed. R. Cohen and J. Middleton (Garden City NY: Natural History Press, 1967) 59.

[64]Lévi-Strauss, *Elementary Structures of Kinship*, 100.

[65]Ibid., xxii.

The diverse gleanings in the book's early part may be viewed as a multiplication of images taken from ethnography that, like Lévi-Strauss's salient images, seem to evoke reciprocity as an interpretive concept. Lévi-Strauss includes among these images data from the "ethnography" of infant thought, which, as a "sort of common denominator for all thoughts and cultures," suggests that reciprocity may be universally sensed and formed into social rules, so as to permeate all the levels of a social group.[66] Once this hypothesis is established, Lévi-Strauss switches from ethnographic gleaning to more careful analysis of kinship systems in South Asia, China, and India, where he seeks confirmation of his hypothesis that there is a controlling "world of reciprocity" behind kinship practices.

The Elementary Structures of Kinship is a long and difficult text that warrants a number of different kinds of analyses. Here it has been cited as the first major product of Lévi-Strauss's fieldwork. Starting with reference to various ethnographic materials, Lévi-Strauss aimed at discerning and ordering the basic mental pattern of reciprocity. In so doing, he claims that

> behind what seemed to be the superficial contingency and incoherent diversity of the laws governing marriage I discerned a small number of simple principles, thanks to which a very complex mass of customs and practices, at first sight absurd (and generally held to be so) could be reduced to a meaningful system.[67]

The nature of this "meaningful system" could be discussed from the perspective of its several mechanisms: incest taboo, maternal and paternal cross-cousin marriage. More important for my purposes here is Lévi-Strauss's insistence that each mechanism of the kinship system "ceaselessly bends itself" to conform to a "whole world," the "world of reciprocity." True, some mechanisms, such as paternal cross-cousin marriage, seem to contribute to a world of reciprocity in only a restricted sense, or sometimes even work against it. This is so because human minds, in the short term, still dare to believe "that one could gain

---

[66]Ibid., 87, 94.

[67]Claude Lévi-Strauss, *The Raw and the Cooked: Introduction to a Science of Mythology: 1*, trans. John Weightman and Doreen Weightman (New York: Harper and Row, 1969) 10.

without losing, enjoy without sharing."[68] Whatever the reality of these short-term temptations, all of his analyses are designed to show that the various kinship practices operate as they do because humans ultimately have little choice but to meet the constraints imposed by a deep-felt sense of reciprocity.

The salient images of Lévi-Strauss's fieldwork, the "faces" remaining in his memory, have been fused with others from ethnography to suggest a "world of reciprocity" that is the most likely explanation for the kinship practices he examines.

A confessing self
and the rise of objectified thought

This "world of reciprocity," posited, searched for, and presented in *The Elementary Structures*, is the whole to which Lévi-Strauss's eye had broadened and the whole that filled him "with rapture" when, at the end of his major field expedition, he discerned his "mistake" and that of his profession: to believe that men are not always men.[69] This whole world now becomes the primary subject of his investigations. Not only is it "subject matter" for him, it is also posited as interpretive device. The structures of the world of reciprocity become a "principle of interpretation."[70] As such, his interpretations of various ethnographic reports begin by assuming a "complex union" of institution, terminology, social customs, and beliefs. This is the "whole" that is "given before the parts" of that which he interprets.[71]

With Lévi-Strauss now sensitive to this whole, after publication of *The Elementary Structures*, his method of explanation becomes less predominantly ethnographic or social science-oriented, and more literary-critical. What is important now are not so much the other peoples and worlds in which Lévi-Strauss immerses himself by ethnographic techniques. Rather, the crucial elements are his own texts, which demonstrate ways to render others out of himself so as to reveal a new world

---

[68]Lévi-Strauss, *Elementary Structures of Kinship*, 497.

[69]Lévi-Strauss, *Tristes Tropiques* (Eng. ed.), 333.

[70]Lévi-Strauss, "History and Ethnology," in *Structural Anthropology*, 1:21.

[71]Lévi-Strauss, *Elementary Structures of Kinship*, 100.

transcending his own and others' societies.[72] As testimony to this shift, which may also be viewed as the expected outcome for a "surrealist" ethnographer, is the text Lévi-Strauss wrote six years after *The Elementary Structures: Tristes Tropiques.*

In *Tristes Tropiques* the impenetrability of the Mundé savage culture is presented as an occasion for Lévi-Strauss's "confession" in a twofold sense. In a negative sense, there is what one might term Lévi-Strauss's "contrition," his awareness of a mistaken attitude that permeated his earlier explorations: "to believe that men are not always men . . . that some are more deserving of interest and attention because they astonish us by the color of their skin and their customs." *Tristes Tropiques* is also a confession in a second sense, as a positive, thoroughgoing acknowledgment of the precariousness of all particular inhabitants in some "objective" existence that would make field research the primary route to knowledge of them. Truer to a surrealist spirit, Lévi-Strauss's literary-critical method is used to demonstrate an overriding unity of experience, subjective and objective.[73]

The shift through a typically social-science method of ethnography to a more properly literary-critical one is evident through examining the fate of ethnography in *Tristes Tropiques.* James Boon suggests that *Tristes Tropiques* is not an ethnography.[74] Perhaps more precisely, in this text the ethnographer's images, significant for Lévi-Strauss's anthropology, are attached more self-consciously by him not only to the "faces" of Brazil, but also to his own memory. Boon himself states this ably when he likens *Tristes Tropiques* to "Symbolist narrative"—a literary precursor of twentieth-century French Surrealism[75]—wherein "objects described exist only in relation to the particular mind of the artist and his

---

[72]On the possibility of such a textual approach being explanatory, see Paul Ricoeur, "The Model of the Text: Meaningful Action Considered as Text," in *Interpretive Social Science: A Reader,* ed. Paul Rabinow and William M. Sullivan (Berkeley: University of California Press, 1979) 95, 99.

[73]Cf. Edward B. Henning, *The Spirit of Surrealism* (Bloomington: University of Indiana, 1979) 37.

[74]James A. Boon, *From Symbolism to Structuralism: Lévi-Strauss in a Literary Tradition* (New York: Harper and Row, 1972) 141.

[75]Jean Peirrot, *The Decadent Imagination: 1880-1900* (Chicago: University of Chicago Press, 1981) 121, 190.

persona."[76] *Tristes Tropiques* is an open acknowledgment, a "confession," of the way Lévi-Strauss constitutes his world. One of the more striking features of the book is that it is a "temporally and spatially collapsed world." Lévi-Strauss's multiple crossings of the Atlantic, for example, are merged by him into one narrative segment in almost indistinguishable form.[77] The encounter with the Bororo is similarly described and collated with recollections of encounters with the Kuki that occurred in the far-removed Chittagong Hill tracts of Pakistan fourteen years later. In this latter spatial and temporal collapse, especially, it is difficult to know whom Lévi-Strauss is discussing. Indeed, part of his point is that it doesn't matter.

This "confession" by Lévi-Strauss, employing a literary-critical method of explanation, initiates the most recent and most ambitious task of his horizontal hermeneutic: his *superrationaliste* integration. Lévi-Strauss, as confessing self, turns to the "text" and to texts of mythology and loses himself, as he claims all inquiring subjects must, in a larger constituting world. Ethnography, as a pool of referents holding his own and others' salient images, will now include reports about social practice, ritual, belief, myths, and versions of myths. His images are now lost in this ocean. And given the integral relation of these images to himself, Lévi-Strauss, the surrealist investigating subject, is also dispersed in that ocean. One may anticipate the outcome of Lévi-Strauss's hermeneutic: by losing himself in the ocean of ethnography that he explains semiotically by structural analysis, he displays an "objectified thought" that constrains people everywhere, but that itself will vanish, closing in on itself, signaling the predominance of "nonbeing" over "being." The journey to this final outcome is through the four volumes of *Mythologiques*.

How does the semiotic or literary-critical method of explanation proceed in these volumes? Lévi-Strauss understands his method as a form of "aesthetic contemplation" different from what he learned at the Sorbonne, which was "contemplation of consciousness by itself." In contrast, he insists on starting with the pool of ethnographic experience that presents "empirically collective forms of understanding" in their

---

[76]Boon, *From Symbolism to Structuralism*, 146.

[77]Lévi-Strauss, *Tristes Tropiques* (Eng. ed.), 24-25.

most divergent form. These are "referents" for his aesthetic contemplation, and unlike the "dangerous," ethnocentric *gymnastique* of philosophical aesthetes at the Sorbonne, Lévi-Strauss, the ethnologist, proposes a "supreme form of mental gymnastics" that allows every joint of a cross-cultural "skeleton" to reveal a "general pattern of anatomical structure."[78]

Lévi-Strauss's aesthetic contemplation approaches these referents in a distinctive way. As he wrote in *La Pensée sauvage*—that "merely temporal halt" between *The Elementary Structures* and *Mythologiques*—his aesthetic contemplation approaches the sensible world of ethnography through the "universal type of the work of art": the small-scale model.[79] The small-scale model, such as the one used by Francois Clouet in his art, effects a reduction of the sensible in its totality.[80] Lévi-Strauss admits that this aesthetic drive for intelligibility occurs at the expense of sensibility.[81] When accused of "going beyond the data," therefore, he readily admits that tendency, arguing, however, that such "going beyond" is an anticipation necessary for future ethnographic work. Lévi-Strauss's general intent is indeed to go beyond ethnographic *sensibilité* by integrating it into an ever-widening system of *intelligibilité*.

There is a particular kind of aesthetic contemplation that maximizes this super-rationalist integration of sensibility and intelligibility. This contemplation is music, the "supreme mystery of the sciences of man."[82] Lévi-Strauss's aesthetic, literary-critical method of explanation will be a "musical" one in that he will "play" the structures of various mythic versions like so many instruments. Playing mythic versions in a musical way is crucial to his super-rationalist integration of feeling and reason for two reasons. First, it is crucial because music exploits both nature's "organic rhythms" and culture's "scale of sounds." The natural and cultural play of music can unite sensibility and intelligibility. Second, music is significant for Lévi-Strauss because it unifies him

---

[78]Lévi-Strauss, *The Raw and the Cooked*, 10-11.

[79]Lévi-Strauss, *The Savage Mind* (Chicago: University of Chicago Press, 1966) 23.

[80]Ibid.

[81]Ibid., 24.

[82]Lévi-Strauss, *The Raw and the Cooked*, 18.

and his subject in the same way it unifies listener and composer. As Lévi-Strauss actively "listens" through structural analysis to the myths that South and North American peoples "compose," those myths have their being in him, just as a composer's work is not complete until it has its being in the listener.[83] The musicality of Lévi-Strauss's explanations causes his dispersal into his subject. It is finally the myths that think and play themselves out through him.

The final aim of this method in anthropology, however, is not merely the loss of the investigating subject, necessary as that is, but rather a better knowledge of "objectified thought and its mechanisms."[84] For this purpose it is "in the last resort immaterial" whether this thought is displayed through Lévi-Strauss's thought or through that of the South and North American Indians. Lévi-Strauss's literary-critical or semiological display of this thought is modeled after his understanding of structural linguistics; it seeks to relate the basic elements of myths, "mythemes," according to the elementary rules that linguistics applied to the systems of signs that underlie the use of language.[85] Lévi-Strauss dissects, combines, redissects, and recombines these basic units of myths within ever-widening contexts so that objectified thought and its mechanisms are displayed.

Structural analysis of the various mythic units builds up a "total semantic field" that presents the "architecture of the human mind" as a set of mutually convertible codes. These codes provide the "layered logic" of the field, and it is the task of his four-volume *Mythologiques* to show how an increasing number of codes are mutually convertible: meteorological, alimentary, sociological, anatomical, geographical, vestimentary, ethical codes.

While the alimentary code, or "cooking," seems to dominate throughout,[86] the major point is the codes' mutual convertibility. If Lévi-

---

[83]Ibid., 17.

[84]Ibid., 13.

[85]Lévi-Strauss, "The Structural Study of Myth," *Structural Anthropology*, 1:211. Lévi-Strauss stresses that analysis of mythemes presupposes language's constitutive units: morphemes, lexemes, phonemes. Mythemes are found at "a higher more complex order," on the level of the sentence.

[86]Claude Lévi-Strauss, *The Origin of Table Manners, Introduction to a Science of Mythology: 3*, trans. John Weightman and Doreen Weightman (New York: Harper and Row, 1968) 479, 495.

Strauss elevates one code over others, it is because such an elevation allows the reader to view the reciprocal convertibility of all the codes in a single "total semantic field." Thus, occasionally, it may be the acoustic code, for example, that dominates the alimentary code.[87]

The semiotic method for displaying the convertibility of codes in a total semantic field, as practiced in *Mythologiques*, relates mythemes drawn from eight hundred myths and mythic versions. He begins with a Bororo myth due to a "certain impressionism," intuitive feeling, and "contingence of personal circumstance."[88] Any selected myth, and his Bororo myth is no exception, exhibits a "syntagmatic chain" that seems arbitrary at first, having no meaning. In other words, all the myth provides to the uninitiated reader is a sequence of parts, linked without apparent logic or continuity. Such a "syntagmatic chain" can only take on meaning when it is placed in the context of a "semantic field."[89]

The first such context is provided, as Lévi-Strauss has all along insisted, by ethnography. It is impossible to interpret myths structurally "without an exact identification of plants and animals" referred to, and without an exact identification of mythic elements' position in a specific culture.[90] Ethnography's ability to provide the contexts for a myth's syntagmatic chain, however, quickly "reaches a ceiling."[91] Then, it is only other myths that give a myth its meaningful context. The overall context for any one myth "consists more and more of other myths and less and less of the customs, beliefs and rites of the particular population from which the myth in question derives."[92]

It is in this movement from a myth's syntagmatic chain, to its ethnographic context, and then to the context of other myths, that the codes become important. The codes are a logic of "tangible qualities" by which

---

[87]Claude Lévi-Strauss, *From Honey to Ashes, Introduction to a Science of Mythology: 2*, trans. John Weightman and Doreen Weightman (New York: Harper and Row, 1966) 471-72.

[88]Lévi-Strauss, *The Raw and the Cooked*, 2, and idem, *The Savage Mind*, 66.

[89]Lévi-Strauss, *The Raw and the Cooked*, 307.

[90]Lévi-Strauss, *The Savage Mind*, 45, 55.

[91]Lévi-Strauss, *From Honey to Ashes*, 356.

[92]Ibid.

the mythologizing mind unconsciously swings from context to context through different "paradigms." When Lévi-Strauss analyzes the two American continents' myths, he claims to be charting these moves, these transformations of the human mind in its world. When the display of this layered or coded logic of sensory qualities is complete, his analyses then have given rise to "objectified thought."

One of the codes, discussed at the end of his third volume, is significant for Lévi-Strauss because it especially testifies to the existence of this world of objectified thought that constrains mythologizers even though they may not consciously reflect on it. This is the "ethical code." The notion of correct behavior implicit in this code Lévi-Strauss terms "deference to the world."[93] Mythologizing subjects, the South American Indians who create and pass on these myths, know that the world constitutes them. They thus protect the world, knowing that as they are dispersed into it, so they are also constituted by and dependent upon it. These mythologizers lose themselves in the codifications made possible by their world. This is the "implicit ethic" that the myths tell.

Lévi-Strauss's claim, however, is not just that mythologizers lose themselves in their world, but that the mythologist also does, and indeed already has in the "musical" act of structurally displaying the mythologizer's "total semantic field." His explanations, his structural analyses of myths, entail *"l'effacement du sujet"* as a "methodological necessity."[94] He seeks what David Peirce terms the "final erasure" of himself.[95]

> Having arrived at the evening of my career, the last image that myths leave for me and, across them, this supreme myth that the history of humanity tells, the history also of the universe within which the other is unrolled, rejoins therefore the intuition which, at my beginnings and as I told it in *Tristes Tropiques,* made me look for in the phases of a sunset (. . . which is progressively complicated up to the point of undoing and abolishing itself in nocturnal nothingness), the model

---

[93]Lévi-Strauss, *The Origin of Table Manners,* 507.

[94]Lévi-Strauss, *The Naked Man, Introduction to a Science of Mythology: 4,* trans. John Weightman and Doreen Weightman (New York: Harper and Row, 1981) 628.

[95]David Peirce, "Lévi-Strauss: The Problematic Self and Myth," *International Philosophical Quarterly* 19 (1979): 381-406.

of facts that I was going to study later and of problems that I would
have to resolve in mythology: a vast and complex edifice, itself also
iridescent with a thousand tints, which displayed under the analyst's
eyes, slowly flowers and closes itself in the distance as if it never existed.[96]

Lévi-Strauss, the confessing self, having poured himself out into a world
that constitutes others, ultimately testifies to the eclipse of even the world
that constitutes him.

The conclusion of the *Mythologiques* volumes was anticipated in the
earlier "confession" of *Tristes Tropiques*. There, both individual and
collective being are "no more than a semblance." "Anthropology," he
suggests, might best be termed "entropology":

> The world began without man and it will end without him. The in-
> stitutions, morals and customs that I shall have spent my life noting
> down and trying to understand are the transient efflorescence of a
> creation in relation to which they have no meaning, except perhaps
> of allowing mankind to play its part in creation.[97]

Consistent with this anticipation in the 1955 work is the conclusion he
wrote for his entire four-volume *Mythologiques*. There, all his oppositions may be reduced to Hamlet's fundamental one between being and
nonbeing.

> With his [the human's] inevitable disappearance from the surface of
> a planet which is itself doomed to die, his labours, his sorrows, his
> joys, his hopes and his works will be as if they had never existed, since
> no consciousness will survive to preserve even the memory of these
> epiphenomena, only a few features of which, soon to be erased from
> the impassive face of the earth, will remain as already cancelled evi-
> dence that they once were, and were as nothing.[98]

Commentators on Lévi-Strauss have termed this ultimate development of his thought an example of many twentieth-century thinkers'

---

[96]Lévi-Strauss, *The Naked Man*, 628.

[97]Lévi-Strauss, *Tristes Tropiques* (Eng. ed.), 413.

[98]Lévi-Strauss, *The Naked Man*, 694-95.

proclaimed "eclipse of the self."[99] Others dismiss it as a sure sign that
Lévi-Strauss has become enmeshed in "pure metaphysics" or a structuralism with "religious overtones."[100] These various interpretations will
not be discussed here. I have wished to display Lévi-Strauss's horizontal hermeneutic as a complex set of factors, taking the form first of a
social-scientific method of explanation, which then develops into a semiotic, literary-critical one. This intercultural dialogue, of course, does
not occur apart from an intracultural one. Before looking at Lévi-
Strauss's intracultural, vertical hermeneutic, however, I must sketch the
horizontal hermeneutic of Marvin Harris.

Marvin Harris: Ordering Human Nature

Harris's horizontal hermeneutic also pursues the explanatory ideal.
Unlike Lévi-Strauss, however, whose shift through ethnography to semiotic explanation displayed objectified thought, Harris aims at a stra-
tegic intersubjectivity among anthropologists based on an interface of
operationalized anthropological categories with "nature."

Interpreting urban folk at Minas Velhas

Harris's anthropological knowledge displays its distinctive form in
his early fieldwork experience among the societies and peoples of Bahia
in northern Brazil (July 1950-June 1951) and in Mozambique in south-
east Africa (June 1956-May 1957).[101] My major concern will be with the
Brazilian experience because it shows most clearly the ethnographic
context for certain features of his later "science of culture." The Mozambique fieldwork, though it cannot be ignored, need not be a major
concern since Harris himself admits that Mozambique was such an arena
of political conflict that only with difficulty could successful anthro-

[99]Peirce, "Lévi-Strauss: The Problematic Self and Myth," 398-99.

[100]Elizabeth Kurzweil, *The Age of Structuralism: From Lévi-Strauss to Foucault* (New
York: Columbia University Press, 1980) 29.

[101]Marvin Harris, *Town and Country in Brazil: A Sociological-Anthropological Study
of a Small Brazilian Town* (New York: Norton, 1956) i; idem, *Portugal's African Wards:
A First-Hand Report on Labor and Emigration in Moçambique,* Africa Today Pamphlets
(New York: American Committee on Africa, 1958).

pological work be carried on there.[102] The Mozambique experience, like fieldwork Harris did briefly in a number of other places, either resulted in brief articles or served as a reference in texts devoted to other matters.

Harris began fieldwork in 1951 in the province of Bahia in northeastern Brazil at the age of twenty-three, after having done undergraduate and graduate studies at Columbia University.[103] As an undergraduate, Harris met anthropologist Charles Wagley and, reportedly "intrigued by a discipline that called more for field trips than office work,"[104] decided to pursue anthropology at the graduate level. Wagley later invited Harris to be a part of a field team for South American research in Bahia.

Absent from Harris's corpus are texts that, like Lévi-Strauss's *Tristes Tropiques,* are replete with autobiographical comment. Even more important is Harris's reluctance in his ethnographic accounts to attend to his own personal background, reactions, or interactions in the field, except insofar as they are necessary to reveal to his readers his particular investigative methods. Even Harris's descriptions of the Bahian mountains and terrain—while reading "like a novel" and offering a "spectacle" taking one out of the present to that other place—are set forth with an air of "the strictest objectivity."[105] It is an unspecified "traveler" who journeys to that place and views its scenery.[106] This attitude contrasts with the reactions of Malinowski or Lévi-Strauss, for example, who were fascinated by the scenery of *their* tropics.[107] From Har-

---

[102]Marvin Harris, "Race, Conflict and Reform in Moçambique," in *The Transformation of East Africa,* ed. Stanley Diamond and Fred G. Burke (New York: Basic Books, 1966) 157, and *Portugal's African Wards,* 5.

[103]See Marvin Harris, *Cultural Materialism: The Struggle for a Science of Culture* (New York: Random House, 1979) 383.

[104]Ibid.

[105]Such is the impression related by one reader, Fernand Braudel, in *On History* (Chicago: University of Chicago Press, 1980) 165.

[106]Harris, *Town and Country,* 9.

[107]Bronislaw Malinowski, *A Diary in the Strict Sense of the Term* (New York: Harcourt, Brace and World, 1966) 11-12. For Lévi-Strauss, note *Tristes Tropiques* (Eng. ed.), 90-92.

ris's texts, then, one gains little knowledge of him as investigating anthropologist and of how he as an individual responds to his ethnographic situation.[108] An understanding of Harris, the investigating subject, is available only indirectly through delineation of the other contexts in which he worked.

The investigated subjects of Harris's fieldwork experience were some 1,500 residents of 270 domiciles of a small Brazilian town, Minas Velhas. It exists in such a lonely, isolated setting, surrounded on all sides by rugged hills, that many people in the nearby capitol of the province had never heard of it. At one time in Brazil's history, it was important as a mountain region where the mining of gold and diamonds caused Brazil's second important economic cycle of boom and bust. In 1951 Harris found it lonely and isolated, "one of those increasingly rare places still immune to the penetrations of Coca Cola."[109]

The people of Minas Velhas are primarily "of two races—Negroe and White—and the results of their intermixture."[110] There are some "Amerindian characteristics," but persons who are clearly of pure American Indian descent are not found in Minas Velhas. The residents are descendants of those earlier sophisticated adventurers who founded the town and were later joined by autocrats and bureaucrats who consolidated the town for its role as administrative center. It is this historical legacy, providing the people an "urban ideal," that defines who they are, and not so much their "racial make-up." It is their ever-present "ethos" as "townspeople," historically bestowed and functionally maintained in the present, that defines these inhabitants of the walled town of Minas Velhas.[111] Harris's designations of his investigated subjects in terms of "ethos" and "townspeople" involve concepts and distinctions inextricably embedded in both the investigated subjects' and

---

[108]In some of his Mozambique articles, Harris's personal involvement is more evident. This involvement, however, is not considered a tool of ethnographic research. His personal involvement takes the form of discharging a "moral obligation" that follows "objective and non-partisan" research. See Harris, *Portugal's African Wards*, 1-2.

[109]Harris, *Town and Country*, 6, 10.

[110]Ibid., 112.

[111]Charles Wagley and Marvin Harris, "A Typology of Latin American Subcultures," *American Anthropologist* 57 (1955): 437, 439.

in the investigating anthropologist's sociocultural contexts. To show how this is true, one needs to describe Harris's ethnographic situation by referring to the remaining components of the quadratic.

One can set forth the "context for investigated subjects" by referring first to Minas Velhas's local individuals, groups, and institutions, and then proceeding outward to the wider networks of relations in the Bahia province and Brazil.

Most determinative for this context is the relation between Minas Velhas and immediately surrounding villages and farming clusters. From "the natives' point of view," this relation is crucial. Within it they define themselves as "townsmen" in juxtaposition to the country dwellers, valuing life in the town and devaluing that of the country.[112] Harris can accept this "native point of view," though only in a qualified sense. Because he does accept it, much of his ethnography tells what it means for a resident to be in an urban context.[113]

After sketching the town's *movimento*—its bustling municipal life— Harris presents the community of Minas Velhas in chapters on economics, class and race, family and individual, government and politics, religion, and folk beliefs.[114] More important, however, for characterizing the town as urban are its pervasive "heterogeneity, individualization, and secularization." These terms are also rooted in the investigating anthropologist's own sociocultural context. Harris uses them to summarize his presentation of Minas Velhas as urban.

In contrast to the peasants of the country, Minas Velhas features the heterogeneity of occupational specialization, differences of rank, and political schisms.[115] Individualization appears in townspeople's "weak sense of community *esprit de corp*," in economic matters, and in the

---

[112]Harris, *Town and Country*, 22, 279.

[113]Ibid., 32.

[114]This ordering of Harris's chapters, which he does not explicitly discuss, generally reflects his later theoretical view of the determinative dynamics of a sociocultural system. In terms of his later *Cultural Materialism*, one can see in this sequence of chapters the basic, causal movement that Harris will theoretically defend: from "infrastructure" to "structure" to "superstructure."

[115]Ibid., 44-45, 96-112, 186-207.

"dominance of capital" as the organizing factor in group labor.[116] Secularization is evident in the civil authority's dominance of the ecclesiastical, in religion's impotence for serving as the town's cohesive force, in the widespread disdain for religion among male residents.[117] Add to these three the predominance of nonagricultural occupations in Minas Velhas, a strong development of political institutions, and unfamiliarity with natural surroundings, and Minas Velhas appears as an "urban complex."[118]

It is especially the town's faith in political institutions, at the province and national levels, that spawns an urban ethos. Unlike the peasants, who view the government with suspicion, the townsmen view it as the producer of progress and habitually regard it as a potential source of outright gifts.[119] The arm of the government in Minas Velhas employs more people than any private enterprise there. These and other factors produce not only an urban *movimento* in Minas Velhas's heterogeneous, individualized, and secularized community, but also a people who turn their backs on the peasants of the country and face toward the urban governmental elites of the Brazilian coast. The residents of Minas Velhas are "away, dreaming of the city."[120]

Harris's fieldwork situation can be more fully displayed by returning to Harris, this time as viewed within his own particular context. Harris's own sociocultural context, insofar as it bears upon the ethnographic situation, may be set internationally and institutionally.

A clue to what I call the international aspect of his sociocultural context, the relation of his own nation's interests to those of other studied nations, may be found in Harris's ethnographic text, *Town and Country in Brazil*. At the end of that text, he includes himself among "those who are interested in improving living conditions in the Brazilian interior."[121] The people of Minas Velhas are potential administra-

---

[116]Ibid., 64-71, 275.

[117]Ibid., 208, 241.

[118]Ibid., 276.

[119]Ibid., 183-84.

[120]Ibid., 288-89.

[121]Ibid., 288.

tors of such improvement, especially among the surrounding peasant and agricultural communities. Yet because of the "urban ethos," which leads townspeople to despise farming as a profession and keeps them "away, dreaming in the city," Minas Velhas is an obstacle to effecting the improvements that Harris values. The townspeople's ethos works against their own and others' "future benefit."

Harris's commitment to improve Latin American living conditions may be placed within the context of American national interest in Latin America. Such national interest included government-sponsored research and publication on Latin America. As one observer puts it, the catalyst for this sponsorship was the interest in Latin America expressed through the New Deal before and during World War II.[122] One result of such government sponsorship was Julian Steward's *Handbook of South American Indians,* produced by the Bureau of American Ethnology of the Smithsonian Institution with the cooperation of the U.S. Department of State. Arnold Strickon, in his historical analyses of the early years of this research, places this research within the context of a basic "need to know" about Latin America at its grass-roots level so as to inform United States policies and activities.[123]

Harris's anthropologist teacher, Charles Wagley, discussed this confluence of anthropological research and United States national interest some years after his own and Harris's anthropological field studies: "The future of Latin American nations and of those rapidly expanding peoples is crucial to our way of life."[124] The United States scholar of Latin American life, according to Wagley, focuses

on operational problems in a "ten-minute to midnight" atmosphere.

---

[122]Arnold Strickon, "Anthropology in Latin America," *Social Science Research in Latin America,* Report and Papers of a Seminar on Latin American Studies in the United States, held at Stanford, California, 8 July-23 August 1963, ed. Charles Wagley (New York: Columbia University Press, 1964) 136.

[123]A similar context for this early research is suggested by other sources, even when they combine their historical analyses with vigorous criticism of the ways in which this confluence of United States national interest and social-science research was effected. See James Petras, ed., "Latin American Studies in the United States: A Critical Assessment," in *Politics and Social Structure in Latin America* (New York: Monthly Review Press, 1970) 327-44.

[124]Charles Wagley, Introduction to *Social Science Research in Latin America,* 1.

In any case, he will learn that Latin America provides the well-trained and original social scientist with an opportunity to break new ground, both substantively and theoretically, as well as to contribute to the welfare of millions to the south.[125]

It is this "welfare" that Harris frequently seems to have as his concern not only in the final pages of his ethnography, but throughout the volume when discussing, as he does, the "degradation" of artisans who are not able to produce a satisfying product, the "malfunctioning" that results from lack of cooperative labor groups, the "urban discontent" generated by family situations in which husband and wife feel "trapped into a life of unrewarding drudgery." Harris's concern for the welfare of his investigated subjects throughout *Town and Country in Brazil* is at least suggestive of the general national and international context sketched by Strickon. His ethnographic presentation of the community life of Minas Velhas, one might say, helps fulfill the "need to know" by which a nation like the United States might, in Wagley's words, "support those forces in Latin America which promote economic, social and political progress by peaceful and democratic means."[126]

Harris's ethnographic work is no simple reflection of this international context or of United States national interest. It is mediated and shaped institutionally. Harris's connection to Columbia University's anthropology department must therefore be considered.

This institutional mediation is particularly evident in Harris's acknowledged indebtedness to two of his former teachers, Wagley and Julian Steward. Wagley, the one from whom Harris "first learned how to think anthropologically," also articulated an international need for social-science research in Latin America. Harris hopes that his own theoretical approach in his introductory text, *Culture, Man and Nature* (1971), will be recognized by Wagley as his "spirit grandchild that here awaits embodiment in future generations of the anthropological tribe."[127]

The other former teacher, Julian Steward, also warrants attention. Steward, who taught at Columbia University from 1946 to 1952, pro-

---

[125]Ibid., 29.

[126]Ibid., 2.

[127]Marvin Harris, *Culture, Man and Nature* (New York: Thomas Crowell, 1975) x.

vided Harris with a theoretical orientation that throughout his career influenced his interest in the study of causality, evolution, and ecology in anthropology.[128] Steward envisioned a synthetic science of society, a theory of cultural ecology that appealed to the immediacy of the concrete conditions of life.

At Columbia University's anthropology department, within the context of New York City, Steward's anthropological, scientific vision provided an "intellectual format" for students who often had experienced or witnessed historical and economic disruption. As Robert F. Murphy tells it, Columbia students in this period had come of age during the Depression, "troubled by the demise of their parents' world, prone to economic anxieties and driven to succeed." In comparison to earlier decades, a higher proportion of the student body represented the low and lower-middle classes. Moreover, many had seen combat and its results. They manifested a political affinity for the world's victims of war. Such "overseas experiences must surely have whetted their appetites for other cultures."[129] This confluence of anthropology and political interests was not just Steward's doing. Franz Boas's interest in political change had also attracted students of this sort in an earlier period. Steward's own context was an academic department with a tradition of this confluence, drawing students "enured to a hardscrabble, uncertain existence, cognizant of the economic realities of life, and attuned to a critical view of their social milieu."[130] In this period, also, there were spirited discussions at Columbia about whether Steward's cultural ecology might be given a Marxist interpretation, a discussion that Harris himself takes up in his *Rise of Anthropological Theory*.

---

[128]Ibid. See also Harris, *The Rise of Anthropological Theory: A History of Theories of Culture* (New York: Thomas Crowell, 1968) 654-87. Julian Steward wrote a letter to Harris congratulating him on the publication of *The Rise of Anthropological Theory*. See *History of Anthropology Newsletter* 7:2 (1980): 5-8.

[129]Robert F. Murphy, "Introduction: The Anthropological Theories of Julian H. Steward," in *Evolution and Ecology: Essays on Social Transformation by Julian H. Steward*, ed. Jane C. Steward and Robert F. Murphy (Urbana: University of Illinois Press, 1977) 9; for further discussion of Columbia University in this period, see Robert F. Murphy, "Julian Steward," in *Totems and Teachers: Perspectives on the History of Anthropology*, ed. Sydel Silverman (New York: Columbia University Press, 1981) 177.

[130]Murphy, "Introduction," 8-9.

In the theories of Julian Steward at Columbia, then, are signs of institutional mediation to Harris of the confluence of anthropology, politics, and ecology. Harris, to be sure, pursued his own interests and agenda; however, along with several other anthropologists, his project manifests a more widely held "elemental and general kind of materialism" rooted in a basic assumption identified by Robert Murphy: "a premise and axiom, that social thought emanates from social action and that the imperatives of work, power and sex are prior to the symbolic forms that encapsulate them."[131]

Both the international and institutional aspects of Harris's sociocultural context might be further discussed for their own intrinsic interest.[132] The primary concern here, however, is to understand how they bear upon Harris's ethnographic situation. One needs to direct one's attention, therefore, to the more immediate context of Harris's research: the Columbia University/Bahia State Community Study Project. Columbia University contributed to this project not only by providing funds from its Council for Research in the Social Sciences but also by supplying one of its three directors: Charles Wagley. Two other directors were supplied by Brazil, and they were sponsored by Brazilian institutions.

The "cultural-ecological" approach of this Columbia University project was evident in its very organization. The project consisted of intensive community studies strategically located according to different ecological zones: coastal, sugar planting, semidesert, and central mountain.[133] Harris's Minas Velhas study was situated in the central mountain region. Harris was at once a member of a large research team headed by Wagley and also the head of a smaller team focusing directly on Minas Velhas. The primary concern of this project's studies was "the process of social and cultural change now under way in three different areas of the State of Bahia."[134] This primary concern dovetailed well with

---

[131]Murphy, "Julian Steward," 181-82.

[132]For further discussion of the Columbia University anthropology department, see, for example, *History of Anthropology Newsletter* 2:2 (1975): 16, and 7:2 (1980): 5-8.

[133]Wagley and Harris, "A Typology of Latin American Subcultures," 442.

[134]Charles Wagley, ed., *Race and Class in Rural Brazil* (Paris: UNESCO, 1952) 3. For more detailed statements of the plans and purposes of the project, see Charles Wagley, Thales de Azevedo, and Luís A. Costa Pinto, *Uma Pesquisa sôbre a Vida Social no Estado de Bahia* (Bahia, Brazil: Publicações do Museo do Estado, 1950).

the national "need to know" in order to benefit Latin America, and with the cultural-ecology perspective at Columbia that tended to fuse anthropology and sociopolitical concern.

As a member of the large research team, Harris was supervised by Wagley. Wagley had guided Harris before, during, and after the fieldwork in its writing phase.[135] Wagley's supervision also meant that Harris's work was coordinated with studies done in the other ecological zones.[136] Harris apparently met with these other researchers and with Wagley during the fieldwork in the nearby province capitol of Salvador, Bahia.[137] This was one way to facilitate coordination in the project without laying down a "rigid outline" for each researcher. Late in 1950, this field team was visited by Alfred Metraux, who suggested that they expand their research to include the study of race relations in Bahia, an emphasis that would otherwise have been made only as it related to their main research interests.[138] Race and class in Brazil formed an area with which both Wagley and Harris would become very much concerned.[139]

If one turns now to consider Harris not so much as one part of the larger team, but as head of the smaller research team that studied Minas Velhas, one gains a better understanding of his fieldwork situation. In Wagley's words, the anthropologist in relation to his particular community of study is the "field scientist who knows the community intimately and thoroughly after almost a year of residence and scientific research."[140] Harris's opportunities for participant observation in this community were achieved with the help of early contacts provided by the Museo Nacional do Rio de Janeiro.[141] Harris's own field team was

---

[135]Harris, *Town and Country*, iii.

[136]These other studies were carried on by Columbia University anthropologists Harry Hutchinson, Benjamin Zimmerman, and Anthony Leeds. Harris, ibid., iii.

[137]Wagley, *Race and Class in Rural Brazil*, 4.

[138]Ibid., 3.

[139]Ibid. See also Charles Wagley and Marvin Harris, *Minorities in the New World: Six Case Studies* (New York: Columbia University Press, 1958), and Marvin Harris, *Patterns of Race in the Americas* (New York: Norton, 1964). Harris conducted several special research projects to study racial identity in Brazil.

[140]Wagley, *Race and Class in Rural Brazil*, 4.

[141]Harris, *Town and Country*, iii.

made up of three Brazilian students, about whom Harris says little except that one was from the provincial capitol of Salvador.[142]

From Harris's reports about his team's investigations, it is evident how his own sociocultural context, with its national and international aspects, interplays with that of his investigated subjects. Harris's own context engages that of his investigated subjects in two ways: first, in the established connection of Columbia University to the state government of Bahia; and second, in the encounters of Harris and his research team with the residents of Minas Velhas.

This play of contexts is best seen in Harris and the roles and statuses that are ascribed to him or that he ascribes to himself. This process of role and status ascription displays the complexity of the conditions that shape Harris's fieldwork situation. Sometimes it is the investigated subjects who ascribe roles to him, and sometimes Harris ascribes roles to himself seeking to counter roles he does not want. Sometimes, it is his connection to Columbia University that indicates the nature of roles and statuses taken; at other times it is his connection to the Bahian government. On still other occasions, it is the relation to both that accounts for a particular role or status that can shape the anthropological knowledge emerging from his fieldwork.

When Harris's team first arrived in Minas Velhas, for example, its members were immediately identified by the investigated subjects as minerologists, geologists, or engineers. Early in his fieldwork, "a week rarely passed without some townsmen appearing in the doorway to ask the 'ethnologist' to identify some strange-looking rocks."[143]

This role of "minerologist" that residents sought to ascribe to Harris—on the basis of a heritage of contacts with officials mainly interested in mineral wealth—Harris sought to counter with a self-ascribed role. This desired role was based on the fieldworkers' connections with the Bahian state government.[144] Both upper- and lower-class people within Minas Velhas seemed to accept the team's explanation that "these strangers represented the State's desire to help improve living conditions." Within Minas Velhas only bureaucrats seemed suspicious of the

---

[142]Ibid., iii, 144.

[143]Ibid., 75-76.

[144]Ibid., 207.

explanation, wondering if they were being investigated by the Bahian state. To explain his role in this way was to win acceptance and rapport by appealing to the residents' cultural expectation that the government brings progress, improvements, and gifts.[145]

Outside the town, however, in the villages where the urban ties to government and politics were weak, this self-ascribed role was a "serious handicap." In spite of the team's concerted effort "to gain information pertaining to basic subsistence, there was dogged resistance."[146] The investigated subjects in the villages ascribed to the ethnologist the role of "State Tax Collector" on several occasions, and before contacts with village informants could be established and maintained, word spread that the state government, represented by Harris's team, was going to seize the land outright. Other villagers feared military conscription.

These instances of the investigated subjects' and investigating anthropologist's ascribing roles and statuses influenced what was or could be learned in the fieldwork situation. Harris's tie to the Bahia state government had both prohibitive and facilitating effects. The facilitating effect, as Harris admitted, was most prevalent in the town, which is the major focus of his study. Presumably, the townspeople accepted his explanation that he was there from the government and, hence, was there to help "improve living conditions." Their acceptance facilitated the acting out of his self-ascribed role as "ethnologist" or "field scientist," two of the terms Harris applies most frequently to himself in his ethnographic text.

How does Harris practice his role as "field scientist"? Harris little reflects on the place or nature of his residence in and around Minas Velhas as, for example, Malinowski reflects on the location of his tent, or Lévi-Strauss reflects on the nature of his hut among the Bororo and the placement of his campfire among the Nambikwara.[147] Harris's lack of reflection is unsurprising given his reluctance to speak about himself in the ethnographic situation.

---

[145]Ibid., 183-84.

[146]Ibid., 207.

[147]Malinowski, *A Diary in the Strict Sense of the Term*, 167, and Lévi-Strauss, "La Vie familiale et sociale," 48.

The impression given in *Town and Country in Brazil* of Harris's way of being a "field scientist" is that of a carefully surveying ethnologist, moving about the community of Minas Velhas with his field team. Passing references are made to the field team's "taking up residence" in one of the outlying villages,[148] but again, Harris ascribes little importance to such residence. Harris's major concern is with techniques of surveying, measuring, and collecting, although other references hint that the field team's "personal familiarity" or "the writer's impression" modifies or supplements such techniques.[149]

That Harris's role as field scientist has this character of "surveying ethnologist" is evident from the nature of his ethnographic text. That text features thirty-two different tables providing data about, among other things, the population and number of domiciles per village, monthly cash income per head of family, actual and ideal distributions of racial types per economic group, church attendance, and the fears of school children.[150]

The field-survey approach is also displayed in Harris's use of informants. He does not base his work on the narratives and reports of a few "well-informed informants," with whom he as anthropologist builds a rapport or special relationship.[151] Rather, when discussing "ideal racial grading," for example, Harris speaks of "ninety-six informants" who were controlled according to color, sex, class, and age.[152] This particular use of informants will, in Harris's later works, be justified epistemologically: "An informant's descriptions of behavior stream events are seldom satisfactory."[153] Informant accounts need to be surveyed, collected, and statistically analyzed. The method of explanation evident

---

[148]Harris, *Town and Country*, 144, 252.

[149]Ibid., 107, 224.

[150]Ibid., vii-viii.

[151]Similarly, in Mozambique, Harris says he learned the benefits of not founding his data on a few "well-informed informants," *The Rise of Anthropological Theory*, 585-86.

[152]Harris, *Town and Country*, 119.

[153]Harris, *The Nature of Cultural Things* (New York: Random House, 1964) 164.

in Harris's ethnographic text relies heavily on statistical data gathered by a team in Minas Velhas.

In sum, Harris's own sociocultural context has been set internationally and institutionally. Internationally, Harris's research partly reflects the concern of a North American nation to support research in Latin America that would, while serving the welfare of Latin American peoples, also serve United States national interest. This concern was also an important context for the research of an institution like Columbia University's anthropology department, which had a history of viewing anthropological research as valuable for dealing politically with social and cultural change. Although this institutional interest might cooperate in this way with national interest, it was not merely a reflection or justification of national interest and policies. The institutional aspect of Harris's sociocultural context, however, did work within this national interest, and then promoted its distinctive professional approach in the ethnographic situation.

Under Wagley's direction, Harris undertook intensive community study consistent with the aims of the cultural-ecological "science" influential at Columbia University and displayed in the thought of Julian Steward. Columbia University's research project related him to Minas Velhas according to ecological zone, and also to the Bahian state government. Stressing his role as one who was there from the Bahian government to "improve living conditions," Harris freed himself partially from other roles ascribed to him (at least within the town where progress and government were valued) so as to conduct research as the "field scientist" that the expectations of his Columbia University context encouraged. As field scientist, or carefully surveying "ethnologist," Harris's method of explanation is demonstrated in his tabular data and descriptions of the urban life of Minas Velhas in its economic, class, racial, familial, political, religious, and folk aspects.

Ambiguities
and a "strong dose of operationalism"

In spite of the clarity sought in the statistical analyses and descriptions of his *Town and Country in Brazil*, some striking ambiguities persist for Harris. I will isolate two of these as salient images from the interplay of contexts manifested in his ethnographic experience. These images indicate the problems addressed by *The Nature of Cultural Things*

(1964), which is the first major theoretical text in Harris's horizontal hermeneutic. Just as discerning salient images in Lévi-Strauss's fieldwork displays the relation between his fieldwork and *The Elementary Structures of Kinship*, so will Harris's salient images illumine the connection of his field experience with *The Nature of Cultural Things*.

The first salient image centers on the dichotomy of town and country. There are ambiguities here for Harris, which stem from both what his Brazilian informants and what his fellow anthropologists say about the dichotomy.

His Brazilian informants stressed the absoluteness of the dichotomy, between a *"vido do campo* (life of the fields)" and a *"vido do commercio* (life of the business district)." Scorn and distrust existed between these two groups, and Harris's "objective" analyses of this urban complex—as opposed to peasant life in the villages—often confirmed the cleavage that was "subjectively" expressed by his informants.[154] But not always was this confirmation forthcoming. He noted striking similarities between town and country life. The peasant villages were only "slightly more cohesive," and only slightly less heterogeneous, individualized, or secularized. What Harris sees between town and country is more a difference of degree than an absolute contrast as reported by residents.[155] Harris's response to this ambiguity is to see his informants' positing of absolute contrast as "deliberate magnification" or "valuation," which he terms their "ethos." When townsmen radically demarcate themselves from the country, they do so because of an "urban ethos" by which they "consciously or unconsciously, abstractly or concretely, value, endorse and seek to perpetuate the various urban traits of . . . culture."[156]

But this anthropological concept of ethos is not a sufficient explanation.[157] Why does Minas Velhas have an ethos that is urban? Harris

---

[154]Harris, *Town and Country*, 140-46, 279. The terms *subjective* and *objective* are used differently in his later works.

[155]Ibid., 278.

[156]Ibid., 279-80.

[157]In his doctoral dissertation Harris cites Alfred Kroeber for this notion of "ethos" as "the direction in which a culture is oriented, the things it aims at, prizes, and endorses, and more or less achieves." See Marvin Harris, "Minas Velhas: A Study of Urbanization in the Mountains of Eastern Brazil" (dissertation, Columbia University, 1953) 3.

answers that the subsistence of the town, as historical analysis shows, was based on mining. Urban values most likely emerge in a community based on mining subsistence.[158] In short, the ambiguities surrounding his informants' contrast of town and country are explained by the concept of an ethos that is rooted in the town's subsistence.

Earlier anthropologists' reflection on the town/country dichotomy also made the dichotomy a salient image for Harris. Harris's anthropological discipline, like others in the history of Western thought, had employed contrasting categories of urban and rural.[159] When studying urban folk at Minas Velhas, Harris encounters ambiguity when he finds traits that anthropologists had often termed urban in a place where anthropologists would not expect to find them, that is, in a town so geographically isolated and low in population. Minas Velhas was in fact more isolated and lower in population than communities that anthropologists had termed classically rural.[160] How does one explain an urban complex found in an isolated area, consisting of a community low in population?

Harris's response is to relegate "degree of isolation" and "population" to a less significant role in determining whether a community is urban or rural. What matters instead is, again, the people's ethos rooted in subsistence. Minas Velhas testifies to the tendency of the subsistence type, in this case mining, to foster urbanism even when a high degree of isolation and low population would seem to suggest rurality.[161] Harris's invocation of the notion of ethos rooted in subsistence—a cultural-ecological notion—enables him to explain the Brazilians' magnification

---

[158]Harris, *Town and Country*, 281.

[159]Ibid., 274-75.

[160]Ibid., 276-77. Harris sees Robert Redfield's *The Folk Culture of Yucatan* (Chicago: University of Chicago Press, 1941) as representative of anthropology's general use of the rural/urban dichotomy. Harris's dissertation on Minas Velhas makes it clearer than his published ethnography that Redfield is a foil for his refinement and correction of the folk/urban categories.

[161]Ralph L. Beals cites Harris's ethnography as a book that no student of urbanism can afford to ignore because of its new perspective on the subject. See Beals, "Review of *Town and Country in Brazil* by Marvin Harris," *American Anthropologist* 60 (1958): 596-97.

of the dichotomy, and to refine his own discipline's use of the dichotomy.[162]

This town/country dichotomy is not only salient in that it dominates the ethnographic text, but also in that it causes Harris to reflect on one of his major concerns: the construction of anthropological classifications in relation to those offered by studied peoples. In particular, Harris highlights the need for anthropologists to "operationalize" the concepts they invoke to cope with intercultural ambiguity. More and more, this need will entail Harris's attempt to justify his own invocation of the concept of ethos rooted in subsistence. This concern to operationalize, or to provide anthropologists with a conceptual framework or a taxonomic system, is expressed in his early essay written with Wagley, "A Taxonomy of Latin American Subcultures."[163] His concern for operationalized concepts, which are especially rooted in subsistence analyses, is evident in his defense of the notion of "economic surplus."[164]

Another salient image, this one concerning the ways Minas Velhas's residents classify racial types, also feeds Harris's drive toward an "operationalized anthropology." Once again, it is ambiguity stemming from both his informants and the anthropological discipline that makes racial classification a salient image. His white, Brazilian informants, particularly one named "Carlos," display an inconsistency between what they say about their relation to "Negroes" and how they act towards them. Whites hold a "stereotype" of blacks as "subhuman" and "subservient" to whites, and see them as easily dismissed and ignored through verbal abuse.[165] In the actions toward blacks that Harris observes, however, whites frequently grant status to encountered blacks and show them great respect. Hence Harris speaks of a contrast between his informants' "ideal" and "actual" behavior.

As Harris further studies the problem in *Town and Country*, and in later studies, he becomes convinced that what his fellow anthropol-

---

[162]Harris, *Minas Velhas*, 2, 3, 10.

[163]Wagley and Harris, "A Typology of Latin American Subcultures," 428-51.

[164]Marvin Harris, "The Economy Has No Surplus?" *American Anthropologist* 61 (1956): 185-89, 197.

[165]Harris, *Town and Country*, 121-22, 125.

ogists' categories overlook and what explains the discrepancies between ideal and actual behavior, is that the Brazilians act not according to their ideal stereotype but according to a "cognitive calculus" that is more complex, one in which race is but one of many other criteria such as wealth, occupation, and education. Physical features are but one element of this calculus. A person black and wealthy, therefore, may be termed "white." "Money whitens."[166]

His anthropologist and social-scientist colleagues then compound this ambiguity by overlooking the main reason for the ideal/actual discrepancy. There is a discrepancy because the terms *white* and *black* denote clear-cut, identifiable physical groups only for the anthropologist.[167] Physical and cultural anthropologists, unfortunately, have studied Brazilian racial classification using the all-too-neat classifications of white, black, mulatto, and sometimes *caboclo* (a mixture of caucasoid and Indian).[168] Harris even refers to his own early testing as "faulty" for using such terms.

Further studies of racial classification in a small fishing village and throughout Brazil's other provinces convince him that this cognitive calculus is so complex that researchers cannot state its general formula, and certainly cannot approach study of it with a few simple categories.[169] Harris argues that the ambiguity of Brazilian racial categories is endemic to those categories and should be accepted as such. Given that acceptance, the challenge is to account for the persistent ambiguity.

Harris's method of explaining this ambiguity again resorts to ethos rooted in subsistence. In the fishing village, for example, ambiguity built into racial terms is "probably an ideological manifestation" of the equalitarian patterns that the fishing industry of the village requires for supplying the subsistence needs of the community.[170] Similarly, in other

---

[166]Ibid., 127.

[167]Ibid., 126.

[168]Ibid., 113, 122.

[169]Marvin Harris, "Racial Identity in Brazil," *Luso Brasiliean Review* 1 (1964): 21-28, 23.

[170]Ibid., 27-28.

provinces of Brazil, Harris tentatively suggests that Brazilians may in fact nurture ambiguity in their calculus of racial identity for a "conservative structural reason." This conservative ideology is meant to counter the rise of any racial ideology that would upset Brazil's highly stratified class society, which is viewed as essential for the elitists' subsistence needs.[171]

In the early essays treating the salient image of racial identity, Harris insists on the need for explanations of ambiguity that use objective categories. Harris means that anthropologists' categories should reflect the knowledge of geneticists and physical anthropologists who have properly discerned that "social races" cannot be neatly distinguished from one another. If an anthropologist adopts categories of "white, mulatto, black" to work with, they are "faulty" because they do not reflect "true" genetic complexity. Instead of being objective, these three categories are only subjective to the "non-biological, culture-bound perspective of the U.S. population."[172] United States residents tend to identify "social races" by such a simple cognitive calculus. If anthropologists work with categories that are subjective to the United States population, they not only fail to be objective, they also fail to report the racial categories subjective to the Brazilian population. Thus, one who uses the above three simplistic categories for Brazil "reports neither the prevailing subjective concept of social races nor the objective opinions of biologists."[173] Anthropologists who use categories that are not objective follow a procedure that is faulty in at least three senses:

1. They fail to represent the best of the United States population's knowledge (that of geneticists and physical anthropologists).

2. They fail to represent accurately the knowledge and cognitive process of another society, that is, the Brazilian one.

3. Consequently, they fail to make possible a knowledge that is subjective to both the United States and the Brazilian populations, that is, intersubjective.

---

[171]Marvin Harris, "Referential Ambiguity in the Calculus of Brazilian Racial Identity," *Southwestern Journal of Anthropology* 26 (1970): 1-14, 12.

[172]Harris, "Racial Identity in Brazil," 22-23.

[173]Ibid.

In Harris's handling of the salient images of his fieldwork experience, then, is evident his movement toward the operationalism that he believes his discipline needs.[174] Harris's reflections upon those salient images are further clarified in his theoretical and epistemological text, *The Nature of Cultural Things* (1964), and restated and defended in his *Cultural Materialism* (1979). The cross-cultural theory and epistemology characterizing Harris's anthropology may be viewed as an interpretation of ambiguities similar to those encountered in his fieldwork.

Operationalism is facilitated by an increasingly rigorous application of a distinction between "etic" and "emic" points of view. The final form of this distinction is a refinement of what in his ethnography and early essays he termed "objective" and "subjective" viewpoints. The "etic" is the point of view of observing anthropologists. Any "etic operations" of research are ultimately judged for adequacy by the observers. The "emic" is the point of view of observed actors or participants. Any "emic operations" employed by the anthropologist seek to elicit the natives' point of view, making them the ultimate judges of the observer's descriptions elicited emically.[175]

Harris first employed this distinction between "etics" and "emics"—which he borrowed and converted from linguist Kenneth Pike[176]—in *The Nature of Cultural Things;* he then systematically developed it in *Cultural Materialism*.

In *The Nature of Cultural Things*, emics/etics is the crucial distinction in a larger operationalist strategy that Harris advances for cultural-anthropological research.[177] According to *The Nature of Cultural Things*, cultural anthropology has as its object "cultural things" that are known

---

[174]Harris, *Cultural Materialism*, 15.

[175]Ibid., 32.

[176]Pike coined these terms from the linguistic terms *phonemic* and *phonetic*. See Kenneth Pike, *Language in Relation to a Unified Theory of the Structure of Human Behavior* (The Hague: Mouton, 1967) 10. For further discussion of Harris's appropriation of the terms, see Marvin Harris, "The History and Significance of the Emic/Etic Distinction," *Annual Review of Anthropology* 5 (1976): 329-50; M. Durbin, "Linguistic Models in Anthropology," *Annual Review of Anthropology* 1 (1972): 383-410; and R. Burling, "Linguistics and Ethnographic Description," *American Anthropologist* 71 (1969): 817-27.

[177]Harris, *Nature of Cultural Things*, 19.

units of the human behavior stream. Because, by definition, cultural things are *"known* units," any theory about them is also an epistemology of how those units are known: "Culture and cultural things must be defined in terms of instruments, calibrations, processes and activities—the operations by which observers can get to know about them."[178]

Much of this simultaneously theoretical and epistemological text presents neologisms (actones, episodes, nodes, paragroups, endogroups, idioclones) as names for these known units by which anthropologists and ethnographers abstract from or condense their field of inquiry, human behavior.[179]

The discovery of these known units, upon which an operationalized anthropology depends, itself rests on a crucial decision by anthropologists to condense the behavior stream by criteria established from the observer's point of view.[180] This is an etic point of view, which conflicts with the views of social-science researchers who simply abstract from human behavior whatever units strike their fancy and with those who select units that the studied actors regard as important. This latter is the emic standpoint.[181] The emic approach is, Harris grants, valuable for studying the verbal behavior of a population, since one can assume that the actor possesses some knowledge of the "cognitive map" by which he converses.[182] When, however, there are conflicting reports about this cognitive map, then the anthropologist must employ the etic standpoint, examining situations of native discourse to resolve the ambiguity. The emic standpoint may also be helpful as a starting point for study even of nonverbal behavior. But here actors are much less reliable as informants; therefore, anthropologists should again employ their

---

[178]Ibid., vi.

[179]Ibid., 45.

[180]Ibid., 77.

[181]Ibid., 75. Harris suggests that abstraction by fancy seems most common, while attempts to abstract based on the actor's point of view is the position of social theorists who claim to be able to understand human action through the "purposes," "meanings," or "intentions" articulated by actors. Harris doubts that anthropologists can or have developed criteria for discerning "purpose," "meaning," or "intention." On this latter doubt, see Harris, *Nature of Cultural Things,* 76-77, 136-48.

[182]Ibid., 148.

etic standpoint. The etic perspective is advantageous because the observer

> stands "far enough away" from or "outside" of a particular culture to see its separate events, primarily in their similarities and differences, as compared to the events of other cultures, rather than in reference to the sequence of classes of events within that one particular culture.[183]

In *Cultural Materialism*, the emic/etic distinction is more systematically developed. Here the decision for the etic standpoint is advanced as a research strategy that not only makes etics primary for the anthropologist, but also shows what principles observers are to use in approaching sociocultural phenomena. Again, in spite of Harris's preference for etics, emic operations function positively in the study of both mental and behavioral phenomena. Emic studies, as long as they are "purely descriptive," or "merely posit functional relationships" between elements in the actors' models of thought, are appropriate. Emic studies of behavioral phenomena may also confirm an observer's point of view on behavior or clue the observer about how to develop his or her point of view further.[184]

According to Harris, however, etics are most important to anthropological explanation. His attitude is reflected in his admonition that the emic standpoint, whether applied to mental or behavioral phenomena, cannot explain the causes of similarities and differences in sociocultural phenomena. Emic views of mental phenomena are "purely descriptive." Emic views of behavioral phenomena may correspond to that of the observers but frequently vary from it, indicating that natives or actors are "mystified" about their behavior and about events taking place around them.[185]

Harris's preference for etics is fundamentally rooted in his belief that emicist operations alone, which formulate and display the natives' points of view, do not achieve the ideal of explanation: to explain the similarities and differences of sociocultural phenomena. His belief is

---

[183]Ibid., 138.

[184]Ibid., 39.

[185]Harris, *Cultural Materialism*, 39.

clear from an important article written in 1974 and later incorporated in *Cultural Materialism* (1979).[186] In this article Harris argues that

> even if one has a perfect knowledge of all the rules that one must know to act like a native—that is, even if one has been brought up as a native, a privilege which all human beings enjoy with respect to at least one culture—predictions based on a knowledge of those rules alone cannot in principle predict the great bulk of behavior stream events.[187]

Harris supports this claim with five propositions. First, he suggests that all emicist renderings of "rules" allegedly governing behavior are not merely taken by the observer from informant reports. To the contrary, these rules require and are based on the observer's input.[188] Second, based on his studies of race in Brazil, Harris attributes a recalcitrant ambiguity to all emic rules. There is no "finite set of emic rules" in a community for an ethnographer to elicit.[189] This recalcitrant ambiguity grounds his final three propositions: that "for every emic rule there is an alternative," that authorities who make rules never go unchallenged by community members, and that rules vary from one generation to another according to conditions inaccessible to the emic standpoint.[190] The native's point of view cannot be trusted as an anthropological explanation of sociocultural similarities and differences.

In Harris's view it is the observer, rarely the studied native or studied other, who has access to the principle that facilitates explanations for an operationalized anthropology. Natives and studied others may explain if they are part of the community of observers using explanatory principles.

The most important principle for the etic standpoint is that of "infrastructural determinism," the kernel of which Harris finds in Marx's claim that

---

[186]See Marvin Harris, "Why a Perfect Knowledge of All the Rules," *Journal of Anthropological Research* 30 (1974): 242-51, and *Cultural Materialism*, 269-78.

[187]Ibid., 242.

[188]Ibid., 270.

[189]Ibid., 271-73.

[190]Ibid., 273-78.

the mode of production in material life determines the general character of the social, political and spiritual processes of life. It is not the
consciousness of men that determines their existence, but on the contrary, their social existence determines their consciousness.[191]

"Behavioral infrastructure" is the "base" to which the observer can
refer for explanation of similarities and differences in sociocultural
phenomena. Rather than discuss Harris's argument for what "infrastructure" properly includes, one can note that he includes in it both
"mode of production" (production of food and forms of energy for subsistence allowable by ecological habitat) and "mode of reproduction"
(the expansion, stimulation, and maintenance of population size through
technology, social practice, and production of children).[192]

Making this infrastructure the reference point for sociocultural explanation enables anthropologists to be "scientists of culture." Infrastructure is presented as nearer to nature; and when anthropologists refer
to it for explanation, they "incorporate the lawful regularities in nature" into their anthropology.[193]

Infrastructure, in other words, is the principle interface between culture and nature, the boundary across which the ecological, chemical,
and physical restraints to which human action is subject interact with
the principle sociocultural practices aimed at overcoming or modi-
fying those restraints.[194]

The preeminence of this infrastructure for explanation of the causes
of similarities and differences in sociocultural phenomena constitutes
Harris's "cultural materialism" or his "techno-environmental determinism."[195] This infrastructural principle, though not as fully devel-

---

[191]Ibid., 55. Harris is citing Karl Marx, *A Contribution to the Critique of Political
Economy* (1859; rpt., New York: International Publishers, 1970) 21.

[192]Ibid., 52, 66. Harris felt that his categorization of the production of children as
a "mode of reproduction" was a refinement of Marx.

[193]Ibid., 56.

[194]Ibid., 57.

[195]For the meaning of materialism in Harris, see *Cultural Materialism*, x-xi; for determinism, see his qualifications and arguments for a mainly "probabilistic" determinism. Harris, *Cannibals and Kings: The Origins of Culture* (New York: Random House,
1977) xiii, 291.

oped as in *Cultural Materialism*, was evident also in the earlier *Nature of Cultural Things*. There, Harris qualified the extreme form of operationalism[196]—which states that things have no existence apart from operations employed in knowing them—by insisting that any empirical science must hold that there are things "outside of the observer" that no logical manipulation can completely create or destroy.[197] While the principle of infrastructural determinism is not explicit in this early text, it does refer to a "material world" that gives observers their bearing, especially when they work in strange speech communities where the only way out of the referential ambiguity spawned by conflicting informant reports is by discerning a consensus "made possible by the fact that *in its local habitat*, a given population is not confronted with all the empirically extant grades and intergrades of physical, biological, and cultural phenomena."[198]

Harris's preference for etics and infrastructure rests on his valuing explanations of sociocultural similarities and differences. Dependence on etics and infrastructure is the only way, for Harris, by which anthropology may be the science it desires to be.[199] In *The Nature of Cultural Things*, to operationalize anthropology in this way is a response to science's "ultimate aim," or its "scientific ethic," that is, to formulate "the lawful principles which govern the behavior of empirical things."[200] The commitment to formulate lawful principles, and so reveal "orderly relations," constitutes an anthropological science's "value position." If nothing is revealed but chaos, an anthropological theory is worthless and judged "bad." If order is displayed, it is "good." Cultural scientists' data language, theory, decisions about whether to work emically or etically and with or without the infrastructural principle are all "prag-

---

[196]Harris takes the early Percy Bridgeman's *The Logic of Modern Physics* (New York: Macmillan, 1927) as an illustration of an unqualified operationalism that he and others seek to qualify. See Harris, *Nature of Cultural Things*, 3-8.

[197]Harris, *Nature of Cultural Things*, 169-70.

[198]Ibid., 158. The emphasis is mine and is added to stress the somewhat hidden infrastructural reference in this early text.

[199]Ibid., 3.

[200]Ibid., 13.

matic affair[s]," "urgent practical problem[s]."[201] Scientific practice
demands a constant questioning, "What works to produce order?"

Why it is urgent to ask this question and to maximize order becomes clearer in later portions of *Cultural Materialism,* in which Harris
defends his strategy, principles, and theories in light of alternatives in
the social sciences. There, it becomes evident why maximizing order is
a scientific ethic for attaining not only truth, but also love. In this section, I have presented Harris's attempt to administer to his discipline a
"strong dose of operationalism" as part of a general, scientific quest for
ordered truth. It is necessary to note how this quest is related to still
broader concerns.

"Science of culture"
as ethic for truth and love

Harris claims that an operationalized anthropology, in which anthropologists opt for an observer's point of view guided by the materialist or infrastructural principle, founds a "transcultural community of
scientific observers." This community's "science of culture" is committed to an ethic of orderliness that fosters both truth and love. This
final section focuses on how Harris fuses the scientific "truth" he claims
to maximize through cultural-materialist explanations with "love," a
term Harris uses occasionally to include all that his texts imply to be
valued by the transcultural community of observers.[202] One may probe
the connection between pursuit of truth and pursuit of love by turning
to his specific cultural-materialist theories.

Harris's anthropology of explanation, his "science of culture," is
best seen in its theories. Cultural-materialist theories may be used to explain various "riddles of culture" (witchcraft, messianism, countercul-
ture, pork taboos),[203] but the heart of this corpus is a "set of theories
dealing with the origin of the principal varieties of pre-state societies:
the origin of sexism, classes, castes, the state, and the origin of principal
varieties of state-level systems."[204] I will not here present Harris's

---

[201]Ibid., 14, 15.

[202]Harris, *Cultural Materialism,* 341.

[203]This is the subject of his *Cows, Pigs, Wars and Witches: The Riddles of Culture*
(New York: Random House, 1974).

[204]Harris, *Cultural Materialism,* 78.

lengthy discussions of each of these. Suffice it to say that Harris the observer explains each phenomenon—from different hunting and gathering societies' social structures to forms of European parliamentary democracy, from infanticide and male-supremacist complexes to twentieth-century feminist movements in the United States—by referring to conditions of infrastructure, the technoenvironmental or ecological base.[205]

What is crucial for Harris is that these cultural-materialist theories allow anthropology, again, to be an operationalized endeavor. These operationalist advantages of cultural materialism are especially apparent in contrast to other strategies of theorizing: sociobiology, dialectical materialism, structuralism, structural Marxism, cognitive idealism, eclecticism, obscurantism.[206] In contrast to structuralism, for example, which explains reciprocal exchanges of goods and women between Australian peoples in terms of an unconscious "sense of reciprocity," Harris's cultural materialism claims to show more parsimoniously that there is an infrastructural, ecological need to share and engage in reciprocal exchange.[207]

But there is more at stake for Harris in this comparison of strategies than mere notation of what best utilizes operationalized social science. His critique of the unoperationalized status of alternative strategies[208] is fused with a consideration of the moral consequences of

---

[205]Ibid., 77-113. For a contemporary example, directed toward lay readers, of this explanatory procedure, see also Marvin Harris, *America Now: An Anthropology of a Changing Culture* (New York: Simon and Schuster, 1981).

[206]Any strategy shows its worth, according to Harris, by being compared to others. See *Cultural Materialism*, 24-25.

[207]Ibid., 80-81.

[208]Sociobiology, for example, because it refers mainly to genetics, leaves many human responses unaccounted for. Dialectical materialism has never been able to show dialectic in history, especially because it empirically cannot identify the "determinative negations." Structuralism, especially that of Lévi-Strauss, is unable to consistently explain food habits, taking them instead as "mental components of digestion." Structural Marxism doesn't have an operationalized notion of infrastructure. Cognitive idealism cannot account for behavior as long as it assumes that "values" (Parsons), or a "system of symbols and meanings embedded in normative structure" (Schneider), or a "semiotic field" (Geertz) determine behavior. Eclectic strategies lack operationalist capacities because their theories are contradictory. Obscurantist strategies (broadly including those of Castaneda, Alfred Schutz, Bob Scholte, Alvin Gouldner) fail to even value operationalist science because they "glorify subjectivity."

his own and alternative research strategies for explaining sociocultural phenomena.

It is in Harris's critique of alternative strategies that one can note two ways by which he relates his science of culture to morality. First, he presents his science of culture as the condition for any morality.

> Morality is the acceptance of principled responsibility for the way in which one's actions or lack of actions affect the well-being of other members of the human species. The absolute precondition for any kind of moral judgment is our ability to identify who did what to whom, when, where and how.[209]

Science as the "precondition" for a moral life is a recurrent theme in his texts. There can be "no freedom and economic equality without objective knowledge."[210] "To subvert objective knowledge" is a form of "moral duplicity" because it is "to subvert the basis of moral judgments."[211]

Second, Harris often appeals to a "moral sensibility" in his readers, which, he argues, should lead them to prefer his cultural-materialist science of culture over other strategies. Here, the morality of his readers functions as the condition for his science of culture. Thus, Harris can speak of an existing "moral imperative" to expand "scientific objectivity" into the domain of sociocultural phenomena.[212]

Alternative strategies in anthropology and social science often counter "moral sensibility" and hence, Harris argues, ignore the "moral imperative." Structuralism, for example,

> mocks the hungry living and dead by transforming the struggle for subsistence into a game of mental imagery. The idea that cooking is primarily a language is food for thought only among those who have never had to worry about having enough to eat.[213]

Similarly, dialectical materialism, by perpetuating belief in a historical

---

[209]Harris, *Cultural Materialism*, 324.

[210]Ibid., 142.

[211]Harris, *Cows, Pigs, Wars and Witches*, xiv.

[212]Ibid., 228.

[213]Harris, *Cultural Materialism*, 189.

dialectic that promises to benefit exploited classes, only deceives these classes and provides a new exploitative ideology for totalitarian elites.[214] Cognitive idealism's grammarians and ethnoscientists are enchanted with rules, codes, and structures, which, like so much institutionalized social science of the "Parsonians," tend toward a conservatism that accepts the system "as given and seeks to account for its stability."[215] Structural Marxism offends moral sensibility, according to Harris, because its earlier-mentioned failure to operationalize infrastructure applies also to its term *exploitation*. Structural Marxists cannot say what exploitation is and thus cannot identify who is exploiting whom.[216] Obscurantism, which denies the values of science in its "glorification of subjectivity," should be abhorrent to the moral sensibilities of even its own advocates. For, argues Harris, without science, their own worst fears of a police-military control, retreatism, and nuclear confrontation are more likely to be realized.[217]

The offenses to moral sensibility caused by failure to operationalize science is most evident to Harris in the "epistemological anarchy" of Paul Feyerabend, who writes that "flexibility, even sloppiness, in semantical matters is prerequisite of scientific progress." In response, Harris not only points out the "logical contradictions" of this position, to which Feyerabend himself should object, but also suggests its "moral" offensiveness.

> It cannot be a matter of taste whether you believe or do not believe that pollution is a menace, that the underdeveloped nations are getting poorer, that the multi-nationals are promoting an arms race, that war is instinctual, that women and blacks are inferior, or that a green revolution is a hoax. Let Feyerabend stand before the ovens of Dachau or the ditch at Mylai and say that our scientific understanding of sociocultural systems is ultimately nothing but an "aesthetic judgment."[218]

---

[214]Ibid., 158.

[215]Ibid., 284.

[216]Ibid., 236-37.

[217]Ibid., 326.

[218]Ibid., 23.

Just because there is this twofold relation between science and morality in Harris's texts does not mean that he explicitly formulates a notion of "the good" as the content for his morality. From his statements on the relation of his science of culture to "moral problems," or to "social pathologies," it is evident what Harris does and does not value. In general terms Harris expresses passing disapproval of such pathologies as war, exploitation, poverty, sexism, consumerism, pollution, and "all the weird driving forces of our competitive capitalist economy."[219] Harris values as a remedy for such pathologies a restoration of the "ecological and cultural configuration that led to the emergence of political democracy in Europe."[220] Such a restoration demands the decentralization of the United States' mode of energy production and the breaking up of cartels and monopolies. These acts may restore the European and American democracies' "march toward freedom" that was a "rare reversal of that descent from freedom to slavery which had been the main characteristic of the evolution of state for 6,000 years."[221]

These matters of content are not central to Harris's discussions. He mainly assumes a certain consensus about the good life that he then suggests his science of culture facilitates. The suggestion usually is that to be moral is to accept and think according to the science of culture. Or more precisely, the cultural-materialist science of culture is to serve as an ethic that informs a moral life capable of meeting the challenges posed by the moral problems faced by humankind.

But how can the science of culture inform the moral life? The clue may be found in understanding Harris's medical-science metaphor for morally troubling sociocultural phenomena: "pathologies." Sociocultural problems are viewed primarily as diseases that are rooted in the recalcitrant forces of nature and that unfortunately determine human nature through the technoeconomic and technoenvironmental conditions of infrastructure. The moral agent faces great difficulty in alleviating the morally disturbing pathologies: "Free will and moral choice

---

[219]Ibid., 285, and idem, *Cows, Pigs, Wars and Witches*, 227.

[220]Harris, *Cannibals and Kings*, 264, 288.

[221]Ibid.

have had virtually no significant effect upon the directions taken thus far by evolving systems of social life."[222]

The moral agent's hope in face of the social pathologies may be grounded, for Harris, only in knowing that this determinism is not rooted in human nature, but outside of it, in infrastructural conditions. Harris therefore argues against interpretations of war as "instinctual" or "natural."[223] War and other pathologies will always seem instinctual as long as agents refuse to consider soberly the "cultural and ecological restraints" that render their free will impotent for avoiding war and other pathologies.

Here Harris's science of culture makes its contribution. It claims to offer the knowledge that moral agents need to take account of the cultural and ecological obstacles to healing this "pathological" world. "To change social life for the better, one must begin with the knowledge of why it usually changes for the worse."[224] With this knowledge, room can be made for moral choice, because now moral agents, armed with knowledge of infrastructural causality, not only know their limitations but will also be able to take advantage of certain "open moments" in the evolution of infrastructural conditions. These moments are opportunities for effecting "improbable alternatives to probable evolutionary changes" and for "persons with deep personal commitments to a particular vision of the future" to struggle toward their goal.[225] In these senses, then, Harris's science of culture is an ethic that informs moral agents not only about "who did what to whom, when and how," but also about when—in what open moments—their moral actions might have the best chance of initiating some modicum of change.

The science of culture, which may serve as an ethic for moral agents, must be the practice of a "transcultural community of scientific observers." Only as such does it have the capacity to "demystify" particular groups' or societies' explanations of sociocultural phenomena, especially explanations of morally disturbing phenomena like war, which

---

[222]Ibid., xix.

[223]Ibid., 53-54.

[224]Harris, *Cannibals and Kings*, xix.

[225]Ibid., 288-89, 291-92.

are often viewed as instinctual to the human species. A community that explains sociocultural phenomena by referring to nature is able to be transcultural because its science attends to conditions that press upon all societies, even though the effects of the nature system take different forms in the infrastructural bases of different societies.

Though Harris's anthropology is transcultural, he does not present it as opposed to the science of Western tradition. Quite to the contrary, his cultural materialism amounts to a defense of Western science. If science remains committed to its unique contribution—encouraging doubt and hostile scrutiny of its own conclusions—then it has a "uniquely transcendent value for all human beings." Science is a significant feature of Western culture that can be affirmed with no "ethnocentric puffery." For, it is designed

> to transcend the prior belief systems of mutually antagonistic tribes, nations, classes and ethnic and religious communities in order to arrive at a knowledge that is equally probable for any rational human being.[226]

Harris can admit, therefore, that scientific truth is a social product, but deny that scientific theory necessarily differs from culture to culture.[227]

Thus, Harris's proposed anthropological community stresses its observer's point of view and transcultural character, while pursuing the explanation of sociocultural others in order to alleviate morally disturbing sociocultural pathologies. Those who "struggle for a science of culture" possess needed resources both for understanding and for improving the welfare of distant others, whether these others be found in the "ecozone" of a central mountain area or in that of a tropical forest. The truth sought by Harris's transcultural community of scientific observers may be

> both the object and means of expressing love. To erect a barrier between truth and love is to wantonly degrade and limit human nature. There are many, but not enough, for whom objectivity is the path that leads to both.[228]

---

[226]Harris, *Cultural Materialism*, 27-28.

[227]Ibid., 318.

[228]Ibid., 341.

Chapter IV

Interpreting Anthropology's Ancestry: Two Vertical Hermeneutics

If in some small measure an anthropologist may become a member of another culture and perceive the world anew, he can do so only through the lens of his native heritage.

Kenelm Burridge
Encountering Aborigines

Under "Interpreting Brazil," I have treated Lévi-Strauss's and Harris's horizontal hermeneutic: their interpretive reach toward contemporary others. Their system for explaining these others consisted of an inter-related set of factors that were explicated by a fundamental quadratic. Within that set of factors appeared the salient images that unified the anthropologists' interpretations and more fundamental perspectives. I shall return to that "unity" and those "fundamental perspectives" in the final chapter.

A proper display of Lévi-Strauss's and Harris's anthropological inquiry requires, first, attention to the vertical, intracultural dimension of their hermeneutics, which interplays with horizontal intercultural interpretations. "Interpreting Brazil" was for Lévi-Strauss a movement from a field of ethnographic images of "reciprocity," to a "world of reciprocity" subjacent to all known kinship and marriage practice, and finally, to a semiotically constructed "total semantic field" in mythology in which a "totalized" world of beings and things, and levels of beings and things, were placed in reciprocal relation or made mutually convertible in one displayed whole of "objectified thought." For Harris,

"Interpreting Brazil" was a movement from ethnographic images of intercultural ambiguity, to metataxonomic systems giving anthropological knowledge a "strong dose of operationalism"; it finally included a principle of infrastructural determinism providing theories in a "science of culture" both to explain and to reform human nature. Lévi-Strauss's and Harris's attempts at "Interpreting Brazil" must now be related to their methods of "Interpreting Anthropology's Ancestry."

Lévi-Strauss: Retrieving Rousseauan *Pitié*

Lévi-Strauss's interpretation of his discipline and its ancestry does not produce a text like the one by Harris, which purports to be a "history of theories of culture." Lévi-Strauss's book, *Totemism*, however, may be taken as his historical-critical explanation of his discipline.[1] This work can be combined with several shorter essays to display his vertical hermeneutic. First, I will summarize Lévi-Strauss's historical-critical method of explanation and then show how his retrieval of Rousseau's philosophy of *pitié* unifies the other historical sources he draws from and integrates his anthropological enterprise.

Pitié in historical-critical explanation

Lévi-Strauss's text, *Le totémisme aujourd'hui*, as historical-critical analysis, takes twentieth-century anthropological theories of totemism as its theme. Lévi-Strauss's intent is "to retread pace by pace"[2] the history of these theories, identifying totemism's emergence as "hysteria" and its subsequent attenuation and "liquidation" in later anthropological thought. Classical totemism, or the "totemic illusion," as he now calls it, held that societies could be differentiated by relegating some of them (the "primitive" or the "savage") to nature, as illustrated by the term *Naturvolker*. Moreover, such peoples betray their "natural attitude" by connecting themselves with animals through linking their social units to natural species: bear clan, eagle clan, and so on. As classical totemism has it, the propensities of natural peoples contrast with those

---

[1]Claude Lévi-Strauss, *The Savage Mind* (Chicago: University of Chicago Press, 1966) xi.

[2]Claude Lévi-Strauss, *Totemism*, trans. R. Needham (Boston: Beacon Press, 1963) 15.

of "civilized man," who purportedly has outgrown the natural attitude.[3]

Beginning with James G. Frazer's classical totemism, Lévi-Strauss discusses the development of major anthropological theories of totemism, showing how anthropologists have recently arrived at a better understanding of primitive thought's tendency to identify humans with species of animals or vegetables. Lévi-Strauss claims, however, that Jean Jacques Rousseau had arrived at this same better understanding more than a century earlier.

According to Lévi-Strauss, it was the American school of cultural anthropology that first began demolishing the totemic illusion. Anthropologists of this school did so by questioning the alleged "natural" attitude of nonliterate peoples and the Western tendencies to differentiate societies on the basis of that attitude.[4] English anthropologists, such as W. H. Rivers, also contributed to its demise. The proper understanding of totemism as a phenomenon universal to humans was recognized by Durkheim; but, Lévi-Strauss laments, Durkheim rooted totemism, along with myth and religion, in the affections.[5] Boas also glimpsed that totemism was an example of a universal phenomenon and not just a property of the *Naturvolker*. He saw too, where Durkheim had not, that totemism was a manifestation of a "classificatory tendency" rooted in the human intellect, rather than in only the affections. His analysis, however, did not take this insight far enough.[6]

It was left to A. R. Radcliffe-Brown in the later years of his career—after several British functionalists had tried to explain totemism in utilitarian terms (natural species, for example, are identified with because they are "good to eat")—to point the way toward explanation of the "totemic" tendency to connect human social structure to animal species. Radcliffe-Brown, according to Lévi-Strauss (who admits that Radcliffe-Brown might take issue with this interpretation of his work),

---

[3]Ibid., 2.

[4]Lévi-Strauss begins with A. A. Goldenweiser's criticism of 1910 and shows the skepticism about the "totemistic phenomenon" emerging in the textbooks of American anthropology by Lowie, Kroeber, and Boas. Lévi-Strauss, *Totemism*, 4-8.

[5]Ibid., 71.

[6]Ibid., 12.

challenges his functionalist precursors to show "why any particular species is selected rather than another." Instead of asking, as many anthropologists had, "Why all these birds?" Radcliffe-Brown asks, "Why particularly eagle, hawk, crow and other pairs?" Asking this question opens the way to structural analysis of relations in primitive thought generally, revealing what another social anthropologist, Evans-Pritchard, had earlier discerned about the thought of Nuer peoples in particular: that the basis of totemic phenomena lies in the interrelation of natural species with social groupings according to logically conceived processes of metaphor and analogy.[7] To thus anchor totemism in such "logically conceived processes" allows the savage mind's totemic propensities to be viewed as one form within a universal, intellectual process.

This is the insight that, according to Lévi-Strauss, was earlier offered by Rousseau. Rousseau knew that

> the apprehension by man of the "specific" character of the animal and vegetable world [was] the source of the first logical operations, and subsequently [the source] of a social differentiation which could be lived out only if conceptualized.[8]

This "apprehension by man," according to Rousseau, takes the form of "repeated attention of various beings and things to themselves and to each other." This repeated attention "must naturally have engendered in man's mind the perception of certain relations."[9] Lévi-Strauss's use of Rousseau not only makes the savage's totemic propensity an instance of a universal process, it assigns primacy to *intellect* in the process. "The advent of culture thus coincides with the birth of the intellect." Culture, though affected by the technoenvironmental conditions that Marvin Harris would stress, does not emerge unless the

---

[7]Ibid., 81, 86. Cf. Alan Jenkins, *The Social Theory of Claude Lévi-Strauss* (New York: St. Martin's Press, 1979) 98.

[8]Lévi-Strauss, *Totemism*, 99.

[9]Ibid., 100. Lévi-Strauss is citing Rousseau's *Discours sur l'origine et les fondements de l'inégalité parmi les hommes*, ed. with intro. and marginal summaries by Henri François Muller and René E. G. Vaillant (London: Oxford University Press, 1922).

"modes of livelihood" and a people's multiple relations with nature "become objects and means of human thought."[10]

This "intellect," discussed by Rousseau and later defended by Lévi-Strauss as crucial to anthropological theory, is best understood as a "faculty" or "psychic state" of "compassion" or *pitié*. It is the mind placed in relation to its world of beings and things. It is *pitié's* founding identification with others that makes the metaphors and analogies of the totemic mind possible.

> It is because man originally felt himself identical to all those like him (among which, as Rousseau explicitly says, we must include animals) that he came to acquire the capacity to distinguish *himself* as he distinguishes *them*, i.e. to use the diversity of species as conceptual support for social differentiation.[11]

The philosophy of *pitié* not only has this theoretical consequence for anthropology's study of primitive mind, it also has an epistemological consequence of which, to Lévi-Strauss, Rousseau is the prime exemplar. Not only is *pitié* a theory of primitive mind, it also is a mode of procedure for the inquiring anthropologist. Rousseau especially displays *pitié's* dual usage in the way he himself arrived at the theory of the human's "original identification with all other creatures"—that is, by a "process of internalization" that involved "trying on himself modes of thought taken from elsewhere or simply imagined."[12]

Due to such an epistemology, the process of internalization, Lévi-Strauss takes Rousseau as his major philosophical spokesman. He applauds Rousseau for doing in philosophy what he had done in his own move from philosophy to anthropology: upset Western philosophical traditions by stressing the integral relation of self and other, the individual and society.[13] Rousseau's peculiar process of internalization is further clarified when Lévi-Strauss discusses the "double-paradox" of

---

[10]Lévi-Strauss, *Totemism*, 100.

[11]Ibid., 101.

[12]Ibid., 103. Bergson, though to a lesser degree, is also credited for making a similar move.

[13]Claude Lévi-Strauss, "J. J. Rousseau: Founder of the Sciences of Man," *Structural Anthropology*, 2 vols. (New York: Basic Books, 1976) 2:37.

Rousseau's thought. First, Rousseau advocated that to study human-kind, one must look into the distance at remote people, and yet Rous-seau gave himself to studying the closest of people: himself. Second, while subjecting himself to this self-scrutiny, he nevertheless refused to identify with the self; rather, he systematically willed to identify with the other. This double paradox issues in the principle that alone grounds the "sciences of man": "to attain acceptance of oneself in others (the goal assigned to human knowledge by the ethnologist), one must first deny the self in oneself."[14]

Lévi-Strauss believes that, with regard to the history of philoso-phy, Rousseau corrects the "introspective philosophy" of Descartes' *cogito*. Descartes "imprisoned" philosophy within the "hypothetical evidences of the self."[15] Descartes could attain universality, but only by remaining psychological and individual in a "transcendental retreat." Lévi-Strauss warns all philosophers, "He who begins by steeping him-self in the allegedly self-evident truths of introspection never emerges from them."[16] Rousseau demonstrates his belief in this statement by his tendency to speak of himself in third person (even splitting himself in the *Dialogues*), and Lévi-Strauss sought to heed this warning—in the "confessions" by which he poured himself out into a world of others, and in search of a world of mutually convertible truths.

Rousseau's notion of *pitié* is crucial to an understanding of Lévi-Strauss's use of other sources from Western cultural tradition in his own theory and epistemology. His use of many sources has caused consid-erable confusion and debate.[17] Without entering into the several treat-ments of whether and how Lévi-Strauss is indebted to Freud, Marx,

---

[14]Ibid., 36.

[15]Ibid.

[16]Lévi-Strauss, *The Savage Mind*, 249. Lévi-Strauss also has in mind here Sartre, whose studies he says apply well to his own Western, French culture, but do not take adequate cognizance of "others."

[17]See, for example, the discussion of "influences" by Ino Rossi, ed., *The Uncon-scious in Culture: The Structuralism of Claude Lévi-Strauss in Perspective* (New York: E. P. Dutton, 1974) 7-9; Bob Scholte, "The Structural Anthropology of Claude Lévi-Strauss," in *Handbook of Social and Cultural Anthropology*, ed. Bob Scholte and John Honigman (Chicago: Rand and McNally, 1973); and Jenkins, *The Social Theory of Claude Lévi-Strauss*, 1-2.

Gestalt theory, structural linguistics, cybernetics, and so on, I suggest that Rousseauan *pitié* functions in his vertical hermeneutic as an integrating principle for what he frequently admits is a selective borrowing from these several sources. Each provides him concepts analogous to *pitié*, or procedures that enable him better to display *pitié* in human thought and life.

Pitié as a "faculty"[18] or as a "psychic state"[19] of original identification with all creatures and things, borrows heavily from Freud. According to Lévi-Strauss, *pitié* is a psychic state that "precedes and governs consciousness." Some have emphasized Freud's influence on Lévi-Strauss more than Lévi-Strauss himself has.[20] Lévi-Strauss more modestly states that from Freud the major lesson gained was that "what is not conscious is more important than what is conscious," and that "true meaning is not the one we are aware of, but the one hidden behind. it."[21] The unconscious, however, does not take on its particular Lévi-Straussian character until other sources are integrated with it by *pitié*. These other sources give Lévi-Strauss's theory of the unconscious a form and content that corrects what he takes to be Freud's largely "affective" unconscious.[22] Lévi-Strauss's unconscious is a psychic state that precedes consciousness but that operates through symbolic laws by which nature and culture, levels of nature and culture, affectivity and cognition are all related in a total, *superrationaliste* whole.

Of these other integrated sources, some of the most significant are those of ethnologist and sociologist Marcel Mauss. Durkheim might also be considered, but, according to Lévi-Strauss, his work was too early for dealing with the new fusion in anthropology of sociology, psychol-

---

[18]Lévi-Strauss, "J. J. Rousseau," 37.

[19]Lévi-Strauss, *Totemism*, 101.

[20]Thomas Shalvey has ably shown the dependence of Lévi-Strauss upon Freud, yet in a way that acknowledges his revision of Freud and his incorporation of other sources. See Shalvey, *Claude Lévi-Strauss: Social Psychotherapy and the Collective Unconscious* (Amherst: University of Massachusetts Press, 1979) 7-20.

[21]Claude Lévi-Strauss, "Réponses à Quelques Questions," *Esprit* 322 (1963): 628, and Ino Rossi, "The Unconscious in the Anthropology of Claude Lévi-Strauss," *American Anthropologist* 75 (1973): 26.

[22]Lévi-Strauss, *Totemism*, 69-70.

ogy, and linguistics.[23] On the contrary, as Mauss's students used to say, *"Mauss sait tout."* Lévi-Strauss finds in Mauss the ethnological expression of Rousseauan *pitié* in both its theoretical and epistemological forms.

Lévi-Strauss sees the philosophy of *pitié* theoretically expressed in Mauss's notion of the "total social fact." According to this notion, human life is characterized by integration into a whole of different "modalities of the social (judicial, economic, aesthetic, religious)," different "moments of individual history (birth, childhood, education, marriage)," and different "forms of expression" resulting from physiological phenomena, that is, reflexes, secretions, decelerations, accelerations. These three kinds of integration constitute the "tri-dimensional" character of the "total social fact," or the *complementarité* of the social, the psychological, and the physical dimensions.[24] Crucial to Lévi-Strauss's anthropological theory, therefore, is the idea that there is one world with which the human mind identifies in all the parts of its existence. Rousseauan *pitié* is evident in Mauss's theories of "totalization."

This "totalization" is dependent upon Mauss's and Lévi-Strauss's understanding of *mana*.[25] *Mana* and mana-like notions are expressions by nonliterate peoples of a "secret power, or mysterious force." Ethnologists have not been able to agree, Lévi-Strauss notes, whether this force is one of action, quality, or state; a substantive, adjective, verb, or all three; abstract or concrete, omnipresent or localized. Lévi-Strauss's own answer is that it is not one but all of these. It is simply "the conscious expression of *une fonction sémantique*, the role of which is to permit symbolic thought to exercise the contradiction that is proper to it."[26] *Mana* is an expression of the human mind's "facing" contradictory and unrelated elements so that they are held together, implying relations between them. *Mana* does not establish *what* these relations are, but indicates *that* relations are called for. As Lévi-Strauss puts it, *mana* "is only the subjective reflection of the need for a totality not per-

---

[23]Claude Lévi-Strauss, "French Sociology," in *Sociology of the Twentieth Century*, ed. G. Gurvitch and W. E. Moore (New York: Philosophical Library, 1945) 520.

[24]Lévi-Strauss, "Introduction à l'oeuvre de Marcel Mauss," in *Sociologie et Anthropologie* by M. Mauss (Paris: Presses Universitaires, 1950) xxv-xxvi.

[25]Ibid., xli.

[26]Ibid., xlix, 50.

ceived."[27] This notion of *mana*, which makes possible the "total social fact," fills out Mauss's contribution to an anthropological theory of Rousseauan *pitié*.

Lévi-Strauss incorporates Maussian notions because, like Rousseau's philosophy of *pitié*, Mauss's "total social fact" also has epistemological consequences for the anthropologist.

> Que le fait social soit total ne signifie pas seulement que *tout ce que est observé fait partie de l'observation* mais aussi, et surtout, que dans une science où l'observateur est de même nature que son objet, *l'observateur est lui-même une partie de son observation.*[28]

For Lévi-Strauss, this means that any easy dichotomy of subject and object is prohibited (*interdite*). This prohibition is important because Lévi-Strauss has been accused both of a "classical empiricism" that makes too much of such a dichotomy, and also of a "subjectivism" that too little accounts for an "objective" world.[29]

About the epistemological dichotomy, it is more precise to say of Lévi-Strauss what he said of Mauss—and this does more justice to Lévi-Strauss's views throughout his texts—that the dichotomy "corresponds only to a provisional and fugitive level in the development of his [Mauss's] science."[30] Just as in his horizontal hermeneutic, Lévi-Strauss moves *from* an ethnographic dichotomy of himself and his Brazilian objects or subjects *to* a systematic confession of the falseness of this split and of the truth of the unity between inquirers and their subjects ("men are always men"), so now in his vertical hermeneutic, Lévi-Strauss uses Mauss to state explicitly that the ethnologist is epistemologically engaged in a concrete *"entreprise d'identification,"* in which the dichotomy is provisionally posited but slowly subordinated and transcended so that

---

[27]Ibid., 50. In a cosmological system of symbols, then, *mana* has *"une valuer symbolique zéro"* analogous to the "zero phoneme" in structural linguistics. Cf. 50 n. 1.

[28]Ibid., xxvii. The emphasis is by Lévi-Strauss.

[29]Contrast, for example, Alan Jenkins's charge of "classical empiricism" with the contradicting ones of Edmund Leach or David Maybury-Lewis. Jenkins, *The Social Theory of Claude Lévi-Strauss*, 38; Edmund Leach, *Claude Lévi-Strauss* (New York: Viking, 1970) 13; and David Maybury-Lewis, "The Analysis of Dual Organization: A Methodical Critique," *Bijdragen tot de Taal-, Land-, en Volkenkunde* 116 (1): 17-44.

[30]Lévi-Strauss, "Introduction," xxvii.

all the diverse objects are reintegrated into the ethnographer's own subjectivity.[31]

Lévi-Strauss recognizes that such reintegration of studied others into the ethnographer's own subjectivity is plagued by the "tragic risk" of losing any point in common with native peoples' points of view. Such a loss would result in *"malentendu."*[32] This tragic risk, which is real, can be overcome because the opposition between self and other is already surmounted on another level where the objective and subjective encounter one another: the unconscious. The "laws of unconscious activity" are "at once ours and others', conditions for all the mental lives of all men and of all times."[33]

Lévi-Strauss's invocation of the unconscious, amid his interpretation of Mauss, returns to Freud. Indeed, Lévi-Strauss speaks of the epistemology of the ethnographic enterprise as being like psychoanalysis, allowing one to rediscover (*reconquerir*) one's most strange self in one's self, and the most strange other that is, in fact, "an other us (*un autre nous*)." But again, it is not Freud who is the major source. It is the unconscious—as implied by Mauss's "total social fact"—that supports the ethnographic epistemology implied first by Rousseau's "process of internalization."

Other sources in the history of social thought are incorporated into Lévi-Strauss's anthropology of *pitié* and further clarify his display of this faculty of "original identification." Since Rousseauan "compassion" entailed identification not just with other humans but with all forms and levels of life[34] (recall the tridimensional character of the "total social fact"), *Gestalt* theory could also help Lévi-Strauss to argue that human intellectual concepts can "cut across the division of realms of existence, being applicable in each of them."[35] The totalizing mind's presence in all these realms—between which Lévi-Strauss sets up structural rela-

---

[31]Ibid., xxx.

[32]Ibid.

[33]Ibid.

[34]Ibid., 101; and idem, "J. J. Rousseau," 41-42.

[35]Kurt Koffka, cited in *Encyclopedia of Philosophy*, 1967 ed., under the heading "Gestalt Theory," by T. R. Miles.

tions of mutual convertibility—is supported by a *Gestalt* doctrine of iso-morphism, holding that all "our experiences have the same structure as the brain processes that underlie them."[36]

The often-noted kinship of Lévi-Strauss's anthropology and struc-tural linguistics is made possible by Rousseauan *pitié's* embracing, in the human mind, a world of contradictory attributes and oppositions. As Rousseau had stressed, apprehension of oneself and all others en-genders "relations which we express by the words *big* and *little, strong* and *weak, fast* and *slow, bold* and *fearful.*"[37] *Pitié* works by a logic using such binary oppositions.[38] It is this logic that guides Lévi-Strauss's an-thropology of *pitié* to structural linguistics. Lévi-Strauss believes struc-tural linguistics confirms his own turn to the unconscious, for it also, when speaking of *une langue* to be deciphered, emphasizes "the role played in the production of language (but also that of all symbolic sys-tems) by the unconscious activity of the mind."[39] Linguistics not only provides this confirmation, but it is under linguistics' influence that Lévi-Strauss's anthropology of *pitié* becomes also a formal "semiologi-cal science."[40] Once other symbolic systems (kinship or mythology) are placed in analogy with language,[41] then the unconscious increasingly

---

[36]Ibid. Lévi-Strauss's recent stress on the importance of the nervous system for mediating "mind" and "experience" indicates his *Gestalt* heritage (*Myth and Meaning* [New York: Schocken Books, 1979] 8), as do some of his earlier acknowledgments in *The Elementary Structures of Kinship*, ed. R. Needham, trans. James Harle Bell and John Richard von Sturmer (Boston: Beacon, 1969) xxvi, 100. For Lévi-Strauss's own ex-plicit discussion of the role of *Gestalt* theory in the formation of his anthropology, see Claude Lévi-Strauss, "Les limites de la notion de structure en ethnologie," *Sens et usage du terme Structure, Janua Linquarum*, ed. Roger Bastide (The Hague: Mouton, 1962) 143.

[37]Cited in Lévi-Strauss, *Totemism*, 100.

[38]Ibid., 101.

[39]Claude Lévi-Strauss, Preface to R. Jakobson, *Six Lectures on Sound and Meaning*, trans. J. Mepham (Cambridge MA: MIT Press, 1978) xviii-xix.

[40]Claude Lévi-Strauss, "The Place of Anthropology in the Social Sciences and Problems Raised in Teaching It," *Structural Anthropology*, 1:365.

[41]It is a challenge to establish this analogy, and Lévi-Strauss's "Linguistics and An-thropology" is written to meet that challenge by placing linguistics and kinship studies of anthropology in an analogous relationship so that the structural analysis of the former may be applied to the latter. See *Structural Anthropology*, 1:79.

becomes *une langue* in anthropology that—with methods similar to phonological analysis in linguistics—can be defined "by a small number of constant relations whose diversity and the apparent complexity of the phonetic system serve only to illustrate the possible gamut of authorized combinations."[42]

The confluence of Marxist thought with Lévi-Strauss's anthropology of *pitié* has raised difficult questions that cannot here be explored fully. Simon Clarke finds little evidence that Lévi-Strauss had studied Marx or Hegel carefully, and Lévi-Strauss admits that his "Marxist catechism consists of two or three rules, but that renders [one] in no way competent to give judgment of Marx's work."[43] However, Lévi-Strauss took Marx as one of his *"trois maîtresses"* and even suggests that a significant part of his overall intellectual task was "to integrate the anthropological knowledge acquired in the last fifty years into the Marxian tradition."[44]

Lévi-Strauss's contribution here is to draw from anthropological knowledge of societies' "conceptual schemes" and to suggest that these superstructural phenomena mediate "between praxis [the fundamental totality of the sciences of man] and practices." These mediating schemes are "structures" by which "matter and form, neither with any independent existence, are realized." This mediation by structures is a modification of a theory of superstructures and can be advocated, Lévi-Strauss claims, without questioning Marx's "undoubted primacy of infrastructure."[45] Lévi-Strauss's treatment of Bororo spatial configuration and social structure may be taken as an example of the mediating role of structures.[46]

Bororo marriage practices are characterized predominantly by asymmetric and "triadic" social forms of organization. Lévi-Strauss's

---

[42]Lévi-Strauss, "Introduction," xxxv (my translation).

[43]Simon Clarke, "The Origins of Lévi-Strauss's Structuralism," *Sociology* 12 (1978): 405-39.

[44]Claude Lévi-Strauss, Postscript to *Structural Anthropology*, 1:343.

[45]Lévi-Strauss, *The Savage Mind*, 130.

[46]Lévi-Strauss cites the Bororo, along with the Caduveo, as the groups that enable his reintegration of anthropology into Marxian thought. See Lévi-Strauss, Postscript to *Structural Anthropology*, 1:344.

informants, however, reported that there was a predominant dualism of village and social structure within which the Bororo symmetrically married out of one moiety into another.[47] This dualism, Lévi-Strauss finally decides, is really only the "native's image of society." It is "only a 'theory' or 'transmutation' of a reality which itself is of a fundamentally different nature."[48]

This "reality" in which dualist theory is rooted is, again, the unconscious. The reported forms of dual organization are only the celebrations of "dyadism" and "symmetry." The Bororo masquerade, "mystify themselves" in this dyadism, yearning for a reciprocity and equality when, in fact, like Marx's proletariat, their society exists in a state of inequality (a triadic, asymmetrical, endogamous caste system).[49]

Once again, the unconscious sense of the relatedness of all things (*pitié*), and the reciprocity that characterizes the relations among all those things, forces itself from the unconscious into, this time, the social life of the Bororo. This is Freud's lesson, which a Marxist may apply "at a different level of reality," that is, the level of the social instead of the individual.[50]

Without discussing all of Lévi-Strauss's uses of these sources, the basic point has been advanced: Lévi-Strauss turns to each of these sources seeking ways to extend in anthropological knowledge the Rousseauan notion of *pitié*, both for theorizing about other humans' thoughts and experiences, and also for offering epistemological claims about how such theoretical knowledge should be attained. Freud provides the stimulus for affirming the unconscious as more important or more

---

[47]This discrepancy between what Lévi-Strauss's best field studies tell him about the Bororo praxis and what the Bororo themselves articulated (but only occasionally manifested) about those practices is the problem addressed by Lévi-Strauss in his two important essays: "Social Structures in Central and Eastern Brazil," and "Do Dual Organizations Exist?" in *Structural Anthropology*, 1:120-31, 132-63.

[48]Lévi-Strauss, "Social Structures in Central and Eastern Brazil," 121.

[49]Lévi-Strauss, "Do Dual Organizations Exist?" 130-31, 143, 147. See Thomas Shalvey's discussion of Marx and Lévi-Strauss's study of the Bororo in *Claude Lévi-Strauss*, 82-95.

[50]Claude Lévi-Strauss, *Tristes Tropiques*, trans. John Weightman and Doreen Weightman (New York: Atheneum, 1976) 390.

meaningful than consciousness; Mauss asserts an unconscious that is not merely affective but symbolic, characterized by a total exchange between units of individual, social, and physiological realms of life; *Gestalt* theory confirms the possibility of thought's effecting similar operations in all realms of existence; structural linguistics, once language is viewed as analogous to other symbolic systems, provides the formal, semiological method of binary opposition for a "structural anthropology"; and *pitié*'s sense of reciprocity as an unconscious mediating structure between praxis and practices can be integrated into Marxian thought.

In sum, Lévi-Strauss's historical-critical analysis of anthropology, which focuses on the demise of totemism, highlights the emergence of "intellect," or Rousseauan *pitié*, in the social anthropology of Radcliffe-Brown. Once he shows that Rousseau had anticipated this theoretical and epistemological position for understanding others, the notion integrates more recent philosophical and social-science developments: Freud, Mauss, *Gestalt* theory, structural linguistics, and Marx.

In spite of all of Lévi-Strauss's sources, it is as Clifford Geertz has suggested: no one of these many sources (Freud, Marx, *Gestalt*, Jakobsen)—and more than those discussed above might be mentioned—is Lévi-Strauss's "real guru."[51] It is Rousseau who is his "master and brother,"[52] and this relationship, primarily, is achieved through his appropriation of Rousseau's idea of *pitié*. In the next section I note that the idea of *pitié* not only guides his historical-critical study of his own and related disciplines, but also shapes his own anthropological enterprise. The retrieval of Rousseau in Lévi-Strauss's vertical hermeneutic supports the same final form of his anthropology that emerges from his horizontal hermeneutic.

Pitié and Lévi-Strauss's "totalization"

That Rousseau functions for Lévi-Strauss as a means of integrating his own anthropological enterprise becomes clear from the connection between Rousseau's philosophy of *pitié* and Lévi-Strauss's understand-

---

[51]Clifford Geertz, "The Cerebral Savage: On the Work of Claude Lévi-Strauss," in *The Interpretation of Cultures* (New York: Basic Books, 1973) 356.

[52]Lévi-Strauss, *Tristes Tropiques* (Eng. ed.), 390.

ing of who or what an ethnographer is. Rousseauan *pitié* can be invoked as support both for the ethnographer's movement away from the self to studied others, and also for the movement back to the self by means of the other, so that neither selves nor others are known separately. It has already been noted how Lévi-Strauss's increasing awareness of the integral relation between self and other led more and more to an ethnography of "others" produced by a confessing "self."

Rousseau's turning away from himself, his insistence on identifying with the other, is the negative side of a confession that involves going out as ethnographer from one's own world into that of others.

> Every time he is in the field, the ethnologist finds himself open to a world where everything is foreign and often hostile to him. He has only this self still at his disposal, enabling him to survive and pursue his research. But it is a self physically and mortally battered by weariness, hunger, and discomfort, the shock to acquired habits, the sudden appearance of unsuspected prejudices. It is a self which, in this strange conjuncture, is crippled, and maimed by all the blows of a personal history responsible at the outset for his vocation, but which will affect its future course.[53]

These negative experiences of a confessing self, however, can effect the positive side of confession: the discovery of the self as a primary tool for discovery of the other, as well as for greater knowledge of the self.

> Hence in ethnographic experience the observer apprehends himself as his own instrument of observation. Clearly he must learn to know himself, to obtain from a self who reveals himself as another to the I who uses him, an evaluation which will become an integral part of the observation of other selves. Every ethnographic career finds its principle in "confessions," written or untold.[54]

When discussing Lévi-Strauss's horizontal hermeneutic, I showed the negative and positive sides of a confession that occasioned a shift from an ethnographic method of explanation dependent on field encounters with others to a literary-critical one whereby Lévi-Strauss explained others by a semiological method more expressive of his subjectivity.

---

[53]Lévi-Strauss, "J. J. Rousseau," 35.

[54]Ibid., 35-36.

There, however, the confession was not so much Rousseauan. The negative side of the confession discerned in his horizontal hermeneutic was contrition for making too much of the anthropologist's supposition that "men are not always men." This contrition then led him to a certain renunciation of the fieldwork experience of gathering particulars, so that his perspective broadened to include the whole of humanity's world, the structures of which he sought to display in objectified thought. Here, in the retrieval of Rousseau, the ethnographic activity of going out amidst others is affirmed in all its negativity as the means of a self's knowledge of others and of self. The Rousseauan epistemology of *pitié* allows Lévi-Strauss to look back on the ethnographic experience as a necessary moment of his anthropology in which others are encountered, but in such a way that the self is always seeking itself as it seeks to know others. Lévi-Strauss's appropriation of Rousseauan *pitié* tacks back and forth between the negative and positive aspects of anthropological confession: between confession as a self-denying immersion in a world of others, and confession as an appropriation of subjectivity for the knowledge of others.

The interpretation of ethnography according to this twofold sense of confession seems nowhere more evident than in Lévi-Strauss's views on the nature of the anthropological profession as seen within the context of Western culture's exploitation of other societies. Lévi-Strauss says of *l'ethnographe:* "His very existence is incomprehensible except as an attempt at redemption: he is the symbol of atonement."[55] Negatively, the ethnographer goes out as a "symbol of atonement," suffering among the others who have been wronged by his culture, a culture that has overlooked its dependency on other societies, thinking itself superior to them. Positively, the ethnographer seeks redemption, a redress of his culture's neglect of the implications of the "total social fact." Not to make this atonement, or not to attempt this redemption, is to allow a morality based on reciprocity to be lost so that humans ultimately destroy themselves. The "lethal effects" of not living out the "total social fact" are already evident in the waning, indigenous South American cultures that Lévi-Strauss himself studied.[56]

---

[55]Lévi-Strauss, *Tristes Tropiques* (Eng. ed.), 389. For the French phrasing, see Claude Lévi-Strauss, *Tristes Tropiques* (Paris: Plon, 1955) 420.

[56]Lévi-Strauss, "J. J. Rousseau," 41.

As study of Lévi-Strauss's horizontal hermeneutic made clear, he did go out to be among others. And many other ethnographers have done the same, so that their reports are also available to Lévi-Strauss as he seeks to identify with others. If these ethnographers, and Lévi-Strauss as ethnographer, have in their field encounters served as "symbols of atonement," how then do they also "attempt redemption"? This challenge elicits the positive contribution of the confessing anthropologist, and Lévi-Strauss uses his subjectivity to meet that challenge and express it in the complex exercises of his four-volume *Mythologiques* presented above. To understand *Mythologiques* in this context, one must understand more about the redemptive task and its aims.

Lévi-Strauss seeks a model for a "total and concrete humanism" that will be redemptive for a world that has ignored the implications of its existence as a totalized whole. The anthropologist who seeks such a "humanism," however, has an immediate difficulty, which his and others' ethnographic experiences teach: It is not just exploitative, Western society that has ignored the principle of reciprocity, even though its heedlessness has dealt the recent and more lethal blows to New World humanity. There are also other societies, those whose peoples anthropologists have embraced and among whom they have suffered, that "have been tainted by the same original sin."[57] The tendency to see one's own group as superior is not limited to Western culture.[58] Anthropologists, therefore, can attempt no real redemption simply by identifying and suffering with one or many other societies.

Anthropologists must undertake an intellectual program prompted by this situation, which, in fact, is analogous to how a savage mind proceeds when it faces its whole but broken world. The basic schema is discussed throughout *The Savage Mind* via the terms *totalization, detotalization,* and *retotalization.* The savage mind, existing in original identification with all beings and things, begins in a state of totalization: "A unity at the heart of diversity is claimed in advance."[59] *The Savage Mind* goes on to show how, on many different levels, the savage mind,

---

[57]Lévi-Strauss, *Tristes Tropiques* (Eng. ed.), 389.

[58]On this widespread cross-cultural phenomenon of ethnocentricity, see Claude Lévi-Strauss, "Race and History," *Structural Anthropology*, 2:328-30.

[59]Lévi-Strauss, *The Savage Mind*, 176.

or the "totemic operator," also breaks up this totalized world, that is, detotalizes it, but in such a way that this detotalization is actually a retotalization of the whole on a different plane or in a different area of experience.[60]

These phases of the totemic operator portrayed in *La Pensée sauvage*, which provide Lévi-Strauss's theory of how the savage mind operates, may also be applied to his own pattern of intellectual operations as anthropologist. Indebted to Rousseau as "master and brother," Lévi-Strauss himself possesses *pitié* that prompts him to identify with others through ethnography. While his identification is partially a symbolic act of atonement for a Western society that has made absolutist claims for itself, it does not in itself contribute to redemption. For, among these others, thrives also the same absolutizing *"péché originel."* Lévi-Strauss, therefore, further follows Rousseau's enterprise by adding two stages of intellectual operation to the original identification with all beings and things (totalization). These two operations involve, first, the destruction of *all* forms of organization and, second, the discovery of principles that allow one to construct a new form. Lévi-Strauss suggests that Rousseau's major works exhibit this same pattern of operation in his movement from "the ruins left by the *Discours sur l'origine de l'inégalité,* to the ample structure of *Contrat sociale,* the secret of which is revealed in *Emile* alone."[61]

So it is that the *pitié* of original identification (totalization), which leads to immersion in a world of others, is followed first by Lévi-Strauss's detotalizing activity, his demolition of each social order's claims to be the totality or even to be an independently existing entity. In this detotalizing, anthropology participates in what Lévi-Strauss calls "the ul-

---

[60]In this sentence I have, of course, telescoped large amounts of material from *La Pensée sauvage*. I cannot here detail how the movement from totalization to retotalization takes place and varies according to different contexts. But, for example, Lévi-Strauss especially cites the "diversity of natural species" as a manifestation of discontinuity in the savage mind's totalized world. The savage mind borrows from this diversity of nature to create taxonomies that break up the original totality. But retotalization is also evident: species can be so opposed as to represent the universe as a vast continuum of oppositions, or the savage mind can break species down into subdivisions, the oppositions among which also represent, at a more particularized level, the total universe. See Lévi-Strauss, *The Savage Mind*, 136-39.

[61]Lévi-Strauss, *Tristes Tropiques* (Eng. ed.), 390.

timate goal of the human sciences," which is to "dissolve man."[62] It is in this phase of anthropological reflection that reductions have their place.[63] But again, such detotalizations and reductions are followed by the anthropological equivalent of the savage's retotalization. The anthropologist, Lévi-Strauss, seeks to discover "invariants" that constitute an "eternal and universal model."[64] This model's *humanité générale*, which is made possible by ethnological detotalization and retotalization, will display the "truth about man" that can be seen in the system of the many societies' similarities and differences.

It is by means of this model that a redemption can be attempted. As the final product of *la comparaison ethnographique*, this model displays *"un nouveau ordre"* that transcends but is built from all particular orders.[65] Lévi-Strauss aims at a retotalized, theoretical model of humanity that enables an attempt at redemption. Such a model

> does not correspond to any observable reality, but with the aid of which we may succeed in distinguishing between "what is primordial and what is artificial in man's present nature and in obtaining a good knowledge of a state which no longer exists, which perhaps will never exist in the future, but of which it is nevertheless essential to have a sound conception in order to pass judgment on our present state."[66]

By seeking to build such a model, "European earth-dwellers" not only acknowledge their responsibility for the "crime" of destroying New World societies, but also set out to help create a society fit to live in.[67]

Lévi-Strauss's retrieval of Rousseauan *pitié* (which involves an anthropological pattern of operations analogous to the totalization-detotalization-retotalization pattern so painstakingly detailed in *The Savage*

---

[62]Lévi-Strauss, *The Savage Mind*, 274.

[63]Ibid.

[64]Lévi-Strauss, *Tristes Tropiques* (Eng. ed.), 392. The "elementary structures" and "formulae" of kinship systems are also described as "eternally coexistent." See Lévi-Strauss, *The Elementary Structures of Kinship*, 454.

[65]Lévi-Strauss, *Tristes Tropiques* (Fr. ed.), 421.

[66]Ibid., 423. Lévi-Strauss is again quoting Rousseau.

[67]Lévi-Strauss, *Tristes Tropiques* (Eng. ed.), 393.

Mind) enables one to interpret the significance of the exercises earlier summarized as characteristic of the *Mythologiques*. That work's display of objectified thought may be seen as a Rousseauan quest for an intellectual and ethical model to serve as "the unshakable basis of human society."[68] The *Mythologiques* assumes an anthropological totalization or original identification with an intercultural world of beings and things. Its 800 myths and mythic versions, then, are the detotalized parts of the totalized whole that Lévi-Strauss the anthropologist seeks to retotalize. This *superrationaliste* enterprise, is, fundamentally, a retrieval of Rousseau.

Harris: Reviving a Marxist Strategy

In examining Harris's vertical hermeneutic, one has the advantage of possessing Harris's own "history of theories of culture" in which he interprets the thought of his own Western cultural tradition. There, he explicitly treats matters that remained only implicit in his horizontal interpretation of others. Such implicit reference is evident when, for example, in formulating his theory and epistemology in *The Nature of Cultural Things*, he invokes in passing the names of important figures of his tradition: Malthus, Marx, Freud, Durkheim. Given the position forged in his horizontal hermeneutic, the lesson these figures teach is not surprising: the "actor cannot be trusted" to analyze units of anthropological knowledge because these Western cultural thinkers have shown that what actors frequently emphasize are precisely those aspects of behavior that are "psychodynamically" least significant or subsumed by "purposes" of which they are totally unaware.[69]

Harris is conscious of this complementarity between knowledge fashioned in horizontal interpretive experience and knowledge drawn

---

[68]Reference to the schema in *The Savage Mind* allows one to fix the *Mythologiques* volumes in this context. One who reads *The Savage Mind* will no doubt note that many other issues could have been addressed in that text. The major purpose of this project does not require detailed treatment of *The Savage Mind*. Lévi-Strauss himself makes it clear that *The Savage Mind* is not the heart of his anthropology, but rather a "pause" during which he charts and justifies his itinerary for the area of mythology. Careful references to *The Savage Mind* have been provided mainly to clarify the nature of his enterprise. See Lévi-Strauss, *The Raw and the Cooked*, 9.

[69]Marvin Harris, *The Nature of Cultural Things* (New York: Random House, 1964) 91.

from those he selects in a vertical hermeneutic. The fusion of perspectives from his own culture's past with positions hammered out horizontally in encounter with others is what now has to be shown. The intent here is not to draw causal arrows by arguing, for example, that Harris's Western, Marxist position determined his cultural materialism. Whatever truth there may be in such a single perspective, one must first display, as I seek to do here, the combination of factors and perspectives that constitutes anthropological knowledge. The Marxist or Freudian cultural influences examined here must be considered together with the earlier-mentioned ambiguities and reflections that Harris experienced horizontally in the world of others. Before discussing that interplay between vertical and horizontal interpretive experience, I will turn to Harris's historical-critical explanation, summarize its content, and then relate it to the anthropological knowledge already presented.

Marxist strategy in historical-critical explanation

Harris's awareness of links between his methodological claims for an intercultural, operationalized anthropology, and his "history," is evident on the first page of *The Rise of Anthropological Theory*.[70] His history of theories of culture is not an "encyclopedic survey" of all figures who in some way address culture theory. He is out to "prove a point" in his history, a point that is important to human understanding of "where we have come from" and "where we are going."[71] It has been noted how Harris advocated his science of culture as necessitated by a certain intellectual and moral urgency. How is this science of culture derived and defended in intracultural, vertical interpretation?

Harris's historical-critical survey is intended to show the inadequacy of nonscientific, nonmaterialist explanations of sociocultural phenomena and the relative adequacy of materialist approaches, so as "to achieve a fair hearing for cultural materialist strategies." This he attempts to show in a primarily chronological treatment of major Western philosophical thinkers in general and of major Western anthropologists in particular.

---

[70]Marvin Harris, *The Rise of Anthropological Theory: A History of Theories of Culture* (New York: Thomas Crowell, 1968) 3-5.

[71]Ibid., 5.

Take, first, Harris's assessments of the major philosophers and social theorists of his own intellectual tradition. He does not base his assessments on detailed examination of their texts. These thinkers are
usually treated in terms of how their cultural theories fit on materialist/
idealist or nomothetic/idiographic continua. Harris, of course, has little
praise for "idealist" and "idiographic" approaches, but charts hope-
fully the sometimes faltering but nevertheless steady resurgence of a
"materialist" and "nomothetic" science of culture.

Among those of a "materialist awakening," Harris first cites John
Locke, who gave cultural materialism its "metaphysical foundations."
He is the "midwife of all those modern behavioral disciplines . . . which
stress the relationship between a conditioning environment and human
thought and actions."[72] Many other thinkers—Montesquieu, Rousseau, Turgot, Adam Ferguson, LaMettrie, D'Holbach, Helvetius, John
Millar—took steps toward a nomothetic science based on the rooting of
knowledge in conditioning experience. All these members of a materialist, "intellectual awakening" contributed to the affirmation of what
Locke implied, that "differential environmental exposure will produce
both individual and national differences in behavior."

> It is thus possible to discern, scattered here and there in the writings
> of the eighteenth century, implicit in one instance, explicit in others,
> ordinarily strewn at random, among contrary and self-defeating con-
> victions, but occasionally as part of a clear and definite system, the
> raw materials, the conceptual tools, and the first faltering practical
> experiences with the scientific explanation of sociocultural phenom-
> ena.[73]

This materialist orientation, according to Harris, was frequently
sidelined and tainted by the currents of cultural idealism with which it
had to struggle. Most of the social philosophers of the Enlightenment,
in spite of the general differences in program, were united, according
to Harris, in seeking the primary cause of sociocultural differences in
"a variation in the effectiveness of ratiocination." The beliefs of Montesquieu, Voltaire, and Condorcet are examples of this supposition that

---

[72]Ibid., 11.

[73]Ibid., 52.

"rational human mental choice directs history."[74] This supposition was further perpetuated and conveyed to anthropologists through Kantian, Hegelian, and neo-Kantian forms of idealism.

Harris himself does not discuss these major idealisms at great length; here I will only highlight his treatment. Kant was an idealist because he believed that "all that was necessary for Europe's Enlightenment to modify social life was for the public to be given the freedom to think."[75] Because it leaves the conditions of thought unaccounted for, Kant's "non-deterministic idealism," holding that free thought could modify social life, makes it difficult for anthropology to engage in theory building. Even the Enlightenment thinkers' belief in "progress," for example, could not be accounted for, but was a "purely idiosyncratic expression of approval or disapproval of a particular historical event."[76]

Hegel's idealism has the benefit of being determinative, a feature required for a nomothetic science of culture. Hegel also gives greater attention than Kant to cultural conditions of thought, the conditions for the rise of personal genius, for example. Hegel's determinative idealism is "worthless ruin," however, for an operationalized science of culture or science. Hegel's "conditions" of thought, Harris laments, turn out to be further instances of thought ("Spirit") unfolding itself. The dialectic by which this is supposed to happen in history and culture is empirically "unintelligible."

> There is no empirical support for the assertion that the evolution of forms is constrained by the necessity of passing through a series of opposite or contradictory stages. Hegel's attempt to characterize the course of world evolution in terms of upward spiraling negations was the result of an infatuation with word and number magic.[77]

---

[74]Ibid., 39-40. According to Harris, this supposition could and did lead to notions in early anthropology that other noncivilized "races" possessed innately inferior intellects. See Harris, *The Rise of Anthropological Theory*, 80-107.

[75]Ibid., 39.

[76]Ibid., 40. The problem of the *philosophes'* mere hope for "progress" is treated by Harris with the aid of Peter Gay's *The Party of Humanity* (New York: Knopf, 1964) 270-71.

[77]Harris, *The Rise of Anthropological Theory*, 68.

Hegel's dialectic, since it lacks empiricism, is dismissed as "mere poetic analogy" and "poetic thrill." When it is found in Marx, Harris argues that dialectic is the "Hegelian monkey" from which a Marxist strategy for any science needs to be rescued. If one adds to these problems Hegel's "splendidly ethnocentric disdain of all pre-State societies," Hegel's philosophy especially strikes Harris as "worthless ruin."

Neo-Kantianism displays its idealism when it marks off a world of *Geist* from that of *Natur* and then defends two distinct types of study, the *Geisteswissenschaften* and *Naturwissenschaften*. Harris contests this dichotomy throughout his writings.[78] He singles Wilhelm Dilthey out as primarily responsible for this split, although unlike the later neo-Kantians Wilhelm Windelband and Heinrich Rickert, Dilthey still held some nomothetic ideals for the *Geisteswissenschaften;* in this tendency he softened somewhat the harshness of the split between the two "sciences." Laws and regularities might still be discerned, according to Dilthey, in the "human sciences."[79] Harris presents all three neo-Kantians, however, as generally hastening the separation of the natural and social sciences so that researchers tended to study "special attributes of the mind" apart from technoenvironmental conditions requiring an approach through natural-science models.

All of these idealisms, especially as they culminated in neo-Kantianism, are not obstacles to the rise of cultural materialism, according to Harris, simply because they are powerful ideas. Such an account would contradict Harris's claim that ideas are not the primary determiners of history. Rather, he argues that these idealisms are ideologies rooted in the conservative needs of a "highly competitive subcommunity of professional intelligentsia" that was committed to routing radical political movements such as Marxism.[80] When the social structures of Europe and America became vulnerable to "communist and socialist subversion," the intelligentsia increasingly suppressed the possibilities for materialist explanations and argued for the "return of life to mys-

---

[78]Ibid., 230; see also Marvin Harris, *Cultural Materialism: The Struggle for a Science of Culture* (New York: Random House, 1979) 142-54.

[79]Harris, *The Rise of Anthropological Theory*, 270.

[80]Ibid., 271.

tery." With that return, Harris suggests, the "science of culture" fell into neglect and disrepute.

The Marx that Harris believes could be revived, and indeed has been revived in twentieth-century cultural ecology, is a revised Marx. Harris advocates a "de-Hegelianized" Marx rid of dialectic, and a "de-proletarianized" Marx that breaks the hold that political activism has on its science. Moreover, Harris claims that Marx's basic strategy can be appropriated without necessarily accepting any of his specific theories of capitalist and feudal societies.[81] Although some have suggested that such qualifications cancel Harris's claim to Marxism,[82] Harris argues that appropriation of Marx's basic strategy is just as significant as the bioevolutionist's appropriation of Darwin's "law of evolution." Darwin's "law" provides bioevolutionists with a basic strategy that does not necessarily commit them to Darwin's theories.[83]

Harris provides his own view "in retrospect" of what the five major "ingredients" of Marxist strategy are.

1. The trisection of sociocultural systems into technoeconomic base, social organization, and ideology.
2. The explanation of ideology and social organization as adaptive responses to technoeconomic conditions.
3. The formulation of a functionalist model providing for interactive effects between all parts of the system.
4. The provision for analysis of both system-maintaining and system-destroying variables.
5. The preeminence of culture over race.[84]

It is primarily this strategy that Harris's vertical hermeneutic appropriates for contemporary cultural anthropology. Marx did not operationalize this strategy as Harris was led to do in his horizontal hermeneutic, stressing the necessary decision between etic and emic standpoints and the need for careful definition of such terms as *infra-*

---

[81]Ibid., 240-41.

[82]Robert Paul and Paul Rabinow, "Bourgeois Rationalism Revisited," *Dialectical Anthropology* 1 (1976): 121-34.

[83]Ibid., 217, 241.

[84]Ibid., 240.

structure, mode of production, and *mode of reproduction.* Marx left too many of these latter undefined.[85] Yet his strategy is significant. Contrary to idealist currents, it stressed that thought is subject to constraining conditions. Even if Marx failed to operationalize his science, there is in his strategy an attention to the conditions enabling an operationalized anthropology.

When Harris discusses anthropology, he portrays its early growth as a "reaction to Marx." Not only was Marxist strategy therefore neglected, so were the kinds of anthropology having the most potential for spawning a nomothetic science. This neglect is particularly clear in the case of Lewis Henry Morgan, much of whose anthropology was incorporated into "communist doctrine" by Marx. The young anthropological science was therefore pressured to eschew Morgan and the nomothetic perspectives he and others represented.[86] Without the cultural-materialist, nomothetic strategy, as partially embodied in one like Morgan, early anthropology became vulnerable to idealist currents.

Harris characterizes the first half of twentieth-century cultural anthropology as an anthropology of "historical particularism." Led by Franz Boas in a systematic avoidance of speculative evolutionary theory, this approach stressed most the "collection of facts." According to Harris, Boas became less and less confident that from these facts any nomothetic regularities might arise. Out of Boas's neo-Kantian understanding of the *Geisteswissenschaften* grew an idiographic understanding of anthropology that gained ascendancy. Harris consequently presents Boas as the one who prepared the way in anthropology for the "individualist"-oriented "culture and personality school" and for "eclectic" strategies. By spurning theory about the sociocultural conditions for individuals and for collected facts, Boas not only failed to achieve a nomothetic anthropology, but, more important, he lacked grounds for his own valued "fact gathering." Thus, though during his work among the Pacific Northwest coast groups he collected perhaps

---

[85]Ibid., 232-33. Other interpreters do not see this ambiguity in Marx as such a disability. See, for example, Ollman's argument for the positive role played by Marx's ambiguity and the suggested value of his "violations" of ordinary language. Bertell Ollman, *Alienation: Marx's Conception of Man in Capitalist Society,* 2d ed. (Cambridge: Cambridge University Press, 1976) 3-11.

[86]Harris, *The Rise of Anthropological Theory,* 249.

more data than any subsequent fieldworkers, ongoing ethnographic research in that area, carefully embracing and testing hypotheses, continues to uncover Boas's major misunderstandings.[87] Boas collected the wrong things because he had no strategy.

Harris goes on to show the consequences of this "historical particularism" and the ascendance of idiographic understandings of the discipline in American anthropology. Alfred Kroeber, relying on the philosophy of the neo-Kantian Rickert, sought to study "superorganic" patterns and cultural configurations by an "aesthetic method" or a "free play of intuition" that Kroeber himself confessed gave "no evidence of any true law in the phenomena dealt with."[88] Robert Lowie, though not systematically opposed to theory as many Boasians were, did systematically object to cultural-materialist theory. Rarely invoking technoenvironmental factors, Lowie more often turned to "prior norms" that "codetermine" behavior.[89] Anthropology's culture-and-personality school (Benedict, Mead, Kardiner, Whiting), utilizing psychological and personality studies to explain the sociocultural evolution of national character or "patterns of culture," also failed to establish anthropology as a nomothetic science. This school relied too heavily on emicist viewpoints. Harris singles out Benedict's *Patterns of Culture* to show how the "crude psychological portraitures" of the culture-and-personality school spell "the end of explanation" in any scientific sense.[90] Harris notes Benedict's avowed indebtedness to Dilthey and calls her study of "Dionysian" Kwakiutl and "Apollonian" Pueblo misguided, although an "ingenious evocation of Dilthian feeling of understanding."[91]

Harris's interpretations of European anthropology also place anthropological theories against the backdrop of larger philosophical developments—these developments again being situated in science/anti-

---

[87]For Harris's lengthy attempt to document this, see *The Rise of Anthropological Theory*, 249.

[88]Ibid., 279, 327-30.

[89]Ibid., 371.

[90]Ibid., 399-400.

[91]Ibid., 402.

science, nomothetic/idiographic, materialist/idealist continua. In France, Durkheim's "group mind" and "collective representations," Mauss's "unconscious teleology of the mind," and Lévi-Strauss's "structural anthropology" all make up the idealists' world. Lévi-Strauss, especially, is the complete idealist:

> Every substantive report, every choice of hypothesis, every sustained analysis, from his Nambikwara research to his studies of myth, draws its principal sustenance from the mainstreams of French and German idealism.[92]

Never mind that Lévi-Strauss, and other French idealists, claimed fidelity to Marx and concern for the "material." Unlike Marx, Harris counters, Lévi-Strauss neither fought nor overturned any idealisms. "He found Comte, Durkheim and Mauss standing on their heads, and he joined them."[93]

With regard to British social anthropology, Harris is particularly heartened by Radcliffe-Brown's desire to "return anthropology to social science."[94] Under the influence of Durkheim in Britain, however, Radcliffe-Brown compromised this drive toward science by granting priority in explanation to social structure over ecological and economic factors. Radcliffe-Brown himself, Harris believes, must confess the difficulty of deriving "sociocultural laws" in this way.[95] According to Harris, this explanatory failure, in spite of Radcliffe-Brown's aims, opens the door for views in anthropology like those of Evans-Pritchard, who attempted to extract anthropology from the sciences and place it in the humanities. In this change of direction, Harris finds again the hand of the southwest German neo-Kantians.[96] The lesson Harris teaches is clear: either anthropologies of explanation assure their status as such by the cultural-materialist principles of explanation or they will fail to explain and thus allow their discipline to be interpreted by anthropolo-

---

[92]Ibid., 513.

[93]Ibid.

[94]Ibid., 521, 523.

[95]Ibid., 534-35.

[96]Ibid., 542.

gists of Dilthian "understanding." On the British scene Malinowski facilitated an anthropological science no more than did Radcliffe-Brown. For, although he did consider ecological and environmental conditions, he approached those conditions "from the natives' point of view." The "material foundations" for explanation are lost in the natives' "motives and feelings arising from non-economic needs."[97]

According to Harris, these rejections of Marx's strategy for a cultural-materialist program are still alive; therefore, his contemporary defenses of cultural materialism involve a critique of "alternative strategies." Harris's "history" of anthropology, however, is not finished. For, beginning in the mid-1930s the most recent materialist "awakening" began, although its adherents were not explicit about their ties to a distinctively Marxist strategy. This awakening had two phases, both of which were American developments. The first was led by George Peter Murdock, whose statistical form of cross-cultural comparison and nomothetic perspective Harris approves.[98] It is only Leslie White and Julian Steward, of the awakening's second phase, who explicitly embraced a strategy of technoenvironmental and economic determinism, and who can give Murdock's unguided statistical research its "nomothetic payoff."[99]

White and Steward are both portrayed as giving priority in the explanations of sociocultural differences and similarities to technoenvironmental conditions. Steward especially (discussed above as Harris's instructor at Columbia University) made the "first coherent statement" about the priority of environment in relation to culture, while avoiding the extremities of early geographical determinism on the one hand, and the disclaimers of all lawful regularities by "historical particularists" on the other.

> Where Steward triumphed over earlier expressions of determinism linking habitat and social organization was in being able to explain how despite the diversity of environments and technologies associated with band organized societies, there remained underlying eco-

---

[97]Ibid., 563-64.

[98]Ibid., 606.

[99]Ibid., 632-33.

logical commonalities which gave rise to the general type and other commonalities giving rise to the subtypes.[100]

True to his own cultural materialism, Harris's historical explanation of this rise of twentieth-century cultural ecology in White and Steward itself rests on cultural-materialist principles. White and Steward and others of similar orientation are part of a "broad movement" in Western culture "aimed at strengthening the scientific credentials of cultural anthropology within the prestigious and well-funded natural sciences." The rise of cultural-ecological research, which gives priority to studying infrastructural conditions, becomes "almost inevitable" in a period when "high levels of economic support" go to the general medical sciences, biology, nutrition, demography, and agronomy.

Rooting cultural ecology in this broad, cultural movement, however, is only a cultural materialist's explanation of cultural materialism's rise, not an argument for it. An argument for it, though, is explicitly mentioned in the course of Harris's "history." It rests on Harris's claim that cultural-materialist strategies, which continue the cultural-ecology tradition, better account for sociocultural differences and similarities than earlier strategies. Harris's special historical task is to show how this recent cultural ecology has a precedent in Marxist strategy. The rise of cultural ecology is a "slow but unacknowledged rediscovery or reinvention of principles long ago made explicit in Marx's 'Preface' to *The Critique of Political Economy.*" Harris attempts to display this rediscovery by showing how a Marxist strategy, stripped of its Hegelian dialectic and proletarian politics, is similar to recent cultural ecology.[101]

Reviving Marx as a "present-day polemical point"

Above, I summarized Harris's historical-critical explanation of his own tradition. In this final section, I will address the form of this ver-

---

[100]Ibid., 666.

[101]Ibid., 655. While summarizing White's and Steward's recent cultural ecology, Harris tries to strengthen his claim that they have Marx as precedent, theoretically, by noting that they—like Marx—use the "trisection" of sociocultural systems (technoenvironmental, social, and ideological sectors), and, historically, by discussing their periods of study of Marx and Engels. See 637, 639-40.

tical dimension of his anthropological interpretation in such a way that one is returned to the major concerns of his horizontal hermeneutic.

The form of Harris's vertical hermeneutic is characterized by the fusion of his present world of concerns with the past tradition that he explicates and out of which he speaks. This is evident in Harris's own acknowledgment that his history is out to make a contemporary point.[102] Harris is highly conscious of the significance of this "point" for his historical analyses. If other historians of the discipline warn that such "points" obfuscate historical understanding, Harris retorts, "present-day polemical point alone makes historical understanding possible."[103]

By "polemical point," Harris means the cultural-materialist epistemology and theoretical principles that he has been led to defend as a result of his "present-day" encounters with other societies and of his struggle to interpret them in intercultural context. In the contemporary, horizontal hermeneutic previously presented, Harris constructed his anthropological categories across "cultural" boundaries from the standpoint of a "transcultural community of scientific observers." In this transcultural community the horizons of particular cultures are transcended by reference to a common nature system that impinges upon them all at their infrastructural levels. It was also noted that this community of observers believes the study of infrastructural adaptations to basic subsistence needs is urgent, because a society's failure to adapt leads to the rise of "social pathologies" that are disturbing to moral sensibility. While the argument is rarely so boldly formulated by Harris, in his view, only a transcultural community practicing the cultural-materialist "science of culture" can offer hope amid a contemporary world of morally disturbing, social pathologies. All this recalls the major points already summarized under Harris's horizontal hermeneutic. These features are pertinent again, however, because for Harris they constitute the "polemical point" made by Harris's history.

---

[102]Ibid., 5.

[103]Ibid., 216. Harris is responding to Stocking's comment in George W. Stocking, Jr., "Cultural Darwinism and Philosophical Idealism in E. B. Tylor: A Special Plea for Historicism in the History of Anthropology," *Southwestern Journal of Anthropology* 21 (1965): 142. See also Stocking's review of Harris's *Rise of Anthropological Theory* entitled "A Historical Brief for Cultural Materialism," *Science* 162 (1968): 108-10.

These are the contemporary concerns that are fused in his interpretation of his past tradition. The fusion is particularly evident in the similarity between the interpretive procedures of his horizontal and vertical hermeneutic. Just as Harris "horizontally" interprets the salient images of his fieldwork by constructing operationalized concepts ordered by materialist principles, so in his historical text he "vertically" interprets and judges past theorizing about sociocultural phenomena by the degree to which past theoreticians operationalize their concepts by means of materialist principles. In addition, Harris's historical explanation of how cultural-materialist strategies have risen in history is also a cultural-materialist one, holding that twentieth-century cultural ecology is an intellectual program nurtured by technoeconomic conditions of monetary support in a historical period in which *naturwissenschaftlich* orientations are financially rewarded. If one takes seriously this fusion of present-day polemic with his history of the past, then one can detect in Harris's anthropological enterprise an inclusive and complex "hermeneutical circle." The circle begins with (1) Harris's discovery of a cultural-ecological tradition at Columbia University through thinkers like Julian Steward; extends to (2) the situating of Harris's fieldwork under Wagley according to "ecological zone"; includes (3) Harris's interpretation of the salient images of his fieldwork through concepts operationalized by reference to subsistence and habitat; and (4) Harris's interpretation of past figures in the history of anthropology according to the same operationalist and materialist strategies; and, finally, returns to (5) an explicit argument for Steward's cultural ecology or materialism as opposed to other strategies. This circle indicates that in Harris's anthropological interpretation, one is dealing with a set of relations integrated into a whole that not only reaches out to embrace many societies and cultures, but also back to fuse past and present horizons.

The role of Harris's "present-day polemical point" in his vertical hermeneutic means that not only is his contemporary perspective (his epistemology, principles, theories) fused with his history, but so also is the moral sensibility that was earlier described as both founding and expressing his science of culture. There is, then, a moral dimension to his treatment of the history of his discipline and of history generally. Harris not only explicates but also values the "broad movement" in Western culture that places a premium on the "harder" forms of social science, within which are included Steward's cultural ecology and Harris's own cultural materialism. This movement is held to be a fundamentally positive development in human history and one that is best able to explain the causes of sociocultural differences and similarities. In so doing, it provides knowledge for social reformers' moral sensibility about "who did what to whom, when, where and how." Thus, recall the claim used to close the summary of Harris's horizontal hermeneutic: cultural materialism promises to be an objective science that may lead to both truth and love.[104]

Although Harris presents his cultural materialism as a culmination of a movement in the history of culture and ideas—from the Enlightenment to Marx and then to twentieth-century cultural ecology—he agrees that the status of his "panhuman science of society" is by no means secure. It is always threatened by the other strategies of the present. He acknowledges that cultural materialism holds a "subordinate, minority position" within the present-day world of social science.[105] Therefore, Harris wants to refrain from utopian claims for cultural materialism's emergence in history. He doubts that it will gain widespread commitment and support from the practitioners of anthropology and social science. He remains firm in insisting, however, that for humanity not to recognize the value of emergent cultural materialism is to court disaster.

> In view of increasing national, ethnic and class interests in subordinating science to politics and to short-term sectarian benefits, I must confess that the prospects for a pan-human science of society appear dimmer today than at any time since the eighteenth century. . . . I merely ask all those who fear the onset of a new dark age to join together to strengthen the barriers against mystification and obscurantism in contemporary social science.[106]

---

[104]Harris, *Cultural Materialism*, 341.

[105]Ibid., 76.

[106]Ibid., xii.

Chapter V

Two Religious Dimensions in Anthropology

Very slowly and very reluctantly, I have come to the conclusion that most of the principles that we have advanced to order our data bear little resemblance in kind to the systems of theory developed in the older physical and biological sciences. They have far more in common with the equally complex, but often unverified and unverifiable, systems outside the realm of science which we know as mythology or perhaps as philosophy or even theology.

George Peter Murdock
"Anthropology's Mythology"
The Huxley Memorial Lecture, 1971

Murdock's words are both the keynote of this final chapter and its foil. The keynote is the analogy drawn between anthropology's principles and those of mythology, philosophy and theology. Through this analogy, Murdock suggests a religious dimension inherent in anthropology. The foil, however, is Murdock's vision of a future science of anthropology in which "unverified and unverifiable" realms are purged. He represents an anthropological tendency, discussed in the first chapter, to place the religious outside of anthropological inquiry as object or subject matter of study. This tendency makes problematic the claim of this work: that the term *religious* may be applied to a dimension of anthropology's own inquiry.

It is the aim of this chapter to present the religious dimensions in the anthropologies of Lévi-Strauss and Harris. To argue this claim, it is necessary to recall the discussion in chapter 1 of contemporary thinkers in the philosophy of religion (Gadamer, Ricoeur, Lonergan, Polanyi), who together provided a model for discerning a religious dimension to human inquiry. The model had three referents and, hence, my agenda has had to follow three steps:

(1) a portrait of the inquiry
(2) an identification of that inquiry's "limits"
(3) a demarcation of these limits as "religious"

Chapters 2, 3 and 4 dealt with only the first step: portraying anthropological inquiry. After general anthropological inquiry was presented in chapter 2, the particular anthropologies of Lévi-Strauss and Harris were addressed in chapters 3 and 4.

The final two steps of the agenda—identifying limits and demarcating limits as religious—will set the demands for this chapter's presentation. Before addressing these last two steps, however, one major task of construing Lévi-Strauss's and Harris's anthropologies lies ahead.

From Explanation to Understanding

Explications of Lévi-Strauss's structuralism and Harris's cultural materialism have shown more exactly how these two thinkers are "anthropologists of explanation." Their explanatory intentions involve them both in a variety of analyses.

Lévi-Strauss's structuralist anthropology of explanation employed ethnographic, social-science, and literary-critical methods of explanation. Ethnographic methods involved travel and exploration of Brazil, fieldwork among Brazil's inhabitants, and description of these peoples in anthropological literature. Social-science methods involved not only these ethnographic methods, but also analyses of materials in ethnology, sociology, and psychology, which later evolved into *The Elementary Structures of Kinship*. Literary-critical methods involved the placing of "mythemes" in the whole "text" of South American mythology so as to trace in the relation of its parts the structural transformations that make up one semiotic system. In addition, Lévi-Strauss's own historical-critical method, his attempt to "retread pace by pace" the history of his discipline, was noted.

Harris's cultural-materialist "explanation" employed similar methods. His ethnographic methods involved travel to Brazil and fieldwork among its inhabitants, so as to present ethnographic tables and descriptions in the literature. His general social-science methods involved this ethnography as well as methods borrowed from sociology, statistics, ecology, and demography. His historical-critical method is applied not only to the history of anthropology, but also to the history of broader social and philosophical concerns.

As noted from the beginning, Lévi-Strauss and Harris are not and cannot be exclusively committed to an anthropological "science" of "explanation." The display of their explanatory enterprises within the two realms of anthropological interpretation—the horizontal and the vertical—enables one to see the contexts for their several explanatory methods and the relations between these.

These contexts and relations allow one now to view the moments of "understanding" that encompass and support Lévi-Strauss's and Harris's anthropological "explanation." Although these contexts and relations have been attended to during this display, it remains to complete here an explication of the two anthropologies by moving explicitly from explanation to understanding.

To discern understanding in these anthropologists of *Erklären* is to attend to the preunderstandings, grasps, and comprehensions as a whole by which they unfold chains of partial meanings. It is in relation to these wholes that the religious dimension will be articulated. To discern moments of understanding in explanation is *not* to discern the religious. That discernment begins with this chapter's next section, as I move to the further discernment of the limits in anthropological understanding. Here I will discuss the problem of discerning understanding in Lévi-Strauss and Harris; it is a culminating portrayal of their anthropological inquiry, but only a first, albeit a significant, step toward discerning a religious dimension.

There are two kinds of preunderstood, grasped, and comprehended wholes constituting Lévi-Strauss's and Harris's anthropological understanding. These correspond to the two realms in which anthropological interpretation is practiced: the horizontal realm of an intercultural, interpretive reach out toward contemporary others, and the vertical realm of an intracultural, interpretive reach back into the past of their own traditions. In each of these two realms, I discern a whole in their explanatory enterprises that sustains and relates the parts of their inquiries and provides a context for them.

In the horizontal realm of these anthropologists' interpretive experience is a whole evident in their transcendence of varying cultural horizons. By what whole have Lévi-Strauss and Harris transcended, reached beyond their own horizons to that of their studied peoples, and within what whole did they then compare peoples of varying cultural horizons?

In the vertical realm is a whole evident in the fusion of their present horizon with that of the past. With what past traditions in their own cultures did Lévi-Strauss and Harris converse to form a whole within which temporal horizons were fused?

In Lévi-Strauss's and Harris's transcendence of cultural horizons as well as in their fusion of cultural horizons are the two kinds of wholistic thinking invoked in their anthropological understanding.

Transcending cultural horizons

Consider first the transcendence characteristic of Lévi-Strauss's and Harris's horizontal hermeneutic. On what basis do they move out beyond their own cultural horizons to that of others? What whole makes possible Frenchman Lévi-Strauss's interpretations of the Bororo or the Nambikwara? What whole enables New Yorker Harris's interpretations of Bahian townfolk and comparison of these with the Bathonga of Mozambique and others?

For Lévi-Strauss, that whole is a "world of reciprocity." This is what is preunderstood, grasped, and comprehended by him at each stage of his anthropological explanations. The salient images dominating his ethnography—simple kinship, war and trade, chieftainship, graphic art—are interpreted in terms of this world of reciprocity. As he becomes more and more certain of the reality of this world, testified to not only by his own salient images but also by those of others, Lévi-Strauss more regularly posits it as an interpretive device: a whole that is given before the many parts that he must interpret.[1]

One can see the various functions of this whole in Lévi-Strauss's horizontal hermeneutic. As his anthropological explanations move on through his early ethnographic methods, and through the wider ethnographic and social-science methods of *The Elementary Structures of*

---

[1] Claude Lévi-Strauss, *The Elementary Structures of Kinship*, ed. R. Needham, trans. James Hack Bell and John Richard von Sturmer (Boston: Beacon, 1969) 100.

Kinship, to his later literary-critical and semiological methods, his world of reciprocity becomes an increasingly more structured system of objectified thought. Especially in his later, four-volume work on mythology, he practices that supreme form of "mental gymnastics"—a gymnastics that allows every joint of a cross-cultural skeleton to reveal a "general pattern of anatomical structure."[2] The "world of reciprocity" is now not just one involving exchanges of goods, power, and women. It is also the exchange of messages. All those other exchanged goods, in fact, can be viewed as messages, structured transformations of thought that constitute a world of reciprocity transcending but built up from "countless concrete representational systems."

Lévi-Strauss attends to this ever more structured world of objectified thought so that its structural transformations "play" him as a composer's music plays its listeners. More important, it is this world of objectified thought that eventually permits interpretations linking the horizons of the Bororo with that of the Gê, of geographically distant South and North American groups, of Tupi-Kawahib chiefly songs with European Gregorian chant, of Oxford with India.[3] Cultural horizons are interpretively transcended in this whole, structured world of reciprocity.

Even when this world (this "vast and complex edifice" that Lévi-Strauss has devoted his life to construct) closes in on itself "as if it never existed," even then it is its whole, relational structure that works its vanishing. It does not simply suffer a disintegration of parts. It "slowly flowers (*s'épanouit*) and closes itself."[4]

In his horizontal hermeneutic, then, it is this whole world of reciprocity that is evident from the time of Lévi-Strauss's early ethnogra-

---

[2]Claude Lévi-Strauss, *The Raw and the Cooked: Introduction to a Science of Mythology: 1,* trans. John Weightman and Doreen Weightman (New York: Harper and Row, 1969) 10-11.

[3]Claude Lévi-Strauss, *Tristes Tropiques,* trans. John Weightman and Doreen Weightman (New York: Atheneum, 1976) 35, 359; idem, *The Raw and the Cooked,* 209.

[4]Claude Lévi-Strauss, *The Naked Man: Introduction to a Science of Mythology: 4,* trans. John Weightman and Doreen Weightman (New York: Harper and Row, 1981) 694. The French is important. The structured edifice does not disintegrate and crumble. It flowers or "blooms"—stretches to its full extent—as its particular mode of vanishing. See *L'Homme nu* (Paris: Plon, 1971) 620.

phy to the final volume of his *Mythologiques* in which the whole flowers and closes itself. Throughout, it has not been simply humans with whom Lévi-Strauss has been concerned, but "humanity." The "truth about man" resides in the whole world of reciprocity—whether this "truth" is that Nambikwara chieftainship is a reciprocal exchange of consent to power for able rule; or that basic mechanisms of kinship "ceaselessly bend themselves" to reciprocity; or that with the structured world's flowering and closing, all human labors, sorrows, joys, and hopes will be "as if they never existed." The world of reciprocity as a reciprocal system of human differences—explaining chieftainship, kinship, or the final end of the human species—is the whole of understanding that is grasped and comprehended in Lévi-Strauss's horizontal hermeneutic.

By "this world" Lévi-Strauss could increasingly speak of "man," and distance himself from what he viewed as his earlier "mistake": to have supposed that "men are not always men." Particular cultural horizons are transcended for Lévi-Strauss in and by this whole world of reciprocity.

From earlier discussion of Harris's horizontal hermeneutic, it is clear that he too seeks a transcendence of cultural horizons. This search is evident in his early arguments for "objectivity" and for operationalized concepts as ways out of conceptual and terminological ambiguities within and between cultures. It becomes especially explicit in his later work when he affirms the etic viewpoint of scientific observers as a means to transcend prior belief systems, opposed tribes, nations, classes, and different communities.[5]

This transcendence is not possible, according to Harris, for just any scientific point of view, but rather primarily for a cultural-materialist perspective. Its principle of "infrastructural determinism" gives it its transcendent view of sociocultural phenomena. This principle grounds sociocultural analyses in the regular processes of nature. Nature's "lawful regularities" can be incorporated through infrastructural principles into anthropology in order to ground a "science of culture."

For Harris, then, it is nature that enables transcendence of cultural horizons in the horizontal dimension of his anthropological interpre-

---

[5]Marvin Harris, *Cultural Materialism: The Struggle for a Science of Culture* (New York: Random House, 1979) 27-28, 318.

tation. Nature is a "material world"[6] on which humans everywhere depend for their subsistence, and to which anthropologists ultimately refer for explanation in their ecological, technoeconomic, technoenvironmental analyses at the infrastructural level of human societies. Nature, therefore, is an ordering whole that Harris preunderstands and continually comprehends. Nature as this ordering whole founds an ordered inquiry that can be practiced by participants of any culture if they join the "transcultural community of scientific observers" who practice this cultural-materialist research strategy.

Although Harris has become increasingly explicit about the character of this research strategy, he has practiced it from his earliest writings. It was noted how the ambiguities of native classifications (of town and country, of racial identity) and ambiguities in anthropological knowledge of these classifications are resolved for the early Harris only by rooting cultural concepts in subsistence analyses of particular communities. Within speech communities, for example, he argues that a consensus about ambiguous classifying procedures could be discerned by reference to "local habitat."[7] Because nature transcends cultures and makes different but predictable impacts on those cultures, Harris seeks interpretive transcendence of his own culture and of other cultures by reference to nature. Thus, Harris's most recent studies—for instance, his *Cultural Materialism*—explicitly formulate a principle of infrastructural determinism to highlight an interface of nature with culture.

Fusing temporal horizons

Not only wholes of the horizontal realm are invoked in anthropological understanding. There are also Lévi-Strauss's and Harris's fusions of past and present horizons in the vertical realm. Both anthropologists undertake their own historical-critical interpretation of anthropology. In this interpretation they evaluate past positions and appropriate certain strands of anthropology. In this dialogue with anthropology, anthropology is not kept at a distance, in the past. Rather, it is appropriated for present interpretation. Indeed, the past is seen as *their*

---

[6]Marvin Harris, *The Nature of Cultural Things* (New York: Random House, 1964) 169-70.

[7]Ibid., 158.

tradition in its appropriation *for* and *in* their present.[8] Their interpretations of the past are embedded in the present, just as present interpretation is embedded in the past. Present and past horizons are fused.

Consider this temporal fusion in Lévi-Strauss's vertical hermeneutic. It has been shown how his historical-critical analysis of twentieth-century social and cultural anthropology cleared a place in his present for a philosophy of *pitié* that was articulated by a past philosopher, Jean Jacques Rousseau. As Lévi-Strauss "retreads pace by pace" the development of anthropology, Rousseauan *pitié* emerges as a contemporary theory of human cognition and as an epistemology for anthropologists' knowledge of that cognitional theory. Rousseau, Lévi-Strauss's "master and brother," is *le plus ethnographe des philosophes*.[9] He "conceived, willed, and announced this very ethnology which did not yet exist."[10]

Rousseauan *pitié*, once retrieved from the past and fused with the most recent views of Radcliffe-Brown on totemism, also served Lévi-Strauss as a way to integrate a variety of thinkers in his tradition: Freud, Mauss, Jakobson, Marx. After being retrieved and while serving to integrate a diversity of historical sources, Rousseau's philosophy of *pitié* more specifically guided Lévi-Strauss's own anthropological enterprise.

With this guidance, Lévi-Strauss works out the fusion in different ways. Rousseau challenges Western philosophers with the path of self-denial and of identification with a world of beings and things. Lévi-Strauss's ethnography, thus, is part of this identification. His anthropological mind begins in totalization. Rousseau, however, tolerated no merely utopian visions and endorsements of savage societies. Lévi-Strauss then proceeds to detotalize others' life and thought, to "reduce" them to aspects of a larger whole in spite of these others' ethnocentric or self-absolutizing claims. Rousseau also taught the possibility of discerning in all this a "new form." So also, Lévi-Strauss moves through totalization and detotalization to the redemptive task of retotalization

---

[8]For the hermeneutical theory of this dialectic of past and present horizons, see H.-G. Gadamer, *Truth and Method* (New York: Seabury, 1975) 267-74.

[9]Claude Lévi-Strauss, *Tristes Tropiques* (Paris: Plon, 1955) 421.

[10]Claude Lévi-Strauss, "J. J. Rousseau: Founder of the Sciences of Man," *Structural Anthropology*, 2:34.

through which societies can reform themselves by referring to an "eternal and universal" model of what is primordial in human nature.

One discerns in Lévi-Strauss, then, no simple borrowing from Rousseau, nor just an "application" of the past French *philosophe*'s ideas. Rousseau's horizon is one with which Lévi-Strauss's own horizon can be fused. Lévi-Strauss himself is explicit about this (as explication of his vertical hermeneutic indicated). For, in his interpretation of the past, Lévi-Strauss explicitly retrieves Rousseau. The retrieval is more apparent in the striking analogies between Rousseau's and Lévi-Strauss's general programs. These analogies are present even when Lévi-Strauss is not explicit about them. The Lévi-Straussian enterprise—in its theories of the savage mind and in its own epistemology—totalizes, detotalizes, and retotalizes after the manner of Rousseau's development in his major works.

Note also the fusion in Marvin Harris's vertical hermeneutic. As with Lévi-Strauss, the fusion involves the appropriation of a major past thinker: in this case, Karl Marx. Marx is interpreted in a way that sets Harris's appropriation of his ideas apart from those of "structural Marxists" and of "dialectical materialists." But once interpreted, the basic research strategy of this past thinker is presented as the perspective informing contemporary social-science currents, particularly those of twentieth-century cultural ecology and cultural materialism.

At times, Harris refers to Marx as a "precedent" of twentieth-century ecology and materialism; those movements are then said to have reinvented or rediscovered Marx. This language may suggest something short of the fusion of temporal horizons by emphasizing mainly the differences between present and past with only occasional borrowings taking place through knowledge of a distant, past thinker. But Harris himself elsewhere notes that his present relation to the past is more integral than that, and actually more of a "fusion." This is especially so when he reflects on the nature of his vertical hermeneutic and propounds a rudimentary historiography which holds that historical understanding is made possible only by "present-day polemical point." His interpretation and appropriation of Marx, then, is made possible by this modern-day concern.

Harris's rudimentary historiography is not all that suggests this fusion; so also does the overall development of his anthropology. As between Lévi-Strauss and an interpreted Rousseau, so between Harris and his interpreted Marx: there are striking analogies of intellectual program. The "inclusive and complex hermeneutical circle" specified in the previous chapter portrayed the interplay of contemporary concerns and past horizons in Harris's anthropology. Undergraduate and graduate training at Columbia, fieldwork in Brazil, theorizing about fieldwork experience, fashioning a history of culture theory, and arguing for twentieth-century cultural ecology and materialism—in all these operations are different mediating scenes (institutional, ethnographic, theoretical, argumentative) in which the horizons of the past and present interplay.

The fusion was evident also in the way the moral dimension of Harris's polemical defense of cultural materialism in contemporary life crept into his vertical interpretation of past traditions. Harris points to cultural materialism as an ethic not only for present moral concerns over against the implied ethics of other contemporary research strategies, but also as an ethic emerging as a culmination of the history of culture and thought. Cultural materialism strengthens "barriers against mystification and obscurantism," thus checking the "onset of a new dark age."

Toward transcultural and transtemporal understanding

Lévi-Strauss's and Harris's experiences show their interpretive stances to contain a transcendence of cultural horizons and a fusion of temporal ones. In their horizontal hermeneutics, they shape wholes (a "world of reciprocity" or "nature") that enable them to transcend their cultural horizons for knowledge of an alien culture and for comparison of several cultures. And in their vertical hermeneutic, they carry on a dialogue within their present horizon as fused with that of the past (which consists of Rousseau or of Marx).

The interpretive stances of the two anthropologists, then, are both "transcultural" and "transtemporal." This cultural and temporal transcendence, however, is a feature of Lévi-Strauss's and Harris's *particularity*. Their transcendence of cultural or of temporal horizons is no unmediated experience "above" or "apart from" their particular life pilgrimages. It is not a knowledge unfocused by particular sociocultural contexts. On the contrary, this transcendence is fashioned by them through and in studies of particular others in their past tradition. Their transcultural and transtemporal understanding is, therefore, a movement *through* particular mediations.

Because Lévi-Strauss's and Harris's interpretive transcendence is rooted in particularity, I have had to draw from different forms of analysis in order to explicate their anthropological enterprises. I have applied components of historical, sociology-of-knowledge, and philosophical analyses, without depending on any one exclusively. Utilizing components of all of these, I sought to display the *particular* ways in and through which these anthropologists carry on their enterprises and transcend cultural and temporal horizons.

The particularity of their modes of transcendence is evident in, for example, Lévi-Strauss's and Harris's "selectivity" of particular positions and their criticism of other particular positions. Lévi-Strauss seeks transcendence of cultural and temporal horizons in dialogue with a Rousseau but *not* a Descartes or a Sartre. Descartes is criticized for remaining locked in the "transcendental retreat" of the self, and Sartre for too exclusive a concern with only the others of Western culture. Similarly, Harris seeks transcendence of horizons in the materialist research strategy of Marx, rather than that of the idealist Hegel. A transcendence of horizons does not entail a knowledge above or independent from particular contexts; rather, it may occur in and through them. Nor does being rooted in particular cultures and traditions necessarily disallow some transcendence of cultural horizons or a fusion of temporal ones. Both Lévi-Strauss and Harris move toward transcultural and transtemporal understanding in and through their particular situations.

To say that Lévi-Strauss and Harris "understand" as well as "explain," is to say that they invoke these transcending wholes in order to encompass and support the practice of their several explanatory methods. Lévi-Strauss and Harris preunderstand, grasp, and comprehend wholes (transculturally and transtemporally) within which the explanatory character of their laws, theories, and hypotheses takes on meaning. These wholes, though significantly developed by their various forms of explanation, can be distinguished from their explanations. Recalling the language used in chapter 2 for distinguishing between enterprises of explanation and those of understanding, one can note that not only do the two anthropologists "analyze," they also "intuit." Their thought is both "calculative" and "meditative." They offer explanatory "method" and they seek "truth."

Limits in Two Anthropologists' Understanding

This display of Lévi-Strauss's and Harris's interpretive experience
has culminated in discernment of the transcultural and transtemporal
wholes that are preunderstood, comprehended, or shaped by them in
their attempts to explain studied others. In discerning these transcending wholes, one is brought closer to discerning the religious dimension
of Lévi-Strauss's and Harris's anthropologies. To show the religious
character of the transcending wholes, however, one must show how their
employment of such transcending wholes occurs "at the limits" of their
interpretive experience. I am using the notion of "limit" that in chapter
1 was presented as a "key characteristic" of the religious. There I showed
how contemporary discerners of a religious dimension seek the religious in human inquiry by identification of its limits.

The notion of limit

Exactly what a limit is and what makes it a "key characteristic" of
the religious was not extensively discussed in chapter 1. There, it served
mainly as one feature of a model of philosophical theology for explicating religious dimensions in forms of human inquiry. In this chapter it
will not be treated at length either. A few general comments are in order, however, before discussing limits in their relation to anthropologists Lévi-Strauss and Harris.

The notion of limit unfolded here attaches to the wholistic view of
Lévi-Strauss's and Harris's anthropologies that this hermeneutical portrait of their work has made possible. That is to say, the limits of their
anthropologies will be discussed with reference not just to their explanations, but more important, to the understanding that encompasses and
supports their explanations. This plan is not only consistent with Ricoeur's unfolding of limit situations in relation to the understanding
moment, but is also particularly appropriate given the character of these
particular anthropologists' understanding.

I stress the notion of limit as attaching to the wholes of understanding so as to distinguish this use of limit from other ways of articulating
limits in Lévi-Strauss's and Harris's inquiries. One might attend, for
example, to limits imposed on their inquiries by personal or existential
factors characterizing them as individuals, factors that historians and
biographers might seek to explain. Or, one might attend to limits set by

sociocultural and sociohistorical contexts that sociologists of knowledge might explain along with historians and biographers. One could attend to limits set by particular world views and philosophical presuppositions that might be explained by philosophers and philosophers of social science along with the historians and sociologists of knowledge.

From the start I have tried to display the important insights rendered by these various approaches to the limits of Lévi-Strauss's and Harris's anthropological inquiry, and have incorporated them within one hermeneutical explication of the horizontal and vertical realms of their interpretive experience. I have not tried, nor does it seem to do justice to the complexity of their anthropological interpretations, to consistently take a single approach, be it historical, sociology-of-knowledge, or philosophical analysis. The explication in the previous three chapters admittedly has been selective, but this selectivity has been necessary in order to relate important components produced by the several kinds of analysis into a whole set of relations constituting Lévi-Strauss's and Harris's anthropological "careers" or "enterprises."[11]

In this section, then, I am discussing the limits in Lévi-Strauss's and Harris's anthropological understanding that attach to a wholistic view of their interpretive experience as that experience has been displayed in my work. In order to address these limits, I will of course continue to draw from a variety of approaches that enable one to see the limit situations in their particular forms. But the primary aim is to note how particular limit situations relate to the wholes of their anthropological understanding.

In chapter 1 I specified two senses of the word *limit*. In the first sense, a limit restricts or sets a boundary in experience and inquiry. In the second sense, however, a limit not only sets a boundary, but also may disclose that which grounds the experience or inquiry that is lim-

---

[11]This is not to deny, however, the fruitfulness of a rigorous practice of one of these approaches, either in the form of historical-biographical analysis centering on Lévi-Strauss's and Harris's personal lives, or sociology-of-knowledge analysis of their contexts, or philosophical analysis of their presuppositions. No doubt, my own explication of the whole "set of relations" constituting their anthropological "enterprises" could be further developed, enriched, and challenged by the fruits of more singular approaches. From the perspective of this work, however, these developing, enriching, and challenging insights should be evaluated in relation to a whole set of insights drawn from the several kinds of analyses of an anthropologist's inquiry.

ited. A limit, therefore, may be both restrictive and facilitative. Limits "attach" to human interpretive experience both as restricting "borders" and as enabling conditions for the possibility of the experience.

This twofold sense of limit has been stressed by various philosophers and philosophers of religion. Ricoeur's exegesis of the notion of limit in Kant's *Critique of Pure Reason*, for example, distinguishes between limit as "boundary" (*Schranke*) and limit as a more productive function of the "unconditioned" in conditioned knowledge (*Grenze*).

> The concept "limit" implies not only and even not primarily that our knowledge *is* limited, has boundaries, but that the quest for the unconditioned *puts limits* on the claim of objective knowledge to become absolute.[12]

Ricoeur then goes on to suggest that the function of the unconditioned, which Kant held to impose only an "empty" requirement, might be given a more positive function in the indirect presentations of metaphorical and conceptual language.[13] Limits, then, according to Ricoeur's exegesis of Kant, not only bound knowledge but may ground it as well.

These two senses of limit—the restricting one and the productive one—are identifiable in other thinkers' works as well. One may recall, for example, Karl Jasper's "limit-situation" (*Grenzsituation*), in which a boundary "plays its proper role of something immanent which already points to transcendence."[14] Similarly, for Heidegger, a "limit-sit-

---

[12]Paul Ricoeur, "The Specificity of Religious Language," *Semeia* 4 (1975): 142. While Ricoeur does not here cite the pertinent parts of Kant's first *Critique*, he clearly seems to have in mind a passage like that at A255/B310-11. The limiting-concept (*Grenzbegriff*) is there "problematic" for Kant because, while its "objective reality" cannot in any way be known so that it is "empty," such a concept nevertheless contains no contradiction and is also "necessary" in its function to limit (*einzuschranken*) the objective reality of sensible knowledge. Ricoeur "fills" the empty function of limiting-concepts with the functions of poetic language. See Immanuel Kant, *Critique of Pure Reason*, trans. Norman Kemp Smith (New York: St. Martins, 1978) 271-72. For the German, cf. *Kritik der reinen Vernunft*, vol. 1 (Wiesbaden, 1956) 279-82.

[13]Ricoeur, "The Specificity of Religious Language," 129-31, 142-43.

[14]Karl Jaspers, *Philosophie*, Zweite unveränderte auflage (Berlin: Springer-Verlag, 1948) 469-70.

uation" has a restrictive or "closed" character, but also a productive, enabling character that promotes "authentic potentiality-for-Being-a whole."[15] Within other and admittedly different philosophical contexts, Plato and Aristotle foreshadowed this twofold sense of limit. Plato's discussion in the *Philebus* of the "limited," the "unlimited," *and* the mixture of these displayed the manifold meaning contained in the word *limit* (πέρας). Such manifold meaning allows, among other possibilities, discernment of the restrictive and productive achievements of a limit.[16] The twofold sense of limit can also be discerned among the many senses noted by Aristotle. A limit may mean the "last point of each thing . . . beyond which it is not possible to find any part," or "the end of each thing," that toward which a thing moves.[17]

The "bounding" and more productive "grounding" functions of a limit are what I understand David Tracy, in contemporary theology, to be refining in his distinction between "limits-to" human experience and disclosed "limits-of" human experience.[18] Langdon Gilkey's notion of a "conditioned absolute" also is a theological attempt to employ the twofold sense of limit. In Tracy's terms, the limits-to can often be stated, while any limit-of reality is more usually "disclosed," "shown," or "displayed." The limits-to may be articulated for scientific inquiry

---

[15]Martin Heidegger, *Being and Time*, trans. John Macquarrie and Edmund Robinson (New York: Harper and Row, 1962) 356, 400.

[16]Plato, *Philebus*, 23c.26a.b, in *The Collected Dialogues of Plato, Including the Letters*, ed. Edith Hamilton and Huntington Cairns (Princeton: Princeton University Press, 1961) 1100, 1102-1103.

[17]Aristotle, *Metaphysics*, 5.17.10221.3-12. For the manifold meaning contained in Plato's notion of limit; for the way it is terminologically differentiated by Aristotle; and for the appropriateness of relating the manifold meanings in these classical thinkers to more recent uses of "limit," see *Historische Wörterbuch der Philosophie*, 1974 ed., under the heading "Grenz, Schranke," by F. Fulda.

[18]David Tracy, *Blessed Rage for Order: The New Pluralism in Theology* (New York: Seabury, 1975) 70, 93, 103, 109, 111 nn. 11, 13; and idem, *The Analogical Imagination: Christian Theology and the Culture of Pluralism* (New York: Crossroad, 1981) 158, 160-61, 163-65, 173. See also Langdon Gilkey's discussion of limits as one of four elements of "ultimacy" or "unconditionedness" in *Naming the Whirlwind* (Indianapolis: Bobbs-Merrill, 1969) 313.

and moral striving as "limiting questions"[19] and articulated for common human experience as negative senses of anxiety, finitude, contingency, guilt, radical transience, or as more positive senses of fundamental trust, order, joy, justice, wonder, loyalty to the whole.

In the articulation of these limit-to experiences, one might also be able to discern a disclosed limit-of reality: a "horizon to" or "ground of" the experience or inquiry being attended to. The religions, by means of their explicitly religious languages and symbols, may invoke such a limit-of reality.Conceptual analyses of religious thinkers, according to Tracy, may go further to "*partly* state" the character of this founding, conditioning reality that grounds human experience and inquiry.[20] Religions are thus rooted in stated limit-to experiences and a disclosed limit-of reality, with the latter "resonating with" the limit-to experiences. This twofold limit-situation constitutes a religious dimension in human experience that the religions elaborate symbolically, conceptually, ritually, or communally.

---

[19]For the notion of a "limiting question" *in* reasoning but at a point beyond which it is "no longer possible to give 'reasons' of the kind given until then," see Stephen Toulmin's early work, *An Examination of the Place of Reason in Ethics* (London: Cambridge University Press, 1950) 202, 204-11. For the application and extension of Toulmin's notion of the limiting question to scientific inquiry, see Langdon Gilkey, *Religion and the Scientific Future: Reflections on Myth, Science, and Theology* (New York: Harper and Row, 1970) 38-40; Tracy, *Blessed Rage for Order*, 96-100. For similar application and extension to moral striving, see Schubert Miles Ogden, *The Reality of God and Other Essays* (San Francisco: Harper and Row, 1963) 27-43.

[20]Tracy, *The Analogical Imagination*, 160-61. For a vigorous qualification of this theological use of the notion of limit, see Gordon Kaufman, *God the Problem* (Cambridge MA: Harvard University Press, 1972) 50-61. Kaufman cautions that "limit means *limit*" in a restrictive sense, and that it is "both deceitful and inconsistent to talk about God on the ground of our limitedness, and then, on the other, to transcend those limits in order to spell out in some detail the structure of the reality that lies beyond them" (50-51).

Both Tracy and Gilkey, as well as other discerners of a religious dimension, make similar warnings. Both men warn against the prematurity of talk about God on the basis of discerning a religious dimension (see Gilkey, *Religion and the Scientific Future*, 62, and Tracy, *The Analogical Imagination*, 160-61). The difference is that while all agree caution is needed when discussing God, the discerners of a religious dimension see *in* the experience of limits a disclosure that, for all its mystery and possible representation in different symbols and myths, may nevertheless be discerned as productive and not only restrictive.

These distinctions—between the religious dimension and religion, and between limit-to and limit-of—are crucial for this final chapter's discernment of a religious dimension in anthropological interpretation. The distinctions lead one to understand, for example, that to seek a religious dimension in Lévi-Strauss's and Harris' anthropologies is not to seek a religion. The claim is not that anthropological interpretive experience is a religion, nor that it possesses a religion within it. At best, and this is what I try to show, it possesses a religious dimension. This latter is what will then be explicated in relation to anthropological understanding in terms of limit-to and possibly disclosed limit-of experiences.

In the transcending wholes of Lévi-Strauss's and Harris's anthropological understanding is the first clue to the character of their limit-situations. I will here argue that these transcending wholes are partial disclosures of a limit-of reality for Lévi-Strauss and Harris. They are not only their preunderstandings, but are also the invoked realities that ground and sustain their anthropological enterprises. To establish this point, however, one must view these transcending wholes as responses within each anthropologist's limit-situation so that the limit-of realities—the world of reciprocity for Lévi-Strauss and nature for Harris— may be related to certain limit-to experiences in their anthropologies.

Having presented these general comments about the notion of limit, I can turn now to the proper aim of this section of the chapter: to describe the distinctive limit-situations of Lévi-Strauss's and Harris's work, showing how these both restrict and ground their anthropological enterprises. These two anthropologists' limit-situations will be related to both the horizontal transcendence and the vertical fusion characterizing their interpretive experience.

The limit-situation of Lévi-Strauss's anthropological enterprise may be summarily termed a "loyalty to the whole." Harris's limit-situation is best described as a "pursuit of order." These are their limit-situations, which warrant further treatment.

Lévi-Strauss's limiting loyalty to the whole

"Loyalty to the whole" is a phrase that gathers and expresses several related fundamental senses that drive or ground the Lévi-Straussian enterprise. Most important here is his fundamental and persistent sense of "compassion" (*pitié*) wedded to "remorse." These senses involve a repulsion by and critique of Western cultural ethnocentrism, and constitute Lévi-Strauss's loyalty to the whole. This loyalty may take different forms, but it is present throughout his anthropology.

As noted, the senses of *pitié* and remorse are not merely emotive qualities, as might be suggested by a psychology that brackets the emotive as just one faculty of the human mind. To the contrary, though Lévi-Strauss himself may occasionally speak of *pitié* as a faculty, he usually refers to it as a psychic state, an experience of "original identification" that holds all of the human's world together in a totality and is also a principle of research for the anthropologist facing a multifaceted world that yet must be approached as a totality. For the savage, *pitié* is evident in *mana*, that expression of the human mind's "facing" contradictory and unrelated elements so that they are held together, implying relations among them. For Lévi-Strauss, *pitié* is manifest in his identification with remote others, and in his view of the world as a wealth of beings and things.

The limiting loyalty to the whole, driven by fundamental senses of compassion and remorse, especially pervades and nourishes the kinds of interpretations characterizing Lévi-Strauss's horizontal hermeneutic. His interpretations of Brazil—including his practice of ethnographic method and extending to his literary-critical effort to build a structuralist model from these Brazilian peoples' similarities and differences with other peoples—give evidence of this pervasive loyalty.

Lévi-Strauss's very discovery of ethnography, discussed above with the aid of the "confessional" statements in his corpus, is a first example of this loyalty. The expert knowledge he had attained of Western philosophy was no consolation for him when he discerned in Robert Lowie's ethnography a world of others. Immersion in his own culture was a "claustrophobic" experience. Identification (*pitié*) with others potentially encountered in field research was for him to be "refreshed and renewed."[21] *"La révélation"* worked by his first encounter with ethnography may be viewed as an experience in "original identification" (*pitié*) with the anthropological world of others that exhibits the fundamental loyalty to the whole.

---

[21]Lévi-Strauss, *Tristes Tropiques* (Eng. ed.), 59.

The claustrophobia of immersion in Western culture becomes more properly "remorse"[22] when Lévi-Strauss notes the moral consequences of a Western culture that neglects *pitié*, the sense of the mutual relatedness of all beings and things. Failure to live out the "total social fact" may have "lethal effects" for humanity, as was evident in the waning societies of South America that he himself had studied. Both remorse and compassion are evident when he describes the encounter of the Old and New Worlds as a "cataclysm" that lays bare the morally bankrupt "humanism" of Western culture. Western culture was prone to self-absolutization and neglected its place as but a part of a larger pattern and rhythm of existence.

> What wear and tear, what useless irritation we could spare ourselves if we agreed to accept the true conditions of our human experience and realize that we are not in a position to free ourselves completely from its patterns and rhythms.[23]

This loyalty to the whole, expressed through compassion and remorse, pervades Lévi-Strauss's entire corpus. Its presence becomes still clearer if one attends again to the corpus's major phases of totalization, detotalization, and retotalization.

In the totalizing phase, where anthropological research begins for Lévi-Strauss, the anthropologist is in "original identification" with all beings and things. Lévi-Strauss's self is presented as an "inference" from studied others, as must be all senses of self-identity.[24] In this first phase of his anthropological activity, he practices ethnography, and he studies others' ethnographies as a form of self-transcendence that must be the basic principle for the "sciences of man."[25] A loyalty to the whole pervades this totalizing phase.

In the second phase, detotalization, remorse and compassion intensify. Having been prompted by these senses to embrace the others

---

[22]On the significance of the remorse behind Lévi-Strauss's structural anthropology and structuralism, see Jacques Derrida, *Writing and Difference*, trans. Alan Bass (Chicago: University of Chicago Press, 1978) 292.

[23]Lévi-Strauss, *Tristes Tropiques* (Eng. ed.), 123.

[24]Lévi-Strauss, "J. J. Rousseau," 37.

[25]Ibid., 36.

of Brazil's jungles and the others whom he can explore in other anthropological texts, Lévi-Strauss comes up against that other problem discussed above: other selves also make absolute their own cultural views and life ways.[26] His remorse now is not so much due to his own restriction to Western culture, but rather due to his encounter with others' restrictions to their contexts. There is thus an increased sense of the particularity, uniqueness, and seeming separation of all beings and things. Yet, as the remorse is complicated in this way, so also do his efforts to bring all to unity—caused by his compassion, his sense of the original identification of all beings and things—become more intense. Thus, his remorse and compassion lead Lévi-Strauss into the activity of reducing, breaking down, or demolishing all social orders' claims to be *the* totality. He seeks to relate all the particulars among which he has "gone out" in order to "go below" to underlying "structures," which can be the basis of unity. A loyalty to the whole pervades this detotalizing phase of his anthropological activity.

As also noted above, however, Lévi-Strauss moves quickly to a retotalizing phase of anthropological activity, wherein structuralist demolition and reduction enable discovery of the "invariants" of human thought and experience. Lévi-Strauss's arrival at these invariants rehabilitates original identification in the face of the many particulars and, thereby, is a further expression of his own totalizing *pitié*. The remorse of Lévi-Strauss remains so long as humans neglect to refer to the retotalized whole that his structural anthropology seeks to display. But in this phase, Lévi-Strauss's own remorse and compassion have at least resulted in a model of *"humanité générale,"*[27] displaying the "truth about man" that resides in the system of the many differences and common properties.[28]

Thus far I have attended to the ways remorse and compassion, which comprise Lévi-Strauss's limiting loyalty to the whole, pervade his horizontal hermeneutic, his interpretive reach out to others. A few comments show that these fundamental senses pervade also the re-

---

[26]Ibid., 389.

[27]Regarding this "model," see above, 134, 188-90.

[28]Lévi-Strauss, *The Raw and the Cooked*, 1:11; idem, *Tristes Tropiques* (Eng. ed.), 390-91; and idem, *The Savage Mind*, 247.

trieval of Rousseau and the other interpretations of his own tradition
that constitute his vertical hermeneutic.

Not only is Rousseau retrieved as the chief philosophical articu-
lator for his own fundamental sense of compassion (*pitié*), but also Lévi-
Strauss's compassion is itself the basis for his lament about anthropologists who wrought division among beings (separating, for example,
savages from civilized people). Lévi-Strauss writes his history of anthropology as an evaluation of the extent to which anthropologists and
anthropological positions treat and make possible study of one, totalized world of beings and things.[29] His fundamental senses of remorse
and compassion thus pervade the fusion of past and present horizons in
his vertical hermeneutic.

Compassion and remorse are the limit-to experiences of Lévi-
Strauss's anthropological enterprise. They restrict and shape the increasing transcendence of cultural horizons in his horizontal hermeneutic, evident first in his ethnographic experience, then in his social-
science search for "elementary structures of kinship," and finally in the
literary-critical, structuralist effort to construct *un nouveau ordre*. They
also restrict and shape the fusion of temporal horizons in his vertical
hermeneutic. Rousseauan *pitié* resonates with Lévi-Strauss's own compassion and remorse. He abandoned his Western philosophical voca-
tion to lose himself in others' thought, just as Rousseau pointed Western
thinkers in general beyond themselves to identification with others.
Rousseau and Lévi-Strauss share the fundamental senses of compassion and remorse. The past horizon of Rousseau's world serves as the
present horizon for Lévi-Strauss's world.

The transcending wholes of Lévi-Strauss's anthropological understanding, then, resonate with these limit-to experiences. The "world of
reciprocity," the whole that encompasses and supports his transcultural interpretations and that is reinforced and reemphasized in his
transtemporal interpretations, is a limit-of reality disclosed in his anthropological enterprise that corresponds to the limit-to experiences of

---

[29]For example, recall Lévi-Strauss's historical-critical treatment of the theme of totemism, in which Frazer and the "classical" analysts of totemism are criticized for
marking off savage from civilized peoples. On the other hand, anthropologist Radcliffe-
Brown, and occasionally Durkheim and Boas, is commended for glimpsing the one,
universal, intellectual process in which all people are engaged. See above, 172-74.

remorse and compassion. The world of reciprocity that Lévi-Strauss posits—that draws him out of his own society into that of others, that leads him to reduce particular others to "invariant" structures, that prompts his construction of a universal and eternal model—is a reality disclosed for an anthropological self who has the particular limit-to experiences of remorse and compassion discussed. Lévi-Strauss's limit-situation constricts his anthropology but also enables and grounds his anthropology by an invoked reality, a world of reciprocity.

Though Lévi-Strauss's investigations and diverse methods of explanation may contribute to his own presentation of this reciprocal world, it is not solely a result of those investigations, no mere object that has "come into view" for him. Rather, it is a presupposed condition for the possibility of the anthropology forged in the fundamental, limit-to experiences of remorse and compassion. The world of reciprocity (a limit-of reality) and the fundamental senses of remorse and compassion (limit-to experiences) resonate with one another to constitute his limit-situation in which a "loyalty to the whole" predominates.

Although Lévi-Strauss holds in his later work that this whole world of reciprocity will "flower and close itself" so that all creation is but "transient efflorescence," this belief does not lessen the importance of that whole for his interpretive experience as an anthropologist. It is only in the later writings, after the whole world has been structurally displayed, that its basic opposition between being and nonbeing emerges, and that the disappearance of the whole into nonbeing is considered. And even with this future, because the whole disappears only when the whole world has structurally "flowered," the structuring whole can never be ignored simply because it will one day vanish. To the contrary, the vanishing whole, however temporary the reality of its being, gives reason and meaning to Lévi-Strauss's and to all humans' scientific achievements, practiced activities, and daily existence.[30] The impending absence of the whole as a limit-of reality does not detract from its power to ground Lévi-Strauss's anthropology.

Before considering why this limit-situation in Lévi-Strauss's interpretive experience may be taken as a religious dimension, one must

---

[30]Lévi-Strauss, *The Naked Man*, 694.

consider the limit-situation that characterizes Harris's interpretive experience.

Harris's limiting pursuit of order

Marvin Harris's limit-situation may be summarized as the "pursuit of order." This phrase, like "loyalty to the whole" in Lévi-Strauss's case, gathers and expresses several related fundamental senses that drive or ground Harris's anthropological enterprise. The most important of these, as the phrase suggests, is a sense of order, but one accompanied by a sense of the recalcitrant ambiguity plaguing intercultural interpretation. The senses of order and ambiguity are also interwoven with senses of justice and oppression. To discern Harris's limit-situation of pursuit of order, one must be aware of the presence of these several senses and their relation to his interpretive experience.

One may first discern the fundamental senses constituting this "limiting" pursuit of order by recalling features of Harris's horizontal hermeneutic. The senses of order and ambiguity, of justice and oppression, are evident in that hermeneutic, through which Harris seeks an ever-greater and more specific transcendence of cultural horizons. This transcendence culminated in a "transcultural community of scientific observers" who practice an ordered inquiry, presenting the effects of an ordered nature on societies' infrastructural levels.

Recall the drive for clarity and order as exhibited in the tables and statistical analyses of Harris's ethnographic text, *Town and Country in Brazil*. The salient images from his fieldwork situation, those images that set the fundamental problem of his anthropological enterprise, centered on the particular problems of intercultural ambiguity that demanded ordering. Whether these ambiguities concerned the town/country dichotomy or racial identity in Brazil, Harris sought order by referring to the ecological, technoeconomic demands upon the community due to its particular place in nature.

In this early period of his writings, this drive for order—culminating in the taxonomic and operationalist text *The Nature of Cultural Things*—featured a sense of justice and oppression. His ethnography was written in that "ten-minute to midnight atmosphere" of concern for the welfare of Latin America.[31] In his drive toward orderly ethnographic description of Minas Velhas can be seen Harris's sense of the oppressed or disadvantaged status of his subjects of study: their "degradation," urban "discontent," their "unrewarding drudgery."[32]

Harris's limited fieldwork experience in Mozambique displayed the interweaving of his fundamental senses of order and justice. There, his operationalist research, emerging from a so-called objective and non-partisan background, entailed for Harris a "moral obligation" to indict a racial and political system in Mozambique that "demonstrably molds the minds and hearts of men into shapes that are alien to their own traditions and that threaten one and all with unhappy consequences."[33] Harris's later works feature a self-conscious and persistent interweaving of his orderly science with morality. His ordering science is a precondition for moral judgment, as he sees it, and a human "moral imperative" requires the practice of an ordered inquiry.

The concerns for both order and justice, then, are found throughout the texts in which Harris "horizontally" interprets others. And in his later writings this fusion of ordered knowledge and morality is more explicitly articulated, so that the two sides of cultural materialism, both as an intellectual strategy and as a maximization of the good and just life, increasingly coalesce. These fundamental senses pervade his interpretation of urban folk at Minas Velhas; seem to impel his drive for operationalism as a "strong dose" for intercultural ambiguity; and, finally, become explicit in his presentation of his "science of culture" as an ethic for truth and love.

---

[31]Charles Wagley, ed., Introduction to *Social Science Research in Latin America*, Report and Papers of a Seminar on Latin American Studies in the United States, held at Stanford, California, 8 July-23 August 1963 (New York: Columbia University Press, 1964) 29.

[32]Marvin Harris, *Town and Country in Brazil: A Sociological-Anthropological Study of a Small Brazilian Town* (New York: Norton, 1956) 69-71, 174-76.

[33]Marvin Harris, *Portugal's African Wards: A First-Hand Report on Labor and Emigration in Moçambique*, Africa Today Pamphlets (New York: American Committee on Africa, 1958) 1-2. For another example of this interweaving of the moral sense for justice with the intellectual pursuit of order, see Harris, *Patterns of Race in the Americas* (New York: Norton, 1964) 99.

The fundamental senses constituting Harris's limiting pursuit of order are discernible also in his vertical hermeneutic. Their presence is unsurprising given the contemporary character of his historical understanding. Harris justifies the retrieval of Marx in Steward's, White's, and his own cultural ecology or materialism by citing the benefits of Marx's infrastructural principle for ordered inquiry and, hence, for moral striving. In addition, Harris understands this retrieval—which he advocates but which has already partially occurred in cultural ecology—within the context of a general interpretation of history. Cultural materialism and ecology are parts of a "broad movement" in Western culture and cannot be ignored despite their present-day minority status in the social sciences. They are the result of Western culture's placing a premium on the "harder" forms of social science.[34] Harris's intellectual defense of this interpretation of history itself has a moral dimension.

Failure to recognize the intellectual contributions of the emergent cultural materialism, for example, is to court disaster for humanity. It is to allow the "onset of a new dark age" of not only ignorance but also of injustice and oppression, so that "aggressive fanatics" take over who are eager to annihilate each other and the world.[35] Harris's moral concern also accounts for his discussion of the moral consequences of other thinkers' systems when he tells the history of his anthropological discipline. The morally good is at stake, according to Harris, in the ordering of history. Again, the senses of order and justice are fused. A failure of intellect may be a crime against humanity.

These fundamental senses of justice and the need for order, united in one general pursuit of order, are the limit-to experiences of Harris's anthropological enterprise. These experiences, taken together, fundamentally dominate and shape the increasing transcendence of cultural horizons that characterizes his horizontal hermeneutic. In it, a "transcultural community of scientific observers," using its infrastructural principles, forges knowledge amid intercultural ambiguity and thus provides the preconditions for justice in a "pan-human community."

---

[34]Marvin Harris, *The Rise of Anthropological Theory: A History of Theories of Culture* (New York: Thomas Crowell, 1968) 655, and idem, *Cultural Materialism*, 76.

[35]Harris, *Cultural Materialism*, xii, 28.

These fundamental senses also restrict and shape the fusion of temporal horizons in Harris's vertical hermeneutic. Harris appropriates Marx's basic research strategy within his own present-day polemical context of intellectual and moral concern.

It is to these limit-to experiences that the most important transcending whole of Harris's anthropological understanding resonates. Nature, the whole that encompasses and grounds his transcultural interpretations and that is reinforced in his transtemporal interpretations, is a limit-of reality disclosed in his anthropological enterprise; it corresponds to the limit-to experiences or fundamental senses of the need for order and justice. The whole world of nature—with its different ecological zones and its production of different technoenvironmental pressures, and with its many possibilities for resolving the several salient ambiguities of his fieldwork situation and for establishing a "materialist" science—is a reality for Harris, who has the particular limit-to experiences of the senses of order and justice.

As with Lévi-Strauss's "world of reciprocity," Harris's "nature" is not a product of his anthropological fieldwork, methods of explanation, or theoretical formulations. Though Harris's methods and investigations develop, refine, or evidence this world of nature, "nature" is a constructed and presupposed condition for the possibility of the fundamental, limit-to experiences of order and justice that pervade his investigations and explanations. Harris's limiting pursuit of order, then, is a single limit-situation in which nature (a limit-of reality) and the fundamental senses of the need for order and justice (limit-to experiences) resonate with one another.

Harris, especially in his ever more explicit reflections on the notion of an orienting strategy for research, recognizes the contribution to his science of such presupposed or constructed realities. Scientific discoveries, he notes, may be the results of "following either metaphysical or downright irrational beliefs."[36] A cultural-materialist research strategy that employs infrastructural principles may thus depend on an invoked metaphysical reality, such as nature, which is not fully defensible by rational argument from the start. For Harris, however, such "meta-

---

[36]Ibid., 19. He makes this observation while discussing Thomas Kuhn's paradigms.

physical assumptions" can be compared and evaluated. The kinds of intellectual and ethical evaluations that Harris makes have been noted. But the ability, intellectually and ethically, to evaluate competing metaphysical assumptions or paradigms does not dispense with the task of positing or invoking metaphysical realities. In fact, Harris's articulation of cultural-materialist science involved a constant tacking back and forth between overarching metaphysical assumption (research strategy) and investigative refinement and development of the assumed reality, that is, nature and its effects on culture at the infrastructural level.

Thus, Lévi-Strauss's and Harris's limit-situations, generally described as loyalty to the whole and pursuit of order respectively, are made up of fundamental limit-to experiences for which certain limit-of realities function as grounds or horizons.

These are the limit-situations that attach to the wholes of Lévi-Strauss's and Harris's anthropological understanding. True, I can and have cited specific parts of their anthropological enterprises in which these limit-situations are evident. Lévi-Strauss's limiting loyalty to the whole, for example, may be discerned in his personal pilgrimage from philosophy to ethnography, in his sociocultural context of a post-World War I, French surrealist search for an "alternative human world" amidst others, and in his structuralist mapping of a *superrationaliste* world of objectified thought. Similarly, Harris's pursuit of order may be noted in his training under Steward at Columbia University, in his cultural-ecological research in Brazil under Wagley, as well as in his recent texts. All of these are particular contexts for their limit-situations. These contexts are particular mediations of the limit-situation.

Nevertheless, in spite of the possibilities of citing particular loci for these limit-situations, the primary concern here has been with the relation of the limit-situations to Lévi-Strauss's and Harris's interpretive experience wholistically viewed. What has been significant, therefore, is the relation of their limit-experiences to the transcultural and transtemporal understanding of their enterprises. Thus the discussion of their limit-situations began only after revealing the transcending wholes of their understanding. These latter—the world of reciprocity (Lévi-Strauss) and nature (Harris)—are the limit-of realities that, for these anthropologists, resonate with their particularly focused limit-to experiences.

Both "world of reciprocity" and "nature," *in* all their particular forms of mediation, then, are the grounds for transcendence of their particular, restrictive situations, and for their transcultural and transtemporal understanding in anthropology. In these limit-situations of restrictive limit-to experiences that yet invoke and disclose productive and grounding limit-of realities, one notes the kind of limit-situation first discussed by way of the contemporary discerners of the religious dimension presented in chapter 1. In Gadamer's language, for example, I have sketched the particular "finitude" of two inquirers' "historical experience," noted the restrictions of that experience, but then found in their interpretive experience that particular kind of finitude that brings into play a "totality of meaning."[37] In Lonergan's language, I have sketched the restricting contexts of Lévi-Strauss's and Harris's anthropologies, which limit their capacity to attain knowledge; but I have done this in such a way that the limited capacity is mated to an unrestricted, intentional questioning that impels them beyond the restrictions. In Polanyi's language, Lévi-Strauss's and Harris's limit-to experiences of compassion, remorse, sense of order and justice, are "passions" that not only restrict their inquiries, but also provide a "structure of commitment" or universal "matrix" for their thought.

The Religious Character of Anthropology's Limits

Not all limit-situations are *eo ipso* religious.[38] In this section I will address the following question: why can these limit-situations in the interpretive experience of Lévi-Strauss and Harris be taken as key characteristics of a religious dimension? I will offer here a twofold response.

Before offering this response, two terms within the question deserve attention: *key characteristic* and *religious dimension*. To say that these limit-situations are key characteristics of a religious dimension is not to say that the situations' limit-character provides an all-encompassing,

---

[37]Gadamer, *Truth and Method*, 416.

[38]Theologian Gordon Kaufman offers a similar qualification. For Kaufman, the experience of limiting finitude may be the ground of both theological conceptualizing and nontheistic metaphysical schemas. See Kaufman, *God the Problem*, 53, 58-59 n. 15, and Tracy, *Blessed Rage for Order*, 111 n. 11.

single definition of the human phenomenon called religion.[39] Rather, the reference to limit, as specified in chapter 1, is a means of identifying the basic character or "family resemblances" among properly religious perspectives that distinguish the religious from other perspectives such as moral, aesthetic, scientific, or political. The limit-character of Lévi-Strauss's and Harris's situations of "loyalty to the whole" or "pursuit of order," then, does not involve them in religion defined in some single, universally-agreed-upon fashion.

Furthermore, to seek a religious "dimension" does not mean to seek in the anthropologists' interpretive experience a fully formulated religion. Even if one is able to find certain key characteristics of or family resemblances among the phenomena of religion, they will often be discernible only in a rudimentary and often obscure fashion. The term *religious dimension* suggests always an intermingling and interaction between religious and other forms of experience and thought, a hiddenness of the religious, such that the religious rarely emerges with clarity. The "dimensional" character of the religious is, and has been all along, the challenge for this work's presentation of a properly religious dimension in cultural anthropology.

It may appear that focusing on terms such as *key characteristic* and *religious dimension* so highly qualifies this project's presentation of a properly "religious" dimension that its thesis is only minimally significant. This is by no means the case. As I shall argue in this chapter, the necessary qualifications can be duly considered while still allowing, and indeed making possible, the significance of the project's thesis: that there is a religious dimension to these anthropologists' interpretive experience.

The significance of the argument that culminates here remains as first formulated. The presence of a religious dimension in Lévi-Strauss's and Harris's interpretive experience suggests their dependency upon and relation to the religious in spite of their claimed distance from religion.

---

[39]For the problems of defining religion, see also Gilkey, *Naming the Whirlwind*, 285-304; Frederick Ferré, *Basic Modern Philosophy of Religion* (New York: Scribner's, 1967) 30-83; Walter H. Capps, *Ways of Understanding Religion* (New York: Macmillan, 1972) 7-12; Tracy, *Blessed Rage for Order*, 92-93, 110 nn. 4, 9; Clifford Geertz, "Religion as a Cultural System," in *The Interpretation of Cultures* (New York: Basic Books, 1973) 90-94.

They cannot easily claim, as some of the other anthropologists discussed above imply, that the religious pertains to phenomena functionally or pragmatically studied "out there" among others, or "back there" in the past. To use Hallowell's language again, the religious may not necessarily be obsolete in cultural anthropology simply because anthropologists have rendered provincial folk anthropologies obsolete. However qualified the argument may be, therefore, it retains significance as a corrective for those all-too-easy claims to restrict the religious to its own separate domain or to reduce it by various forms of functional and pragmatic explanation.

This significance applies to the cases of Lévi-Strauss and Harris. For, recall that both tend to reduce religion by anthropological explanations, either the structuralist ones of the avowedly agnostic Lévi-Strauss or the cultural-materialist ones of the avowedly atheistic Marvin Harris. As also noted, however, there are ambiguities surrounding their anthropological reductions of religion or their tendencies to mark it off as a separate realm from their own enterprises.

At the same time that Lévi-Strauss, for example, claims that he "has never felt the slightest twinge of religious anxiety" or that he views his structuralism as having no "common ground with theology," he nevertheless suggests that a "religious faith" freed from preoccupation with the "human subject" should understand and appreciate structuralism's final, unified, coherent whole.[40] Thus, in an interview, Lévi-Strauss has accepted an interpretation of his thought that finds in it *"une dimension spirituelle plus ou moins explicite."*[41] It has not been clarified, however, what that dimension is or how it relates to his enterprise.

Similar ambiguities surround Harris's cultural-materialist reductions of religion to infrastructural and technoeconomic conditions of political-economic exploitation. For all his tendencies toward such reductions, he nevertheless grants "authenticity" to "other ways of knowing" like aesthetics and religion.[42] Atheist Harris is less likely than

---

[40]Lévi-Strauss, *The Naked Man*, 687-88. He stresses that "believers" have not capitalized on this understanding because they timorously clutch the human subject.

[41]Lévi-Strauss, "Un anthropologue: Claude Lévi-Strauss," in *Dieu existe-t'il? Non, Repondent Pascal Anquetil et al.,* ed. Christian Chabanis (Paris: Fayard, 1973) 87-88.

[42]Harris, *Cultural Materialism*, 5-6, 315-16.

agnostic Lévi-Strauss to discuss such authentic, other ways of knowing and is even less likely to accept the religious as a dimension of his own anthropology. But the ambiguities accompanying his reductions are enough to lead one interpreter to view Harris's own fundamental presuppositions as "eschatological," so that Harris is portrayed as "operating a millenarian type of revitalization movement."[43] Such a movement would be "religious" even from the point of view of some writers in anthropology.[44]

These ambiguities in Lévi-Strauss and Harris suggest a relation to the religious amidst their suspicious distance from it, and alongside their reductions of religion or their restrictions of it to a separate domain. I will in this section turn to the limit-situations already identified *in* Lévi-Strauss's and Harris's interpretive experience in order to demarcate the religious dimension that is there in spite of the qualifications I attach to that demarcation and in spite of the ambiguities involved in the two men's viewpoints concerning religion. One can now return to those limit-situations and ask why they can properly be taken as key characteristics of a religious dimension.

Limits as universal and elemental

The first aspect of the promised twofold response to questions about the religiousness of Lévi-Strauss's and Harris's limit-situations begins with the "universal" or "elemental" implications of those limit-situations. The limit-situations, in both their limit-to experiences and limit-of realities, attach not just to any feature of Lévi-Strauss's and Harris's anthropologies, but rather to their anthropological understanding. Lévi-Strauss's compassion and remorse and his world of reciprocity, and Harris's sense for order and justice and his world of nature pervade their preunderstood and comprehensive understanding.

Because the limit-situations are related to this understanding, they possess a universal and elemental character. They have a universal im-

---

[43]Donald Edward Curry, "Emic and Etic: The Eschatological Presuppositions of Marvin Harris and Kenneth Pike," Studies in Political Anthropology, Working Paper Number Five (n.p., n.d.). Here Curry can compare Harris with missionary and Christian linguistic anthropologist, Kenneth Pike.

[44]See, for example, Anthony F. C. Wallace, *Religion: An Anthropological View* (New York: Random House, 1966) 157-66.

plication, first, in their invoking of a transcultural understanding in horizontal hermeneutic and a transtemporal understanding in vertical hermeneutic. They refer to a transcendence of spatial or cultural as well as of temporal horizons, and hence aim toward universality.

The limit-situations have an elemental implication, second, in their relatedness to understanding. For, understanding is the founding, preunderstood, fundamental feature in their interpretive experience. Limit-situations invoke what is "basic" to or "at the root" of their anthropologies, and hence aim toward what is elemental.

In the previous section it was necessary to show the integral connection of Lévi-Strauss's and Harris's limit-situation to the transcending wholes of their anthropological understanding. It is in that connection that limit-situations take on their universal and elemental character and so become key characteristics of the religious. Lévi-Strauss's compassion and remorse and Harris's sense for order and justice are not occasional sentiments or ideas; rather, they are fundamental limit-to experiences that pervade their entire enterprises and invoke universal and elemental worlds of reciprocity or nature.

The universality and elementality of their limit-situations are also signaled in how both Harris and Lévi-Strauss urge their readers to acknowledge the transcending wholes to which their limit-situations have provided them access. They both present intellectual and moral reasons for such an acknowledgment. For Lévi-Strauss, the structured world of reciprocity is presented as that which provides intellectual meaning to various myths that, in their separation from all other myths, seem intellectually absurd. Lévi-Strauss also presented his structured world of reciprocity as a "total social fact," the moral consequences of which humans are called to live out. Failure to do so is to risk destruction. Harris too urged his readers to acknowledge the transcending whole of nature, especially its interface with culture at the infrastructural level. Intellectually, such an acknowledged transcending whole would, according to Harris, ground a science of culture that rightly discerns causes of sociocultural similarities and differences. Morally, the acknowledgment would mean attainment of the preconditions for moral judgment and the possibility of restoring the pan-human community. A fused intellectual and moral plea issues forth from the anthropologists' universal and elemental claims.

The universality and elementality of limit-situations does not necessarily entail the explicitly religious, and certainly doesn't indicate a theism. But to take the limit-situation as a religious dimension does mean that such situations are appropriate points of engagement for religious language and conceptualization. This accessibility is especially evident in light of results provided by those who have studied the use of religious language in "ordinary discourse" as well as in theological discourse.

Note, first of all, the implications from ordinary-discourse analyses. Van Harvey has summarized the results of such analyses.

> And of those family resemblances that characterize religions, the chief one is the preoccupation with certain universal and elemental features of human existence as they bear on the human desire for liberation and authentic existence. The most obvious of these elemental features are finitude and contingency, the perpetual perishing of everything that is, the fact of order, and the fittingness of certain kinds of being for other beings (value).[45]

To say that the universal and elemental features "bear on human desire for liberation and authentic existence" is to say that those features have a particular value. This value is further specified in Stephen Toulmin's ordinary-discourse analysis of "religion" and "matters of faith." Toulmin suggests that in its limiting questions, "reason marches on faith," a faith that provides "reassurance" or "confidence" for humans threatened by actual life situations.[46] The most reassuring answers of religious faith, the "better" or more valuable ones, are those that "give us reassurance which will not be disappointed." This kind of reassurance

> will allay our fear of "the eternity before and behind the brief span" of our lives, and of "the infinite immensity" of space; will provide comfort in the face of distress; and will answer our questions in a way which will not seem in retrospect to have missed the point.[47]

---

[45]Van A. Harvey, *The Historian and the Believer: The Morality of Historical Knowledge and Christian Belief* (New York: Macmillan, 1966) 261.

[46]Toulmin, *An Examination of the Place of Reason in Ethics*, 217.

[47]Ibid., 212. Toulmin's quotations are from Pascal, *Les Pensées de Pascal*, disposées suivant l'ordre du cahier autographique, ed. G. Michaut (Fribourg, 1896) 11, 25.

The religious reassurance discerned in ordinary discourse, then, seeks both a temporal transcendence (freedom from fear of "the eternity before and behind") and a spatial transcendence (freedom from fear of the infinite immensity of space). The universal and elemental wholes of Lévi-Strauss and Harris, functioning in both their transtemporal and transcultural hermeneutics, constitute a dimension that can be developed with "reassuring" religious language.

Second, insights drawn from analyses of less-ordinary forms of religious discourse, that of theology and philosophical theology, also suggest the integral tie between the religious and universal and elemental concerns. Amidst the pluralism now characterizing Christian theology, most of the diverse forms of religious expression and language can be viewed as re-presentations, by symbol and concept, of fundamental, universal, or elemental limit-situations pervading human experiences and inquiries.[48] These limit-situations may be those that here are termed "loyalty to the whole" and "pursuit of order." But other equally important ones may be discerned such as mortality, experience of the uncanny, nothingness, fundamental trust, wonder, or a sense of "love that knows no restrictions."[49]

Because of these universal and elemental concerns in the less ordinary as well as in ordinary discourses of the explicit religions and theologies, I have presented similar features as they occur in the discourse of Lévi-Strauss's and Harris's interpretive experience. Compassion and remorse in Lévi-Strauss and the senses of order and justice in Harris are

---

[48]The view of theology as an expressive re-presentation of limit-experience is developed at length in Tracy's *The Analogical Imagination*. See George Lindbeck's critique of this position, which he characterizes as an "experiential-expressivist" mode of relating theology and religious experience (George Lindbeck, *The Nature of Doctrine: Religion and Theology in a Post-Liberal Age* [Philadelphia: Westminster Press, 1984] 16-17, 31-34). Lindbeck is particularly concerned that the "experiential-expressivist" approach inappropriately assumes a "common core experience" that religious language then "expresses" (31, 47). Tracy himself, however, rarely uses the language of "common core experience," and appreciative as he is of contemporary pluralism, he applies "limit" to religious experience only as a key characteristic indicating family resemblances of personally and culturally diverse experiences. Limit-situations and Tracy's limit-to experiences are strikingly different, and hence the theologies that re-present them vary accordingly (see Tracy, *The Analogical Imagination*, 3-31, 164).

[49]Tracy, *The Analogical Imagination*, 164-65.

their experiences of "elemental and universal features of human existence." I also have stressed their elemental and universal concerns by noting the relation of these limit-to experiences to the transcending wholes of their anthropological understanding, those limit-of realities that also feature the universal and elemental concerns.

Again, an argument noting similarities between religion's tendencies to seek reassurance featuring universal and elemental transcendence, and Lévi-Strauss's and Harris's tendencies also to seek transcendence does not warrant saying that Lévi-Strauss's and Harris's anthropological re-presentations and explications are *explicitly* religious. It does warrant, however, typifying their universal and elemental impulses as a religious dimension. Their limit-situations—constituted by limit-to experiences and invoked limit-of realities—are a dimension of their interpretive experience in which they grapple with universal and elemental experiences similar to those whose work, in both ordinary and less-ordinary theological discourse, is explicitly religious.

Religious searches for an adequate limit-language

It is not just the universal and elemental character of Lévi-Strauss's and Harris's limit-situations that allows these situations to be key characteristics of a properly religious dimension to their work. If one turns to the kind of language Lévi-Strauss and Harris use to explicate and re-present their limit-situations, one perceives a rudimentary "limit-language." By "limit-language," I mean their ways of addressing what I have termed their limit-situations.[50] The words, phrases, and rhetorical appeals of their limit-languages further suggest the "religious dimension" character of the limit-situations in their anthropologies.

In order to display this limit-language, I shall need to return to part of my presentation of Lévi-Strauss's and Harris's anthropologies. I emphasize again that this limit-language is rudimentary. What is apparent are components of a limit-language that may not always fit coherently with other components of the same anthropologist's limit-language. It may be that their limit-language, not explicitly reflected upon by either anthropologist, is not the most appropriate for representing the limit-

---

[50]For discussions of limit-language in explicitly religious discourse, see Ricoeur, "The Specificity of Religious Language," 108-22, and Tracy, *Blessed Rage for Order*, 131-36.

situations that restrict, shape, and ground their anthropological enterprises. Extended critiques of the coherence or appropriateness of their limit-languages are not proper here. The attention given here to the rudimentary limit-language is primarily to reinforce the interpretation of their limit-situations as religious dimensions. Identifying limit-languages will show their limit-situations, in all their universal and elemental character, pressing toward more typically religious expression.

Lévi-Strauss's limit-situation, which I have characterized as "loyalty to the whole," is represented in "odd" languages of different types.[51] First note the "play" that Lévi-Strauss wrote while crouching in his hammock at Campos Novos during a bout with depression.[52] Reflecting on the difficulties and nature of anthropological research, this play, "The Apotheosis of Augustus," almost constrains its reader to view it as an allegorical expression of two halves of Lévi-Strauss: a fieldworking self who, like the play's character, Cinna, is "only happy among savages" and nature, and an anthropologist-intellectualist half who, like the other character, Augustus, "amalgamates Nature and Society thus making himself a god among men."[53]

At the time of this play's writing, Lévi-Strauss was undertaking what he would later call the anthropological variant of original identification or compassion with others. At that time, too, he considered himself to be enduring a particular form of suffering characteristic of an ethnographer's *pitié*. In addition, the play introduces the final part of his *Tristes Tropiques* confession, a part in which special consideration is given to the nature of anthropological existence, what I have called his interpretive experience. This "dramatic fable," then, is a re-presentation by an anthropologist-self who has spurned his own society (remorse) to identify with "the most remote and the most alien others" (compassion).

---

[51]For the notion of an "odd" language, see Ricoeur, "The Specificity of Religious Language," 107, 131, and Ian Ramsey, *Religious Language* (New York: Macmillan, 1957).

[52]Lévi-Strauss, *Tristes Tropiques* (Eng. ed.), 377-78.

[53]Ibid., 379-80. See James A. Boon's summary, *From Symbolism to Structuralism: Lévi-Strauss in a Literary Tradition* (New York: Harper and Row, 1972) 144.

Without discussing all aspects of this creative composition or presuming to exhaust its meaning, a meaning that Lévi-Strauss himself has difficulty fathoming, I suggest that this "new version of Corneille's *Cinna*" is a representation of his fundamental limit-situation of compassion and remorse. The allegorical expressions involve twentieth-century Lévi-Strauss in a mythos, a reinterpretation and retrieval of classical myths and symbols already reinterpreted and retrieved by Corneille in the seventeenth century.[54] The religious character of this allegorical limit-language is suggested by the struggle of both the "Cinna" and "Augustus" halves of Lévi-Strauss's anthropological self with explicitly religious concerns: becoming a god among men, attaining the "divine nature," attaining "immortality," becoming a "messenger of the gods."[55] Lévi-Strauss resorts to the distinctively religious elements of this mythos in order to re-present the limit-situation of his anthropological and ethnographic experience.

While, again, there is no warrant for thus making Lévi-Strauss's anthropology a religion, the ability to re-present his limit-situation in such a dramatic fable, with its explicitly religious tones, does give his limit-situation its "religious dimension" character. But there are other limit-language components that also re-present his limit-situation.

If one refers to terms previously noted only in passing, one finds a second form of a re-presenting limit-language. Recall how Lévi-Strauss interprets his anthropological experience with words such as "redemption" (*rachat*), "atonement" (*l'expiation*), "original sin" (*péché originel*). These terms re-present the fundamental senses of compassion and remorse that have already been shown to "limit" (restrict, shape, ground) the formation of Lévi-Strauss's anthropological activity in its totalizing, detotalizing, and retotalizing phases.[56]

Lévi-Strauss's use of these "half-effaced yet still powerful" elements of Jewish and Christian myths, symbols, and ethos does not make Lévi-Strauss "Jewish" or "Christian," that is, explicitly religious. Nor would it be sufficient to link these bits of Judaism's language—"re-

---

[54]See Robert J. Nelson, *Corneille: His Heroes and Their Worlds* (Philadelphia: University of Pennsylvania Press, 1963).

[55]Lévi-Strauss, *Tristes Tropiques* (Eng. ed.), 379, 381, 382.

[56]Recall the important passage in *Tristes Tropiques* (Eng. ed.), 389.

demption" and "atonement"—to Lévi-Strauss's own stance as a twentieth-century Jew and then portray his life as an "ordeal of civility" that is unique to a Jewish "struggle with modernity."[57] Whatever the value of so stressing the specificity of Lévi-Strauss's relationship to the Jewish community, a specificity that Lévi-Strauss himself does not grant much significance,[58] his corpus reveals his use of these Jewish/Christian terms to be one possible response to limit-situations that, for all their particularity, are for him fundamental to human existence as a whole.

These terms might be dismissed as insignificant for this broad context or as incidental features of Lévi-Strauss's text, except that Lévi-Strauss presents these borrowings from Western culture's religious traditions in such an important segment of his *Tristes Tropiques*. His invoking of these terms—*redemption, atonement, original sin*—immediately follows his summary of "The Apotheosis of Augustus," which I have interpreted as a re-presentation—by a revision of religious mythos—of his limit-situation. The terms' immediate context is a further development of his own struggle to interpret anthropologists' existence—their remorseful exits from their own societies, their compassionate identifications with remote others, and the suffering that both exit and identification entail. In fact, the "Jewish" or "Christian" metaphors are situated in a sentence that stresses their reference to the fundamental situation of anthropologists: "His [the anthropologist's] very existence is incomprehensible except as an attempt at redemption: he is the symbol of atonement."[59]

It is in the same segment of *Tristes Tropiques* that the symbol of "original sin" is invoked for the universally encountered problem of "ethnocentricity." As noted above, this problem of universal ethnocentrism—the tendency of all peoples to feel a "tremor of repulsion" when

---

[57]As one of the best-known examples of this latter tendency, see John Murray Cuddihy's psychohistorical thesis in *The Ordeal of Civility: Freud, Marx, Lévi-Strauss and the Jewish Struggle with Modernity* (New York: Basic Books, 1974). For critical discussion of Cuddihy's thesis, see Thomas Shalvey, *Claude Lévi-Strauss: Social Psychotherapy and the Collective Unconscious* (Amherst: University of Massachusetts Press, 1979) 134-36.

[58]See, for example, *Tristes Tropiques* (Eng. ed.), 230-31, and idem, "Un Anthropologue: Claude Lévi-Strauss," 72.

[59]Lévi-Strauss, *Tristes Tropiques* (Eng. ed.), 389.

facing the alien[60]—is an obstacle to Lévi-Strauss's *pitié*, his sense of the identification of all beings and things. It is an obstacle, however, that also defines a major moment of his anthropological enterprise: detotalization, the reduction of all groups' and societies' autonomous claims to be the whole. Original sin takes its place, then, along with redemption and atonement as part of the "odd" language borrowed from the above-mentioned religions for the purpose of re-presenting important moments in the fundamental limit-situation of Lévi-Strauss's anthropological enterprise.[61]

Without claiming that these metaphors are always coherent, one can rightly acknowledge them as components of a limit-language. They are an attempt to re-present the limit-situation that sought a structurally related world of reciprocity outside time and space, which Lévi-Strauss felt to be necessary but which "does not correspond to any observable reality."[62] Although only a "rudimentary" limit-language, these Jewish and Christian terms and their re-presentative relation to the limit-situation further suggest the religious dimension of Lévi-Strauss's limit-situation.

One illustration of Lévi-Strauss's limit-language, then, is a dramatic fable that suggests the generally religious concerns characterizing the limit-situation. The atonement/redemption language of *Tristes Tropiques* focuses especially on the remorseful exit from his own society and the compassionate identification with remote others. When Lévi-Strauss finally reflects on the character of the whole, structured world invoked by him in his limit-situation, his language of re-presentation is articulated from what he takes to be a Buddhist point of view.

As he reflects on the character of his invoked, retotalized whole, the rudimentary limit-language of atonement/redemption and self-denial becomes a "Buddhist" limit-language of "loss of subject" in a vanishing whole—a loss (*l'effacement*) that Lévi-Strauss takes to be a

---

[60]Claude Lévi-Strauss, "Race and History," in *Structural Anthropology*, 2 vols. (New York: Basic Books, 1976) 2:328-30.

[61]For other examples of Lévi-Strauss's use of the language of "expiation" and "atonement," see "J. J. Rousseau," 42, 43.

[62]Lévi-Strauss, *Tristes Tropiques* (Eng. ed.), 392.

"methodological necessity" for the structural anthropologist.[63] This loss of subject that Lévi-Strauss describes most clearly in the final pages of *L'Homme nu* was anticipated in *Tristes Tropiques* when he proclaimed that between Buddhism and himself there could be little misunderstanding.[64] The fundamental senses of compassion and remorse, driving him to ever more specified relations in the structured world of reciprocity, teach, finally, the value of Buddhist insight.

> What else indeed have I learned from the masters who taught me, the philosophers I have read, the societies I have visited and even from that science which is the pride of the West, apart from a few scraps of wisdom which, when laid end to end, coincide with the meditation of the sage at the foot of the tree. Every effort to understand destroys the object studied in favor of another object of a different nature. This second object requires from us a new effort which destroys it in favor of a third, and so on and so forth until we reach the one lasting presence, the point at which the distinction between meaning and absence of meaning disappears: the same point from which we began.[65]

Buddhist teaching re-presents for Lévi-Strauss what was earlier summarized here as the culmination of his horizontal hermeneutic: the triumph of nonbeing over being, the slow flowering of the whole under the analyst's eyes, the inevitable disappearance of humanity from "the impassive face of the earth."[66] Anthropology might thus be renamed "entropology." All the journeying through volumes of myths' structural oppositions and transformations, in order to construct the transcending whole world of reciprocity, is like so many steps on the way to an enlightenment: the realization of the provisionality of collective and especially individual being and the ultimate realization of the absence of meaning.

In this final form of re-presenting the limit-situation of his anthropological understanding, the opposition between his own society and

---

[63]Lévi-Strauss, *The Naked Man*, 628.

[64]Lévi-Strauss, *Tristes Tropiques* (Eng. ed.), 413. This tendency is more recently acknowledged by Lévi-Strauss in "Un anthropologue: Claude Lévi-Strauss," 87.

[65]Lévi-Strauss, *Tristes Tropiques* (Eng. ed.), 411.

[66]Lévi-Strauss, *The Naked Man*, 694-95.

that of others, and the many oppositions that characterize others' worlds all reduce to one final opposition, between being and nonbeing. The Lévi-Straussian compassion and remorse that invoked and disclosed a world of reciprocity, now invoke and disclose, as a "finale," the full flowering and vanishing of that world. This rudimentary, Buddhist limit-language represents the fundamental senses of compassion and remorse as they finally display the "truth about man in a system of differences" that vanishes.

In Harris's anthropology—in which a social-scientific rather than a Lévi-Straussian literary-critical mode of explanation dominates—one should not be surprised to discover little in the way of textual metaphors and dramatic plays as ways of re-presenting his fundamental limit situation. Harris utilizes few terms explicitly borrowed from the great religions, and he writes no mythic plays while crouching in his South American hammock. Nevertheless, Harris's interpretive experience possesses a limit-language. It is marked, however, not so much by an "odd" borrowing of explicitly religious symbols, but by an intense fusion of claims to reality, truth, and value, all of which are typically religious concerns.[67] This fusion is most apparent in his "language of conflict" with other positions in social science. Harris's language amid such conflict re-presents the fundamental limit-situation of his anthropological enterprise. One can speak, then, of Harris's rudimentary limit-language as polemical.[68]

It has been noted throughout my display of his hermeneutic how this polemical language flourishes amidst his comparisons of cultural materialism with other research strategies. On the level of reality, I have depicted Harris as in search of the real causes of sociocultural pluralism, the real causes of its similarities and differences. On a level of truth,

---

[67]For discussion of this fusion as one way of approaching the "extremely elusive," essential character of family resemblances in religious discourse, see Gilkey, *Naming the Whirlwind*, 285-86.

[68]As just one indication—from outside the corpus of his texts—of how defining a feature Harris's polemical orientation is in his anthropology, note the way his primary research interests are listed in the *Fifth International Directory of Anthropologists,* Current Anthropology Resource Series (Chicago: University of Chicago Press, 1975): "Exposure of Eclectic Contradictions; Development of Materialist Theories; Identification of Idealist Tautologies" (153).

Harris always teaches an operationalized, true knowledge of these real causes.[69] On the level of value, Harris advocates the removal of "social pathologies" that disturb an often vaguely defined "moral sensibility."

On each of these levels, Harris compares his cultural materialism to other strategies. I am concerned here not with another summary of his comparisons as they occur on each of these levels, but rather with the manner in which these levels are fused in his polemical treatment of other positions and in his defense of his own.

For Harris, one should seek an isomorphism between the stances of each level, those of reality, truth, and value. And as he develops his polemic by comparing alternate research strategies, it is his stance on the level of value that seems to dominate overall. Harris's arguments about the "real" causes of sociocultural phenomena and about "true" knowledge of them are frequently rooted in what he takes to be universal and elemental concerns on the level of value.

This mode of argument, focused in an appeal to the level of value, is evident in the early pages of his most important theoretical work, *Cultural Materialism*. After an entire chapter devoted to showing how his operationalist, cultural-materialist view of the real causes of sociocultural phenomena possesses the "more acceptable criteria of truth," he closes by asking, "What is the alternative?"[70] In this argument the final recourse is to the level of value. In his view, to subvert the "scientific method," as practiced by the cultural materialism he advocates, is ultimately to allow morally culpable "fanatics" and "messiahs" to destroy each other and others for their own good.[71]

One might recall how this means of defending the scientific method is also applied in his polemical critiques of rival strategies in social science. There, Harris was not satisfied simply to argue that these other positions entail an unoperationalized knowledge of sociocultural reali-

---

[69]Harris's operationalism leads him to soften any contrast between reality (a "cultural thing," for example) and known truth. However, he qualifies his operationalism by insisting that there is a material world outside the operating observer that no logical manipulation can completely create and destroy. See Harris, *Nature of Cultural Things*, vi, 196-97.

[70]Harris, *Cultural Materialism*, 27.

[71]Ibid., 28.

ties; he also buttressed that argument with reference to the moral consequences of their unoperationalized knowledge. As examples, Harris claims that structuralism "mocks the hungry living and dead"; dialectical materialism allows a totalitarianism based on the propagation of false hopes; "Parsonian" cognitive idealism accounts for stability but not needed social change; and structural Marxism cannot define "infrastructure" or "exploitation" and thus cannot expose who is exploiting whom.

For Harris, then, there seems to be a certain dictate on the level of value specifying a cultural-materialist strategy for knowledge of sociocultural realities. This way of fusing reality, truth, and value is particularly evident in the polemic against Paul Feyerabend mentioned above. Harris opposes Feyerabend's "epistemological relativism"[72] on the grounds that such a position on the level of knowledge "poses a grave threat to our survival" and thus has damaging moral consequences. This threat, Harris argues, is especially the case when the social sciences study poverty, classism, racism, pollution, the Holocaust. Harris's argument for a certain kind of knowledge of reality based on appeals to moral sensibility on the level of value is strikingly put in his challenge to Feyerabend:

> Let Feyerabend stand before the ovens of Dachau or the ditch at Mylai and say that our scientific understanding [knowledge] of sociocultural systems [reality] is ultimately nothing but an "aesthetic judgment."[73]

This kind of language, emerging in Harris's polemical criticisms of rival theorists, particularly displays its representative character. It is a language re-presenting what has been explicated throughout this chapter as the limit-situation that restricts, shapes, and grounds his anthropological understanding. In the polemical clash—whether it be with structuralism, dialectical materialism, sociobiology, or Feyerabend's epistemology—those fundamental senses are re-presented, the limit-to experiences of the need for order wedded to a sense of justice.

---

[72]I cannot treat here the adequacy of Harris's reading of Feyerabend, on which his polemic is based.

[73]Harris, *Cultural Materialism*, 23.

Reference to this polemical limit-language is important because it displays the intense fusion of the senses for order and justice in Harris's anthropology. Earlier, when treating Harris's limit-situation, I noted the presence of the two fundamental senses and even their relation in, for example, Harris's ethnography, in which moral concern is evident amidst his descriptions. It is in the polemical limit-language that the fusion of concerns—for reality, truth, and value—is most apparent.

Even though Harris's limit-language lacks a borrowing of symbols from an explicitly religious tradition, his polemical limit-language is typically religious. This limit-language, like that of Lévi-Strauss, can be taken, therefore, as further indication of the religious dimension of his limit-situation. That is to say, his limit-situation is expressed in a language that is significantly similar to that of explicitly religious discourse: the fusion of concerns for the real, the true, and the good.

Although I note this fusion in Harris by referring to a "level of value," the crucial point is that a truly fundamental concern is signaled there, a concern that according to Harris's position ought not to be limited to the level of value but moves beyond it to the whole anthropological enterprise as it works itself out at the levels of reality and truth. It is this "move beyond," characteristic of his polemical limit-language, that signals something more than just an ethical dimension. The ethical is a point in his enterprise at which one can observe the confluence of other major concerns as the expression of a fundamental limit-situation. In that confluence, of the real and the true with the good, is the religious dimension of his anthropology.

These two re-presentative limit-languages—Lévi-Strauss's borrowings from explicitly religious discourse and Harris's typically religious fusion of polemical concerns for value with those for reality and truth—join with the universal and elemental features of their limit-situations to suggest the religious dimension of those limit-situations. These limit-languages are not reflected on by the anthropologists themselves and, as noted above, they are at best rudimentary or fragmentary. That of Lévi-Strauss, for example, is an amalgam of ancient mythos, French tragedy, Jewish/Christian terminology, and Buddhism. Similarly, the polemic of Harris's limit-language not only brings to light its role of re-presenting his limit-situation, but also subjects that language to the varying and at times tumultuous world of controversy. In such a polemical context, a coherent or explicitly formulated limit-language is not found. What is to be found, however, in Harris's as well as Lévi-Strauss's limit-language, is a drive toward symbol and properly religious discourse so as to re-present the limit-situations that restrict, shape, and ground their anthropologies. In this drive both anthropologists move beyond explanation.

Anthropology and theology: toward conversation

Throughout this work, discernment of a religious dimension has depended upon revealing the unities and wholes characterizing Lévi-Strauss's and Harris's interpretive experiences. These unities have been variously manifested. By again attending to the specific character of these, I will conclude with an indication of the common area of conversation between theology and cultural anthropology.

My attention to unities began with the explication of Lévi-Strauss's and Harris's explanatory enterprises in terms of an overarching, supportive, and encompassing understanding. This understanding manifested a transcending wholeness in both dimensions of anthropological hermeneutic: the horizontal and the vertical. In the former is a whole that is a transcendence of cultural horizons. In the latter is the wholeness of a fusion of temporal horizons. Their anthropological understanding, then, featured both a spatiocultural and temporal transcendence.

It was in relation to these two transcending wholes of understanding that I also explicated Lévi-Strauss's and Harris's limit-situations. In them I sought another unity within which were distinguished the restrictive, particularized, limit-to experiences that yet resonated with, invoked, and disclosed limit-of realities that ground and make possible the transcendence of particular restrictions. As attaching to Lévi-Strauss's and Harris's whole understanding, these limit-situations do not simply occupy some segments of their anthropologies; rather, they pervade the important moments of their anthropological enterprises wholistically viewed.

The religious dimension of their limit-situations was then located precisely in their fundamental concerns for these wholes, in the universal and elemental features of those wholes, and in the rudimentary limit-languages by which they attempt to re-present their fundamental experience of such wholes.

The character of the wholes disclosed in Lévi-Strauss's and Harris's hermeneutics is particularly manifest in the terms that they use for the limit-of realities that resonate with their limit-to experiences. By attending to these, one may clarify the character of their religious dimensions and, at the same time, indicate the possibilities for conversation between theology and anthropology.

Lévi-Strauss's invoked limit-of reality is a world of reciprocity or an objectified thought having a dynamic architecture that eventually "flowers and closes" itself. This world, which makes possible both the savage's and Lévi-Strauss's own totalizing, detotalizing, and retotalizing activities, functions as what Langdon Gilkey has termed a "conditioned absolute" or a "conditioned ultimate" in his anthropology.[74] It functions as "a particular vision of the truth of things which is held to be itself nonrelative or hypothetical."

The notion of a conditioned absolute encapsulates again what Tracy has distinguished as limit-to experiences and limit-of realities. Lévi-Strauss's world of reciprocity is "absolute" by reason of its role in his hermeneutic as a nonrelative, transcendence-engendering presupposition. It is a *pressentiment*, as Lévi-Strauss says, postulating a world at the "limit of" his inquiries that makes possible the formulation of his structural anthropology. But that world is also "conditioned" by reason of its particularized limit-to experiences—those fundamental senses that are so much a feature of Lévi-Strauss's own personal pilgrimage, of his French milieu, of particular fieldwork experience, and reflection on the salient images of that fieldwork. His world of reciprocity is part of a vision that is at once conditioned and absolute.

This world of reciprocity, then, may provide a final characterization of Lévi-Strauss's religious dimension. This world, so fundamental for both his horizontal and vertical hermeneutics, postulates for humanity and its world a "law of exchange" to which all life ceaselessly bends. This world, for Lévi-Strauss, was evident from his study of kinship and marriage practice. Finally, though, it was most apparent in mythic thought, wherein the "law of exchange" unites not only familial groupings but the various components of the different levels of exis-

---

[74]Gilkey, *Religion and the Scientific Future*, 52, 54.

tence: cosmological, sociological, vestimentary, culinary, acoustic, anatomical, geographical, ethical.

The world invoked in his religious dimension is a totalized one. It teaches a lesson that for Lévi-Strauss is replete with intellectual and moral consequences: "Just as the individual is not alone in the group, nor any one society alone among the others, so man is not alone in the universe."[75] If the "spectrum or rainbow of human cultures" finally "flowers and closes" or sinks into the void of nonbeing, this too is but the final end of a humanity and a universe integrally related, engaged in a creative "frenzy" that not only valuably relates all being but also works its vanishing.

Jean Paul Sartre worried that a structuralism like Lévi-Strauss's, which points to a world whose forces constitute and transcend man, might be a "surreptitious reintroduction of God into philosophy."[76] Lévi-Strauss's disclaimer of any "common ground with theology"[77] would have to be noted as a word of caution here in response to Sartre's concern. In the terms of this work, however, there is a dimension to Lévi-Strauss's thought that, as his rudimentary limit-language hints, is susceptible to discourse about religious symbols like God, to *theos-logos*. Any theology, however, claiming to re-present systematically the limiting situation of Lévi-Strauss's loyalty to the whole would have to represent not only the relatedness of all being in a totality, but also the Lévi-Straussian *pressentiment* that the total world will undergo the eclipse of humanity.[78] This implied theological discourse about God, the pos-

---

[75]Lévi-Strauss, *Tristes Tropiques* (Eng. ed.), 414.

[76]Shalvey, *Claude Lévi-Strauss*, 123.

[77]Lévi-Strauss, *The Naked Man*, 688.

[78]For one ethicist and theologian trying to account for this possible "eclipse," see James M. Gustafson, *Ethics from a Theocentric Perspective*, 2 vols. (Chicago: University of Chicago Press, 1981) 1:58, 88-99. Theologians who have been influenced by French deconstructionist studies, particularly those of Jacques Derrida, relate this eclipse to Christian discourse about death and incarnation. Cf. Thomas J. J. Altizer, Max A. Myers et al., eds., *Deconstruction and Theology* (New York: Crossroad, 1982) 1-33, and Mark C. Taylor, *Erring: A Postmodern A/theology* (Chicago: University of Chicago Press, 1984) 4-10, 118-48.

sible forms of which cannot be discussed here, would of course involve revisions of classical theism.[79]

Marvin Harris's transcending whole of nature also warrants final comment, for it suggests the general character of his religious dimension. This "nature," which Harris seeks to view in interface with culture and which so founds his "science of culture," may also be viewed as a conditioned absolute.

Like Lévi-Strauss's world of reciprocity, Harris's "nature" is "absolute" by reason of its role in his hermeneutic as the nonrelative, transcendence-engendering presupposition. Just as powerfully as the world postulated in Lévi-Strauss's *pressentiment*, so nature in Harris's strategy is a postulated world at the "limit of" his inquiries that makes possible the formulation of his cultural-materialist anthropology. But again, this strategy is of course "conditioned"—conditioned by his own personal life pilgrimage, by training at Columbia University in the cultural ecology of Steward and under Wagley, by the preoccupying, salient images of his fieldwork that also dominate his writings. But like Lévi-Strauss's conditionedness, these conditions are applied in his interpretive experience to effect transcendence of cultures and fusion of temporal horizons.

Harris's stress on the transcending whole of nature portrays him as a "naturalist" in a sociocultural "science" of cultural-materialist anthropology. As his principle of infrastructural determinism implies, nature tends to be "all that is the case in the widest environment of man."[80] The distinctive place that Harris grants to ideas or to "superstructure" has been noted; however, for his science of culture, these ideas remain subordinate to the technoenvironmental, technoeconomic infrastructure whereby nature interfaces with culture.

In his stress on nature, Harris shares several features with others typically described as naturalists. As has been seen, for example, he shares this perspective's sympathy with the early materialist statements of the French physiocrats and the encyclopedists of the eighteenth cen-

---

[79]On the notion of classical theism, see Charles Hartshorne and William L. Reese, *Philosophers Speak of God* (Chicago: University of Chicago Press, 1953) 15-25, 29-230; Gilkey, *Naming the Whirlwind*, 54-55; and Tracy, *Blessed Rage for Order*, 147.

[80]Gilkey, *Naming the Whirlwind*, 23n.

tury.[81] His retrieval of Marx's materialism, of course, has been noted. Like others of the naturalist position, Harris acknowledges his fundamental indebtedness to David Hume.[82]

Harris also exhibits some of the humanist propensities of the naturalist position, whereby despite humanity's fundamental determination by nature, there can be control over it and thus the pursuit of human hopes. Harris makes room within his "probabilistic determinism" by calling colleagues in his society to operationalized knowledge of nature. Only by such a knowledge will humans both know the limitations imposed on them by nature and also identify the "open moments" in humanity's development where the evolutionary trajectory is most vulnerable to human will and hopes. So it is that Harris himself can state the humanist aspirations of his naturalist or positivist enterprise.[83]

> Positivism was born in the eighteenth century with Hume, not out of despair, but out of hope; not out of a narrow-minded view of the truth, but out of a broad vision of new methods for increasing knowledge; not out of detachment and disinterest in human well-being but out of a passionate belief in the ultimate perfectability of social life; not out of Comte's conservative "order and progress" but out of the enlightenment's search for "liberty, equality, and fraternity."[84]

Such naturalist or positivist positions usually claim, often because of their humanist orientation, to have excluded the concerns of Christian theology, especially those clustering around its symbol, God. Harris's avowed atheism attests to this. Yet, among representative modern naturalists, Santayana and Dewey may be singled out as two thinkers who do not see the naturalist view as opposed to "Christian piety" or to "Christian virtue."[85] Dewey's well-known criticism of "religion," which

---

[81]Ibid.

[82]Ibid. Cf. Harris, *Cultural Materialism*, 9-13.

[83]What Harris calls his positivism can also be called naturalism on the basis of his consistent invoking of nature as the transcending whole for his anthropological interpretation.

[84]Harris, *Cultural Materialism*, 13.

[85]Gilkey, *Naming the Whirlwind*, 23n.

doesn't reject the "religious," also suggests one way to mitigate naturalist suspicions of religion.

By trying to discern a religious dimension in Harris's cultural materialism, one might be questioning, in principle, an anthropological naturalism claiming to be separated and distant from religious concerns. The avowed atheism of cultural-materialist Harris, who shares the naturalist commitment in his fundamental invoking of the transcending whole of nature, need not preclude a religious dimension in his anthropology that is susceptible to re-presentation by theological discourse, even though he himself does not systematically formulate that discourse. The taking of nature as one locus of the religious finds contemporary manifestation in, for one example, theologian and ethicist James M. Gustafson. For Gustafson, nature is one putatively nonreligious arena within which religious affectivities or senses may arise. "Nature elicits piety." From nature, Gustafson finds what for him are particularly "religious" senses of dependence, of gratitude, or of possibility for human development and achievement.[86]

These possibilities for re-presenting Lévi-Strauss's and Harris's religious dimensions in theological discourse have been discussed only briefly. But again, my aim has not been to delineate theological discourses, but to indicate their possibility given the religious dimensions discerned here. Such a possibility returns one, albeit in a more specific form, to the "kinship of interest" between Christian "theological anthropology" and modern "cultural anthropology." What in chapter 1 I intimated as a mere "kinship of interest" between theology and anthropology now has been explicated in terms of the limit-situations of Lévi-Strauss's and Harris's anthropologies. These limit-situations constitute the religious dimension of those anthropologies and can be re-presented by forms of theological discourse.

What, then, can one say about possible conversations between anthropology and theology? One must certainly heed cultural anthropology's various critiques and suspicions of theologies that express and sanction folk anthropologies of Western culture—that is, views of hu-

---

[86]Gustafson, *Ethics from a Theocentric Perspective*, 1:210-11. For this author there are also other arenas (culture, society, and so forth) within which the religious affections may also arise.

manity that make no attempt to encounter others, or to test generalizations about humanity by reference to the diversity of societies, the "rainbow of human cultures." One might affirm, therefore, modern cultural anthropology's transcendence of the Christian West's provincial folk anthropology.

But now—at least on the basis of these analyses of anthropologists Lévi-Strauss and Harris—may one not also grant the religious a role in constituting anthropological impulses? If our structuralist and cultural-materialist anthropologists of explanation unfold their enterprises within preunderstood and comprehensive wholes that have a properly limiting and religious character, must it seem so strange to contemporary inquirers that Augustine would ground a *scientia* in an illuminating, divine *sapientia;* that Aquinas's "active intellect" is finally a participation in the "divine light"; that Calvin claimed that the knowledge of the Ancients and other scholars rests on the "renewal" of a "divine" power; or that Schleiermacher would propose that a human sensuous consciousness and a "God consciousness" mutually give rise to or excite one another?

If Lévi-Strauss and Harris "transcend" their own culture for knowledge of other cultures by means of particular appropriations within their traditions, why must anthropologists be surprised that theological enterprises are quickened by a similar transcending impulse on the basis of particular appropriations of their traditions? As a sensitive theology might self-critically affirm anthropological suspicions of folk anthropology in theology, might not a sensitive cultural anthropology affirm theology's contribution to anthropology's own "limiting," religious impulses?

Might there not be a place, then, even from cultural anthropology's viewpoint, for a "religious" reflection that retrieves, albeit through critical reinterpretation, Augustine's "God," who creates and sustains things different and similar in one whole; or Aquinas's "natural law," which attains universality precisely in its variance according to custom, time, and place; or Calvin's *divinitatis sensum,* which no people are too "savage" to lack; or Schleiermacher's universal God-consciousness, which is established in encounters with others in an ever-widening, multifarious communion of feeling? These theological drives toward universality—despite the particularity of their forms—allow religious reflection a place as a genuine conversation partner with an anthropological understanding whose limit-situations also involve both spatio-cultural and temporal transcendence.

To be sure, religious reflection and its re-presentive theological discourse do well to remain sensitive to the suspicions engendered by anthropology's cross-cultural perspectives. The inevitable particularity of all religious and theological discourse holds the danger that theolog-ical anthropology will appropriate its traditions in the self-absolutizing manner of provincial folk anthropologies, rather than invoke tran-scending wholes that allow others to be encountered, interpreted, and known as other. Acknowledgment of this criticism, however, does not prohibit theology's contribution to genuine dialogue with modern cul-tural anthropology.

Conversation can occur between theology and anthropology, two enterprises seeking in all their intracultural particularity a transcen-dence grounding their intercultural interpretations. In this work I have entered that conversation by explicating religious dimensions in Lévi-Strauss's structural anthropology and in Harris's cultural-materialist anthropology. I have entered a conversation that must remain open— open to further anthropological suspicions, open to further examina-tion of other anthropologists' modes of interpretation, and open to other theologians' articulation of transcendence amid their particular situa-tions.

Index

Names

Adams, J. L., 11
Altizer, T. J. J., 251
Aquinas, Thomas, 33, 59
  on human knowledge, 37-40, 46-47
  view of "alien," 48-49, 52-54
Aristotle, 40, 48, 219
Augustine, 33, 48, 59
  on human knowledge, 34-37, 46-47
  view of "alien," 48, 50-52

Barnouw, V., 106
Barth, Karl, 6
Bartholomeuw, 23
Beals, R. L., 154
Benedict, R., 197
Bergson, H., 175
Berreman, G. D., 79-80, 84
Beteille, A., 102
Bingham, H., 33, 54-55
Boas, F., 94, 173, 196-97
Bonaventure, 35
Boon, J. A., 132-33, 240
Braudel, F., 92, 140
Breen, Q., 42
Brodbeck, M., 22
Buddhism, 243-45
Burling, R., 158
Burridge, K., 25, 51, 59, 84

Calvin, J., 33, 59
  divinitatis sensum, 41-42, 47, 54
  on human knowledge, 40-43
  view of "alien," 49, 54-56
Capps, W., 233
Castaneda, C., 165
Chabanis, C., 97, 234
Ching, Francis K. W., 56
Clarke, S., 182
Clifford, J., 121
Clouet, F., 134
Comte, A., 70, 198
Condorcet, M., 192
Cook, Captain J., 33
Cuddihy, J. M., 242
Curry, D. W., 235

Dallmayr, F. R., 13
Debussy, C., 123
Derrida, J., 223, 251
Descartes, R., 176
Devereaux, G., 76
D'Holbach, P. H. T., 192
Diamond, S., 83, 88
Dilthey, W., 43, 70-71, 72, 194, 197
Dimen-Schein, M., 69
Douglas, Mary, 30
Dumas, G., 113
Durbin, M., 158

Subjects